JOHN SMAILES is a journalist, motorsport commentator and publicist and until recently proprietor of a specialised communications agency. He co-wrote *Climbing the Mountain*, the autobiography of Australian motorsport legend Allan Moffat OBE; was the managing editor of the sixtieth anniversary history of the Confederation of Australian Motor Sport; wrote *Race Across the World*, the incredible story of the 1968 London–Sydney Marathon and a sequel to *The Bright Eyes of Danger*, written with the first Australian Touring Car Champion David McKay. Mount Panorama has been a big influence in Smailes's life. He attended his first-ever motor race at Mount Panorama in 1960—where he first met Jack Brabham; raced in two Bathurst 500s; covered car and motorcycle racing as a journalist for print and TV, publicised the motorcycles and was corporate communicator for the cars.

JOHN SMAILES
MOUNT PANORAMA
BATHURST — THE STORIES BEHIND THE LEGEND

SYDNEY·MELBOURNE·AUCKLAND·LONDON

First published in 2019

Copyright © John Smailes 2019

All rights reserved. No part of this book may be reproduced or transmitted in any form or by any means, electronic or mechanical, including photocopying, recording or by any information storage and retrieval system, without prior permission in writing from the publisher. The Australian *Copyright Act 1968* (the Act) allows a maximum of one chapter or 10 per cent of this book, whichever is the greater, to be photocopied by any educational institution for its educational purposes provided that the educational institution (or body that administers it) has given a remuneration notice to the Copyright Agency (Australia) under the Act.

Allen & Unwin
83 Alexander Street
Crows Nest NSW 2065
Australia
Phone: (61 2) 8425 0100
Email: info@allenandunwin.com
Web: www.allenandunwin.com

 A catalogue record for this book is available from the National Library of Australia

ISBN 978 1 76052 936 9

Diagrams by Midland Typesetters, Australia
Index by Puddingburn
Set in 12.5/17.5 pt Minion Pro by Midland Typesetters, Australia
Printed and bound in Australia by Griffin Press, part of Ovato

10 9 8 7 6 5 4 3 2 1

 The paper in this book is FSC® certified. FSC® promotes environmentally responsible, socially beneficial and economically viable management of the world's forests.

To the founding families:
Arthur OAM and Jan Blizzard
Jack and Tot Hinxman
Ivan and Leonie Stibbard
&
G.T. Jenny

Contents

Diagrams ix
Prologue xi

Part 1: The Legends
1. The Master of the Mountain 3
2. In the Shadow of Brock 27

Part 2: Precious and Precarious
3. A New Era 51
4. Preparing for War 70
5. Police and Politics 88

Part 3: The Golden Age
6. The Golden Age of Motorcycles 115
7. The Golden Age of Cars 140
8. The Tin Tops 161

Part 4: The Races That Stop a Nation
9. A Wild Ride 181
10. Supercars 204
11. Jump Over Your Shadow 224

Part 5: Tragedy, Triumph and Turmoil

12	The Laps of the Gods	241
13	Sky Pilots	265
14	A Day at the Races	285
15	Virtual Reality and Real Legends	304

Epilogue: The Battle of Bathurst	319
Acknowledgements	331
Index	336

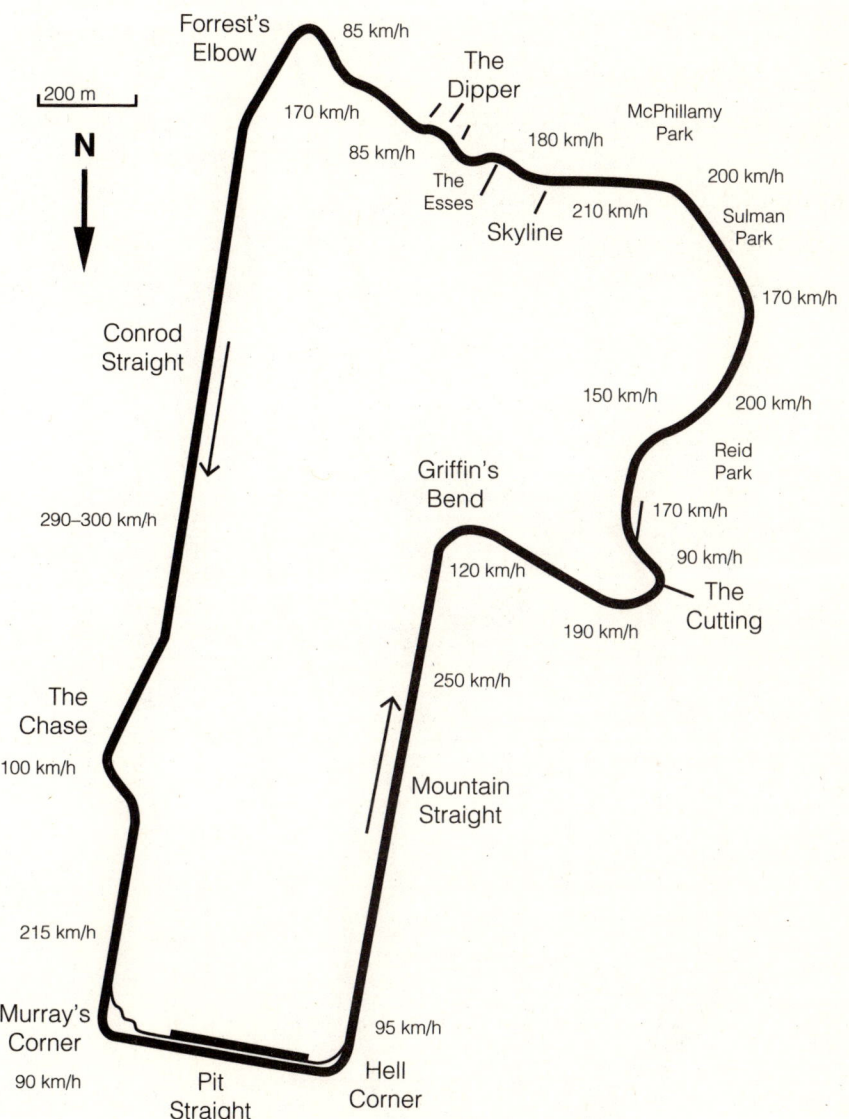

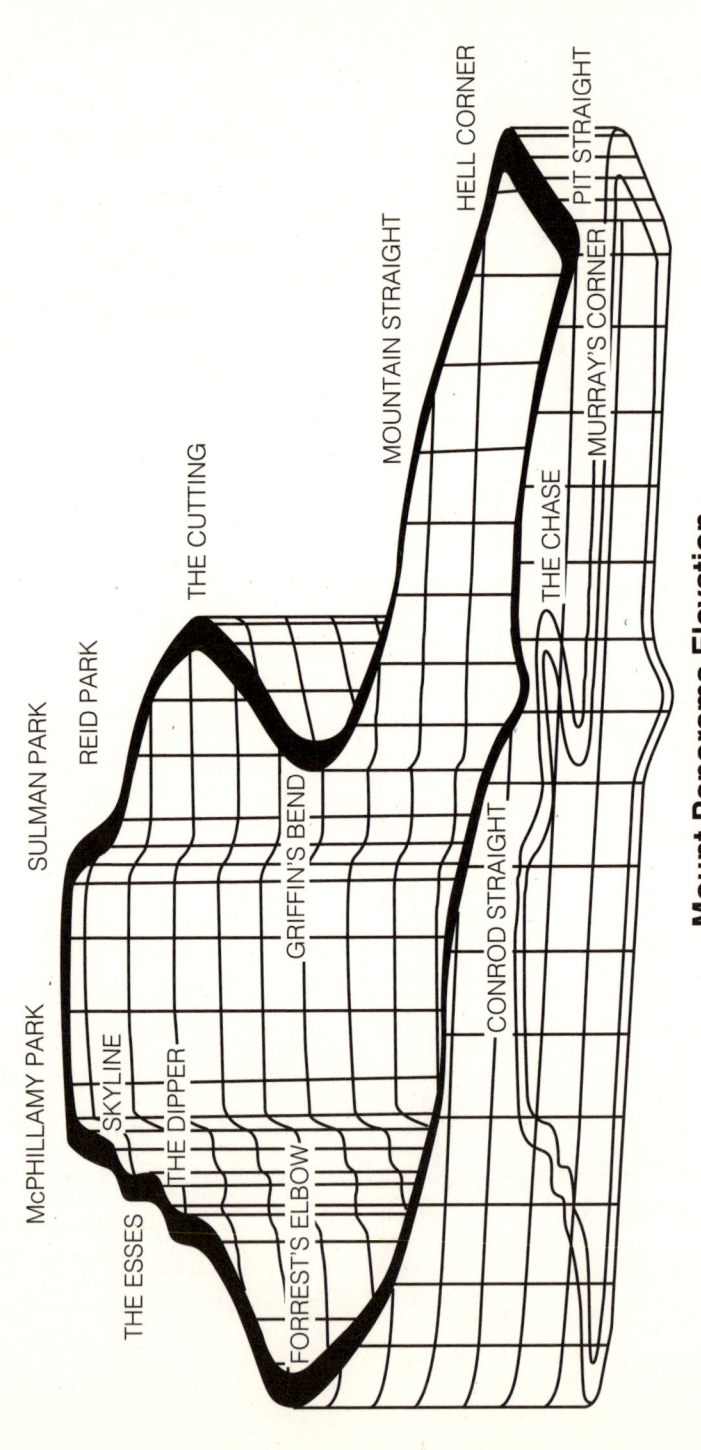

Mount Panorama Elevation

Prologue

Around the world, enthusiasts refer to it as Mount Panorama, the Mountain or simply Bathurst (Victorians pronounce it as Bath-Hurst: two words), the rural city in the Central West of New South Wales, just over the Great Dividing Range, which is as famed for its motor-racing circuit as Indianapolis is for its speed bowl. There aren't too many race circuits named for their city of origin—or vice versa. In 1911 Indianapolis was built with a surface of 3.2 million paving bricks, and with the goodwill and support of America's burgeoning motor industry. Mount Panorama was initially made of dirt, built with the hard labour of the otherwise unemployed and under the deep cover of subterfuge.

Mike Kable, an ambitious young reporter for the *Lithgow Mercury*—he would soon become one of Australia's most revered journalists in the automotive space, the doyen of motoring writers—knew he was onto something. Mount Panorama, the country's pinnacle racetrack, had been built with funds improperly and perhaps illegally obtained from the public purse.

The deception that allowed it to occur involved local government officials, state government ministers and perhaps even a recently deceased prime minister.

It was 1957 and Kable, then 22, had been aware of the story for as long as he could remember. He'd been raised in Bathurst, and as a committed motorsport enthusiast had even been the start-up publicity officer for the Bathurst Light Car Club, formed in 1953 when he was just eighteen.

Mike had served his cadetship on *The National Advocate*, Bathurst's local paper, before being promoted to the *Lithgow Mercury*—part of a stellar career trajectory that just seven years later would see him anointed as the inaugural motoring editor of Rupert Murdoch's flagship national newspaper *The Australian*. He took motoring journalism out of the car-advice section of the classifieds and elevated it to page-1 prominence. He broke stories of national importance and paved a precipitous path between being a confidante of captains of the industry, and maintaining his objectivity and integrity.

'As you probably realise, factual information plays by far the most important part in the compilation of any historical record,' he said in a letter to the town clerk of Bathurst City Council when he decided to unlock the secret of Mount Panorama's conception.

It was a time long before the Freedom of Information Act, but Kable had decided, rightly, to formalise his line of enquiry

PROLOGUE

and to hold the Council to account for the actions that had led to the construction of the racetrack that today is regarded as one of the top six road circuits in the world. He wrote his letter on 27 August, and in three days he had his reply.

Bathurst can lay claim to being Australia's longest-serving home of consistently top-level motorsport. Initially it was all about motorcycles: as early as 1911, they raced on a street track—the Peel circuit—outside the satellite suburb of Kelso. In 1914 the first Australian Motorcycle Grand Prix (GP) was held on a 24.8-kilometre triangular course around Kirkconnell, 25 kilometres to Bathurst's east. Whether it qualified as the national GP or whether it was the first GP held in Australia—a fine distinction—is lost to history; the city of Goulburn also claims the first Australian GP.

This inaugural Bathurst race was nine laps, making it a phenomenal 223-kilometre distance (even today, grands prix don't run that long), and it took more than three hours for competitors to complete it. Even so, nine of the 27 starters made it to the finish. Brothers Edgar and James Meller took first and fourth places respectively on their matching pair of 2¾ horsepower Douglas TT bikes. Breakdowns claimed the non-finishers; only one crashed, into a creek, as he traversed Yetholme, Sunny Corner and Meadow Lea.

The following year, on the same dusty, corrugated track, James Meller returned the favour, winning on his Matchless.

They were pioneers. Kirkconnell was a long way from anywhere then and is not much more accessible now, which is why they've put a gaol there. Seven hundred people turned up to watch that first motorcycle grand prix and it would have been an adventure just getting to the event—especially if they'd come over the Blue Mountains.

There's rivalry between cities for big events and the tourist dollars that come with them. Goulburn, proclaimed Australia's first inland city in 1863, 22 years before Bathurst, stole the Grand Prix away with the promise of easier access, closer accommodation and a challenging circuit. Goulburn staged the state's premier event—sometimes called the Australian Grand Prix or the Australian Tourist Trophy (TT), and other times state-based—until 1930. Bathurst was left with speedway racing at the local showground, and it created champions. Local rider Arthur 'Bluey' Wilkinson honed his skills there before going off to race for British club the West Ham Hammers in the Speedway World Championship. He won it in 1938.

Bathurst struck back with a new 11.5-kilometre gravel track; with some degree of irony it was situated in part on the main Bathurst-to-Goulburn road. It was called the Vale circuit after the creek over which it crossed, and it had the distinction of being only partially closed for racing. While competitors tore down one side of the roadway, motorists would be gathered together by a man with a red flag and guided down the other. Vale prevailed for seven years, and it was only towards its end that the flimsy fence separating the two sides of the roadway was replaced in strategic locations by an earth bank.

Vale was a fast, tough track with average speeds approaching 100 kilometres per hour. For the first three years it ran anti-clockwise, a hazard to riders and spectators as competitors rode towards the setting sun, churning up heavy dust clouds

PROLOGUE

with their speeding bikes and creating a lethal sightscreen. Racing almost stopped right then until someone came up with a brilliant—and logical—idea: run it in the reverse direction. With the sun at the riders' backs, Vale survived another three years.

Racing was spectacular in both directions. The bikes were able to get air either way: designated take-off and landing positions were nominated on the circuit map, a siren call for spectators.

Don Bain, a hugely talented young Sydney rider—slightly built, with prominent ears and a tight mop of curly hair—won the first race, the Junior TT for smaller-capacity bikes in 1931, dominated the years that followed, and won the final race on the circuit in 1937. It was his first and only win in the Senior TT, for larger-capacity machines.

Vale had never been anything more than an interim measure. It was barely acceptable for motorcycles, and never for cars. Cars in the 1920s and '30s raced on open roads, competed in speed trials and set intra-capital records, but police clamped down as speeds increased and the population grew. Superspeedways like Maroubra in Sydney, and Richmond and Aspendale in Victoria (the birthplace of four-wheel motorsport), along with hill climbs and sprints, provided closed-road opportunities. But they, too, were dangerous. Go off the side of the Olympia Motor Speedway bowl at Maroubra and survival was uncertain.

In 1928 the Victorian Light Car Club made a breakthrough. It staged the first Australian Grand Prix on an almost perfectly rectangular 10.4-kilometre closed-road course at Phillip Island in Victoria. One of the four right-hand corners, the only turns on the track, was called Hell; another at the end of a long straight was called Heaven.

The mayor of Bathurst at the time, Martin Griffin, had watched Phillip Island with great interest. Griffin was by some accounts a motorsport enthusiast. What is more likely is that he was a sharp-eyed entrepreneur who only ever saw Vale as a stopgap; his real goal was to attract cars and bikes to a purpose-built motor-racing track that would be Australia's first. Phillip Island was a step in the right direction, but it was makeshift: a public road converted to a racetrack. What if he were to build a racetrack and disguise it as a road?

If he built it, not only would the competitors come, Griffin reasoned, but the spectators would be sure to follow. His audacious plan required such subterfuge—and perhaps even complicity—from public officials that if he'd implemented it in today's world of accountability, it may well have brought down a government.

Once a worker on the railways, Griffin had the gift of the gab. He was regarded by his constituency and parliamentarians in Macquarie Street, home of the New South Wales Government, as one of the finest orators in the land. He became mayor of Bathurst in 1931, the year Vale began operation, and there is convincing evidence that he had already begun planning the circuit's successor.

Griffin saw the stars align. The Great Depression, which shook the world in 1929 and deepened in Australia in the 1930s (GDP declined by 10 per cent and unemployment was beyond 30 per cent) meant that schemes contrived to provide funds for public works were likely to get up, especially if there was a political imperative. And politics were rife in Bathurst. Its representative in parliament at the turn of the 1930s was local man Ben Chifley, who would become Australia's sixteenth prime minister after

PROLOGUE

World War II. Throughout the 1930s he was a staunch Labor Party man, hugely influential in the Bathurst region and vehemently opposed to New South Wales premier Jack Lang's breakaway wing of the party. Chifley was a thorn in Lang's side. If Lang was going to keep Chifley sweet, a bit of pork-barrelling was in order.

Bald Hills was the steeply rising range to the south of the Vale circuit. There were goat tracks joining the two. Even today, committed entry-fee-evaders can find a way into the Mount Panorama track with a bit of cross-country hiking from the Vale road. Griffin was unimpressed with the name. Bald Hills? Hardly inspirational. And he decided its Aboriginal name, Wahluu, known to the Council even then, was less so. In 1934, as his plans unfolded, he held a public competition through *The National Advocate* (later to become the *Western Advocate*), a newspaper partly owned by Ben Chifley's family, to find a new name. Local girl Kathleen Walsh had hiked to the top of what is now Skyline, had a Banjo Paterson moment as she observed the 'sunlit plains extended' and suggested Mount Panorama. The 10 shillings prize she earned then would be worth $50 today—a lot of buying power in an economic depression. (On the other hand, if she'd kept the Riddle/Sheehan 10-shilling note she was given—a rare issue—it would be worth up to $40,000 today on the collectors' market.)

There is every possibility that Chifley, known to be a motoring enthusiast—and the man who later said, 'She's a beauty!' when he saw the first post-war FX Holden at its line-off ceremony, at which he was officiating as prime minister—was well aware of Griffin's scheme to build a racetrack by subterfuge with public money. It's likely also that Eric Spooner, the New South Wales Minister for Local Government and Secretary for Public Works, was in on the scam. But if they were, a pre-internet society and a bureaucracy protected by formal communication allowed them to avoid any hint of collusion.

Mike Kable grew up on the Vale circuit. For years people believed his family owned the grand old home that was on Kable's Corner, one of the trickiest parts of the circuit's track. But on a drive around one day I was dissuaded from that notion when he pointed out a much more modest dwelling set back from the road. There were many Kables in the Central West, all descendants of the First Fleeter Henry Kable. The Kables had been beneficiaries of an initial land grant by the colonial government. They even owned the land on which the Royal Hotel, so much a part of the early history of Mount Panorama, stands. But none of it was Mike's. He simply held the knowledge of how the Mountain came into being and was seeking confirmation.

On 30 August 1957 he received his answer from Bathurst's town clerk K.M. Forrest (not the Forrest of Forrest's Elbow). It was enlightening:

> I enclose herein a copy of information which has been taken from Council's 1936 records and from which you will see that the scheme was first mooted by the late Alderman Martin Griffin, Mayor of Bathurst for a period of 10 years, and the work was put in hand as a scheme for the relief of the unemployed, during the depression years. The road at that stage was intended purely as a scenic road. Mr W. Adams was the Council's City engineer.

PROLOGUE

> On the resignation of Mr Adams, Mr Hugh Reid became responsible for the road and many features were redesigned. The road is not [sic] banked as it is a road racing track.

On the surface it seemed Mike had his story but Griffin had contrived to make it someone else's idea. In 1935, even before works began, a delegation of motorsport luminaries had been invited to a Bathurst City Council meeting to discuss motorsport on the Mountain; they included Ray White, the secretary of the Auto Cycle Union of NSW, and John (J.O.) Sherwood, later to form Empire Speedways and at the time the most powerful member of the Light Car Club of NSW and an enthusiastic and prominent racing driver. They were deliberately scheduled to be last on the agenda, when people were eager to get away. The Council, it is recorded, showed little interest in a racing track—one alderman, a dairy farmer, was quoted by Sherwood as saying that motor racing would cause his cows to run dry. But the seed of the idea had been sown, and the politicians had created distance between themselves and the concept.

'It is understood that Mr John Sherwood, as President of the N.S.W. Light Car Club—which body organised the first races—made the suggestion that the scenic road become a racing circuit,' said Bathurst's town clerk in response to Mike Kable's query. It was an artful reply, in today's terms a fine piece of corporate chicanery.

In December 1936, federal government funds of £7000 (equivalent to $700,000 today) topped up the state government's contribution of £27,830 ($2.78 million today) for the new 'scenic road', and a cautiously worded acceptance from Bathurst City Council to the federal government noted that the Auto Cycle Union, which conducted the Vale races, should be told that the construction of a road to Mount Panorama would soon begin.

The smokescreen had been well prepared.

In fairness, implementing the project as an unemployment relief scheme worked sensationally. Up to 230 men at a time, tightly supervised—even the impact of smokos on progress was factored in—used picks and shovels to clear the ground. In its lower reaches, the area was farmland, but higher up it was almost as impenetrable as the Blue Mountains had been when the early explorers crossed it.

Hughie Reid, who replaced Bathurst town engineer Adams as the designer of the project, appeared to be—on the face of it—a naturally talented race-circuit designer. Viewed through the prism of history, he may have even been one of the best in the world.

During its construction, the 'scenic road' was widened from 18 to 24 feet (5.4 to 7.3 metres), as noted in Council minutes. Corners became more open and progressive. Run-off areas were carved into paddocks. But the biggest giveaway about where the design came from is in an official photograph taken of Mayor Griffin at the top of the mountain. Alongside him is Don Bain, acknowledged racing master of the Vale circuit, and Cec Weatherby, one of Bain's main rivals. The scenic road, obviously, had had expert help.

Mount Panorama rose 862 metres above sea level at Skyline, the highest point of the circuit. There was 174 metres of vertical rise from Pit Straight to the top of the mountain, a rise of about 1:6 in 3 kilometres. The gradient out of the right-hand sweeper at the top of Mountain Straight was greater than

PROLOGUE

11 per cent—difficult even now but murder on the cars and bikes of the time.

Bathurst City councillor Walter J. McPhillamy, landowner and former mayor, gave up 15 acres (6 hectares) at the top of the circuit for what Council minutes recorded as 'a children's playground'. Instead, it provided parking and camping access. McPhillamy was rewarded by having the area—which includes one of the most exciting corners in world motorsport—named McPhillamy Park in perpetuity. Hughie Reid got Reid Park, where a plaque exists to this day, and Mayor Griffin is recognised in Griffin's Bend off Mountain Straight.

Suddenly Mount Panorama was no longer a secret. John Sherwood, who later specialised in giving grandiose names to speedway events (nothing, it seemed, was ever less than a 'world title'), succeeded in securing the actual Australian Grand Prix for the opening car meeting. Ray White took a leaf from Sherwood's book: unable to run the Australian Motorcycle Grand Prix or TT, he invented the Australian 150th Celebrations TT.

Over the Easter weekend in 1938, motorcycles and cars would both compete at the first purpose-built motor-racing track in Australia—each on successive days. When that news got out there was no turning back. Yet those in control of the government voice had had sufficient time to manage the message. There were no protests, and no one seemed aggrieved by the secondment of the public purse.

Mike Kable never wrote his story. In fact, as time passed, he toed the corporate line: 'Officials of the Light Car Club of NSW heard about the new road in 1937'—not so; it was 1935—'and headed by their president John Sherwood conferred with Alderman Griffin about the prospect of turning the circuit into a regular motor-racing venue. The idea appealed to Alderman Griffin,' Mike wrote in 'The Bathurst Story', in a 1974 motor-racing book called *One for the Road*. It's a shame that in the political ducking and weaving necessary even then to avoid damnation for a good idea, Griffin contrived to step aside from the limelight in which he deserved to bask.

Mount Panorama simply became, from its inception, the pre-eminent motor-racing circuit in Australia, and one of the most prominent in the world. It created heroes and legends. Mike Kable was responsible at least in part for their discovery. His newspaper columns provided powerful support to young talent. (In 1999, when Formula One star and former Bathurst racer Mark Webber's Mercedes-Benz crashed not once but twice at Le Mans, it was Kable who stomped down to the incident site in the middle of the night to gather the evidence that proved the car was at fault, not the driver.)

When Mike succumbed to cancer in 2000, aged 65, the Australian Supercars governing body inaugurated its annual Mike Kable 'Young Gun' Award, for the rookie of the year, in his honour.

Part 1

The Legends

Two drivers stand tall among the many who have seized success at Mount Panorama. One won at the highest level on two wheels and four, the only person to do so. The other made his name synonymous with the Mountain. Tragically, both died in the pursuit of their profession.

1

The Master of the Mountain

Gregg Hansford is the only top-line competitor to have won at Mount Panorama on two and four wheels. He won the Australian Senior and Unlimited grands prix on bikes, and the Bathurst 1000 and Bathurst 12 Hour. Hansford's skill and his bravery—on the bikes especially—epitomise the ethos of the Mountain circuit. Yet Hansford came second in the greatest race he ever contested on the Mountain.

It was Good Friday 1974 and the media manager of the first truly independent motorcycle grand prix at Australia's greatest race circuit illegally led a small party of journalists to an out-of-bounds area on Conrod Straight, the fastest and potentially most dangerous place on Mount Panorama—and, in fact, on all racetracks in Australia. Their purpose was to witness a phenomenon that would change the face of racing and elevate motorcycle competition to an entirely new level. If it failed, though, it would bring the sport into public disrepute. On that morning it was an each-way proposition.

A new breed of super grand prix machines was expected to break through the 300-kilometre-per-hour barrier.

Only two months previously, the same bikes—spearheaded by Yamaha's four-cylinder TZ750A and ridden by world champion Giacomo Agostini (he ultimately won fifteen world titles)—had come perilously close to the triple-ton on the banked track of Florida's Daytona 200.

But now, the bikes were at Mount Panorama, ridden not by Agostini but by two young Australians, not untried but not yet proven. One had turned 22 earlier that week; the other was still 21.

Gregg Hansford and Warren Willing were both entered in the twenty-lap, 123-kilometre Australian Unlimited Grand Prix that weekend on the enormously powerful machines, along with nine other riders including internationals Pat Hennen from the United States and Anglo-American Ron Grant. But from the outset, the focus was just on the two Australians—Hansford and Willing were the poster boys of a new breed of motorcycle racing emerging in Australia.

Conrod Straight is a killer. Of the 21 deaths at Mount Panorama since its inception, twelve have occurred on the 1.9-kilometre downhill plunge from Forrest's Elbow at its top to Murray's Corner at its base. As speed builds, the ability of a vehicle—car or motorcycle—to remain in controllable contact with the ground changes exponentially. And aerodynamics in the 1970s was largely a black science, unknown to some and experimental to others.

Two years before, journalists had stood in a relatively safe spectator area at the base of Conrod and witnessed what was said to be the greatest Improved Touring-Car race of all time. It was the third round of the 1972 Australian Touring Car Championship, and five-time champion Ian 'Pete' Geoghegan, in a locally modified Ford Falcon GTHO, battled four-time champion Allan Moffat in his US-built Ford Mustang. They traded position more than twenty times in thirteen laps, their cars perpetually imbalanced as they slipstreamed for advantage on the bumps and corrugations of Conrod. When they returned to the pits, with Geoghegan the hair's-breadth victor, both cars bore the scars of body damage from their 260-kilometre-per-hour grinding, suspension-bottoming contact with the Conrod tarmac. Moffat's Mustang was covered with oil from Geoghegan's car, which had split hoses.

Three years before that, the pits had been silenced when crews looked to the second hump of Conrod—the straight had two distinct lift-off elevations—to see the fatal crash that claimed 22-year-old emerging star Bevan Gibson. One Bathurst race meeting later the veteran Tom Sulman replicated the inversion, in his elderly Lotus Eleven Climax, again with a fatal result.

Some of the journalists who stood in the paddock bordering Conrod on Good Friday 1974 had been at Mount Panorama for all those races and incidents. For the real cognoscenti there is no difference between fast bikes and fast cars. Bravery, skill and mastery over mechanical elements are universally appreciated, and Mount Panorama provided the common ground.

In truth, the spectator crowds were different then. The bikes at the time had a more blue-collar leaning. But Hansford and Willing were changing that perception. Thanks to smart young promoters like Vincent Tesoriero—a real force in the development of the sport—a new breed of motorsport enthusiast was emerging. That was reflected in the journalists at this first modern-era bikes-only meeting at the Mountain.

And now it was the moment of truth.

The journalists gathered at the fence, which was nothing more than a three-strand restraint to keep the cattle out. The media manager pushed them back. 'Leave at least a 50-metre gap,' he implored. It seemed prudent. No one had ever been allowed here before, and he'd lose his job and face a huge sanction if something went wrong. But what an opportunity it would be—what a unique experience—if it all went right.

And then the bikes were there. Even on the first lap of the first practice session they were getting air, their front wheels losing contact with the ground and pawing at the sky. And it wasn't just the sight. The sound was awesome—the in-line four-cylinder two-strokes emitted high-pitched screams like no other bikes did. They were so loud you could hear them coming, and the sound remained long after they'd gone, chasing them down into the braking area.

An assault of air surrounded the bikes. Turbulence creates a physical force field. For every kilometre per hour of speed, the corresponding air resistance on the front fairing of a race bike increases by a multiple of three. If you're standing close enough, it's like a near miss from a punch thrown by a prize-fighter.

No one had ever felt anything like it before, not even from the cars. The slippery open-wheelers that had dominated Mount

Panorama in the 1960s travelled like arrows through the air, and the touring cars were rudimentarily aerodynamic, but the bikes were built like bricks. Their fairings, designed to guide airflow around the rider, still presented a near-impenetrable wall to the atmosphere through which they were passing. Even now, almost half a century on, MotoGP teams are still experimenting with the wings, tabs and winglets that have become the stock-in-trade of Formula One. The Federation Internationale de Motocyclisme (FIM), the world governing body of motorcycle sport, is refusing many of their attempts, partly on the grounds of safety. The winglets impose new dynamics and no one is certain how to manage them.

The Mount Panorama journalists stood in awe of this new sensation, some of them attempting to mark the braking points at the end of Conrod as the bikes tipped left into Murray's Corner. At such increased speeds, the pressure on brakes and the need to find new points of no return for keeping the throttle wide open would become critical. There was a windsock on top of the second hump, an essential guide to the cross-winds that could catch competitors out; strong windage can be fatal, but the windsock that day was almost limp, every now and then catching a playful breeze.

By the third lap, the journalists had become active participants. Some had brought cameras—telephotos with mirror lenses—to diffuse the background. Viewed through a 200-millimetre lens, American Pat Hennen appeared over the second hump and for a split second his front wheel—a good metre in the air—caught a slight gust and he turned sideways, pointing directly at the photographer. The photographer prided himself on his reflexes: the adrenaline hit his stomach with a cold rush and he simultaneously took a step to the side. But Hennen was gone. In the instant that the photographer had reacted, the American—travelling at 75 metres per second—had already sped the length of two football fields past the journalists, corrected his own trajectory and was braking for Murray's Corner.

It was a shocking moment—an indication of the extreme vulnerability of the position.

The media manager gathered up the journalists, who didn't complain as they returned to the pits.

The atmosphere was charged with excitement. With huge grins on their faces, people were describing, more than anything else, the traction—or rather the lack of it—of these new machines. They would wheelspin in every gear. The power band, although reasonably wide, was still brutal. Riders would reach the point at which it lit up—at around 8000 rpm—and they'd enter a new world of control.

While the media pack had been on Conrod Straight they'd missed the action on the opposing Mountain Straight, to the west. For the first time ever, the bikes were monowheeling over the hump halfway up the mountain. Competitors on the 350-cc machines—half the size of the new bikes, but still potent—were seeing the Yamaha TZ750s open 200 metres on them from the entry point at Hell Corner to the exit at Griffin's Bend. Two hundred metres in just under a kilometre! It was phenomenal.

They were going as fast up the Mountain as they were coming down. But the fabled 300 kilometres per hour was out of reach. Not because the bikes weren't capable. With gearing on a long flat road, of course they could do it, but the circuit couldn't provide the playing surface. It would take a foolish rider to hold the thing flat down Conrod. There was no absence of bravery, but all the skill in the world just couldn't provide a 300-kilometre-per-hour result when the chassis and suspension weren't in synch with the track. Two-eighty would have to do. It was still as fast as anyone had travelled on Mount Panorama.

Tyre performance became a major topic of consideration. Wide, slick tyres, now a mainstay of motorcycle competition, were then in their infancy—in fact pretty much unheard of. Dunlop had devised a treaded tyre, quite narrow, for the TZ750, but it was inadequate, especially at Mount Panorama.

Hansford and Willing listened to the comments and quietly smiled. They'd both been at Daytona two months before, Hansford riding one of the TZ750s, Willing acting as his mechanic, and both of them learning from Australia's world 250-cc champion Kel Carruthers, who was running Yamaha's US team. Carruthers had been instrumental in the development of the new bike. He'd risked his life riding the prototype when no one else would throw a leg over it, and had convinced Yamaha to increase the wheelbase of the bike to settle down the death-twitches that threatened to throw riders off during swift changes of direction.

Hansford had been unsuccessful at Daytona, but he'd learned a lot about the TZ750's characteristics. Willing, the quietly spoken race engineer with a prodigious riding talent, had learned a lot too—not from the seat but on the tools. Now at Bathurst he and Hansford were rivals. Willing applied his technical knowledge to his bike. Hansford, not mechanically astute, had the self-belief to ride around most problems and was content to do so.

Both, however, had a secret weapon. They'd brought back to Australia a limited stock of new semi-slick rear tyres that had been developed just for Daytona. While others were talking up, with some trepidation, their lack of traction, Willing and Hansford knew they had an edge.

Gregg Hansford and Warren Willing came from opposite ends of town. Hansford had been born into privilege. His dad Harry had died when Hansford was in his teens and he'd lived with his mum, Edna, in what was essentially Hansford's Compound: six acres (2.4 hectares) in Nestor Avenue in the upmarket Brisbane suburb of Bardon. When Hansford married Julie, a model, when they were both quite young, there was plenty of room and money to build their own home on the same property, with both houses nestled around the swimming pool. Hansford belonged to a motorsport clique in Queensland, and most of its members were wealthy. Charlie O'Brien was one; his family owned quarries and transport companies, and at various times he drove for both Allan Moffat and the Holden Dealer Team. Bruce Allison was another; his dad, Big Col, had multiple businesses that helped fund Bruce's open-wheeler career, ultimately in the fearsome V8-powered Formula 5000 cars both in Australia and the UK. Bruce would marry Julie's twin sister.

Warren Willing, just three months younger than Hansford, was from the Western suburbs of Sydney. His parents, service station owners Barbara and Brian, had a daughter, Rhonda, and three boys—Len, Warren and Glenn—all of them motorcycle mad. The Willings went to school with the Sayle boys Douglas, Murray and Jeff; along with another member of their Macquarie Boys' High alma mater, Joe Eastmure, they comprised the Macquarie Motorcycle Mafia. The Sayle boys' mum Marie knew them all: she worked in the school's canteen. The Sayles sucked the Willings into motorcycling. Harold and Marie Sayle had been going to Mount Panorama and camping in the Bathurst sportsground since the mid-1950s, initially travelling there in a sidecar until the kids came along. The Willing–Sayle link was sealed when Murray married Rhonda Willing.

Between them all, there was a cornucopia of opportunity. Vince Tesoriero, who inaugurated the Castrol Six Hour production race and coined the descriptor 'superbike'—a term now universally used, with a world championship named after it—recognised something special in both Gregg Hansford and Warren Willing. In Tesoriero's view they were the pick of both litters, immensely talented and promotable, and they fitted in perfectly with the youth formula he was developing. Tesoriero was looking for new adventure heroes, determined to turn motorcycling into a sport that would rival surfing for the attention of a young Australian public. As well as circuit racing, he was also active in motocross, and his talent spotting was becoming legendary. As he did for Hansford and Willing on tarmac, he fostered Stephen Gall and Anthony Gunter on dirt—and made them all stars.

'Gregg was a big strapping lad who looked too big to fit on a bike,' Tesoriero recalled. 'He was introverted too.' In 1973, Hansford turned up at Mount Panorama for the first time on a Yamaha TZ350 and with natural ability he'd won the Australian Senior TT, then backed up to win the Unlimited TT as well. It was a stunning debut and had brought him to the attention of the motorcycle industry. His new TZ750 for 1974 came from Queensland distributor Annand & Thompson.

Willing was ambitious, more so than Hansford, but he lacked the funds and the acumen to seek support. In 1974 it was Tesoriero who took the proposition of a new-look motorcycle series to cigarette company Rothmans. Through a haze of smoke at their Granville headquarters, Tesoriero overcame his own non-smoking habit to extract enough funds to run the Chesterfield Australian Grand Prix and to purchase Willing a TZ750 Yamaha on which he could match-race Hansford. The Chesterfield $20,000 Grand Prix, with $1000 going directly to the winner, was the richest Australian motorcycle race ever staged at the time. The Auto Cycle Union of NSW, long-term promoters of the Mount Panorama motorcycle races, could not believe their good fortune.

The Australian Racing Drivers' Club, promoters of the car racing, had in the 1973 off-season decided to concentrate on their burgeoning long-distance production car race in October. With costs escalating well beyond the risk-to-reward ratio, they had decided to abandon their traditional Easter date. The Auto Cycle Union, armed with its cigarette money, leapt right in.

It almost came unstuck on the morning of Easter Saturday. A preliminary race to the Grand Prix, the Bathurst Unlimited, provided a first hit-out for the big bikes. Hansford made a slow start but then surged to the front on lap two while Willing, easing himself into a day of racing in several classes, was content to use the race as a warm-up.

Not so Bryan Hindle. The quietly spoken, lightly framed, deeply religious and incredibly talented Western Sydney chemist had stunned motorcycling back in '71 when he'd beaten Giacomo Agostini fair and square at Sydney's Oran Park. 'Ago' had been brought to Australia by tyre-industry entrepreneur Bob Jane to promote his new MV Agusta franchise, and the Oran Park race was expected to be nothing more than a demonstration run. Instead Hindle took the fight to the Italian maestro and claimed the flag. It's a toss-up which of them was more surprised.

Now at Mount Panorama on Easter Saturday 1974, Hindle was on a new TZ750 and he was challenging Hansford. It was three-time world champion Kenny Roberts who later wrote of the Australian, 'If you pass Gregg Hansford in a corner you know you're going to crash.' The naturally talented Hansford had such an innate feel for the limit of adhesion that he was on it all the time. Roberts' assertion was that to pass Hansford, you had to go beyond the limit, courting disaster.

Hindle had a go—not just anywhere, but around the *outside* at McPhillamy Park, the unsighted left-hand sweeper at the top of the circuit. A few days later, from his hospital bed, Hindle admitted his mistake: 'The last thing I remember is fighting the bike as it went over on its side. I thought I had it back up, but it was too late. It all happened in a tenth of a second and I had no time to think of crashing or to be afraid.'

Hindle and his cartwheeling machine both crashed at 150 kilometres per hour. The energy had hardly dissipated when they collided with the stone wall of the McPhillamy Park entry gates.

The result was that Hindle broke his pelvis in four places, shattered four vertebrae and fractured his left arm in two places. It took months and another operation for the bones in his arm to begin to knit. The Mount Panorama crash was the turning point in what could have been a brilliant career. Hindle was back on a bike in October to win—and be disqualified from—the Castrol Six Hour production race, but after several more crashes he kept a promise to his wife and family to retire from the sport and take up a safer recreational pursuit. He chose powered hang gliding. In February 1978 he died when his glider flamed out, crashing to the ground at an air show near Dubbo, 200 kilometres north-west of Bathurst.

In the final four laps of their battle, Hansford and Hindle had carved more than 5 seconds off the Mount Panorama lap record. Slashing the record had been expected but a reduction of that magnitude was awe inspiring. The next day, in race two of the Unlimited—still warming up for the main event—Hansford reduced the record again by another second, down to 2 minutes 25.89 seconds. Willing, tentative, moved to second behind Hansford but missed his braking mark at Hell Corner on the turn into Mountain Straight, went up the escape road and then chased down and passed Pat Hennen and veteran Ron Toombs to reclaim his runner-up spot at the flag. It was two from two for Hansford.

When the flag was raised for the main event, neither Hansford nor Willing got away well. Rob Hinton, scion of one of Mount Panorama's most revered racing families, won the sprint to Hell Corner. But he was swamped up Mountain Straight. By the time they reached the top of the mountain, Vince Tesoriero's dreams had been realised—Hansford and Willing were sharing the lead. Daylight was second.

Mount Panorama organisers have traditionally been loose with the figures when it comes to estimating crowd attendances. In order to boost numbers and satisfy commercial investors, there have been times when heads have been counted twice; when caterers and officials have found their way onto spreadsheets reserved for paying customers; when a whole weekend's crowd has been condensed into one day's reporting. But that Easter Sunday, 23,394 genuine payers—arguably the largest crowd at any Australian motorcycle meeting up to that point—saw the greatest race of all time.

Gregg Hansford rode his bike like an Austrian ski instructor, shoulders spread broadly like a bird of prey, looming over the machine, his weight and strength bearing down on the fulcrum of contact with the ground. It was not a natural stance for a motorcycle racer but because of his size it was all he could do, and he made the most of it. Warren Willing rode like a ballet dancer. He used his slender, flexible body economically. Every movement was one of beauty, synchronised with his machine, and there was no wasted effort.

For twenty laps Hansford and Willing cut and thrust at each other, eating away at the lap record on virtually every lap. Down Conrod Straight, one of them would slide into the other's slipstream. You didn't have to be close. The vortex created by these new Formula 750s trailed back almost 50 metres behind the rear tyre, like the tail of Halley's Comet, so you'd hold back, picking up speed in this new aerodynamic wonderland, then pull out at the last second with such velocity that you'd rocket past with an advantage the other rider couldn't match.

On the first hump of Conrod they were racing side by side with both wheels in the air . . .

It was unprecedented.

Hansford's advantage was in the braking area. Riders use their bodies as air brakes—sitting up suddenly above the airstream of the fairing to substantially slow the bike. Most of the braking force is on the front wheel, and Hansford's strength and stance gave him an advantage.

On the last lap Hansford led Willing down Conrod into Murray's Corner. He led again to the apex of the corner but then—suddenly—there was Willing beside him, edging millimetres ahead towards the chequered flag.

For years Willing would taunt his good friend about it, saying that it was a planned manoeuvre, that he'd set him up laps before for this one run at the flag. And that could be true. Willing's advantage was his lighter weight; he'd perhaps set his bike up slightly differently, or possibly conserved his trick rear tyre a little more for better traction. Whatever the reason, when it mattered, he'd had greater drive out of the corner. And he won.

Between them the pair had decimated Hansford's lap record, bringing it down 2.5 seconds to 2 minutes 23.35 seconds. That was an amazing effort; it doesn't happen in defensive competition. Like Pete Geoghegan and Allan Moffat two years before, Willing and Hansford had etched themselves into immortality on Mount Panorama. And to a degree it didn't matter who had won. It was the race that counted.

Their battle at Bathurst set up both Willing and Hansford for international careers. Hansford, better connected and more financially assured, joined Team Kawasaki Australia, managed by ace tuner Neville Doyle, and went to Europe where he won ten world championship grands prix in the 250-cc and 350-cc categories, finishing second in the world title for both classes in 1978, and second and third in 1979. He was regarded as one of the most naturally talented riders in the world, perhaps handicapped only by his own laid-back style. 'Win at all costs' just wasn't in his lexicon. There's the oft-repeated story of his bike sitting on the grid at Assen in the Netherlands, ready to go, with Hansford still asleep in his motorhome, discovered only after a frantic search. He won that Grand Prix.

Willing, equally talented but perhaps not as recognised, hit the privateer trail, racing with his extended Sayle family. He never won a grand prix. He crashed in the North West 200 at Coleraine, Northern Ireland, in 1979, on a street circuit so dangerous it made Mount Panorama look insipid. His life was saved by a marshal who clamped his severed femoral artery for several long minutes until help arrived. Willing's brother-in-law Murray Sayle was in the same event. 'I arrived at the scene and there was wreckage over the track and the drain beyond,' he remembered. 'Warren was maybe 20 metres off the track. He was conscious and all I could do was hold him and tell him to hang on until help arrived.'

Willing never raced again. It took eighteen operations to save his leg. But he went on to a brilliant career as a race engineer, working with Kenny Roberts to fettle Kenny Jr to two world championships. Willing passed away in Sydney in 2015, succumbing to prostate cancer.

Hansford's moment of two-wheel truth came at the Belgian Grand Prix on the daunting Spa-Francorchamps circuit in 1981, when a crash badly damaged his knee. It wasn't the stuff of retirement, but Hansford had had enough. He suffered monstrously from homesickness. Although Julie travelled with him and together they'd move about in a luxuriously equipped motorhome to avoid the pain of hotel-room living, Hansford always wanted nothing more than to return home. The adulation of the crowds was one thing, but back home there were tradies who'd line up at the end of each working day on the hilly roads of Bardon and cheer as Hansford popped wheelies just for them. Kawasaki gave him one each of his 250 and 350 grand prix machines, and there are stories of local police turning a blind eye as he gave them a workout near his house.

Besides, he had the next phase of his career waiting.

Hansford would go on to become the only competitor, ever, to win the Australian Unlimited TT, the Bathurst 1000 and the Bathurst 12 Hour all at Mount Panorama. The last two would come in a rush, six months apart and almost twenty years after his motorcycle successes.

Hansford's close friend Charlie O'Brien had given him his first taste of four-wheel action back in the early '70s: a private test day with a Torana at Lakeside circuit in Queensland. He was such a natural talent that O'Brien talked him up to the best in the land. In 1977, four-time champion Allan Moffat, at the top of his game with his Falcon GT coupés, was so impressed that he hired him, without testing, to co-drive with Colin Bond in Moffat's second car in the Bathurst 1000.

But Hansford's motorcycle commitments, and a recurring problem from a crash injury, ruled him out of what could have been the most celebrated debut of all time. The race went down in history—the controversial Ford formation 1–2 finish, where Moffat led Bond over the line by half a car's length. Belgian Jacky Ickx shared the win with Moffat, and it was sports-car and open-wheeler ace Alan Hamilton who co-drove with Bond.

When Hansford returned home from Belgium in 1981, Moffat pounced.

The Canadian–Australian firebrand, winner already of four Bathurst long-distance endurance races—including one with a flag-to-flag solo drive—had taken up with Mazda, forcing through homologation for the tiny RX-7 to be recognised not as a sports car but as a touring car. The year-long battle to win acceptance had been hard-fought, and Moffat now needed drivers capable of guiding the high-revving vehicles to victory on tracks that were purpose-built for big-torque V8s. 'Mazda gave me as my co-driver Yoshimi Katayama, the guy they rated as their grand master,' Moffat said. 'The little veteran was a small capacity motorcycle ace. He'd claimed second for Suzuki in the now defunct 50-cc world motorcycle title and then moved up to 125 cc, where he scored four world championship grands prix victories. He was a person who knew how to maintain pace in the absence of power.

'I matched Yoshi with a motorcycle ace of my own. Some said I was taking a huge risk by giving Gregg his first-ever competitive drive in Australia's biggest motor race. But I wasn't worried. By then I'd tested him and he confirmed what I suspected—he was as good and talented and right-minded as any driver I'd known.'

Hansford drove for Moffat's Mazda for three years. For the 1984 Bathurst 1000, their last race—a rule change had made the car uncompetitive—Moffat had a plan. He entered two cars but only two drivers. Moffat would take the more powerful Mazda with the new peripherally ported 13B engine. Hansford would drive the less powerful car with the older 12A engine. When they got to the point of the race where a driver change was mandatory, they would both swap to the leading car and retire the other.

But fifteen laps into the 163-lap race, Moffat's car seized and he moved back to the less powerful one. For the rest of that long day Moffat and Hansford tore around the course, hopeful that the Holdens of Peter Brock and John Harvey in front of them would fail. They didn't; the Mazda came third. Hansford mounted the cars' podium at Mount Panorama for the first time.

After that, Hansford was a driver in demand. He raced Colin Bond's Alfa Romeos and Dick Johnson's Mustang and Ford Sierra. The Johnson–Hansford relationship ended with some acrimony: ahead of the 1988 season, Hansford found out he no longer had a drive only when he learned from a third party that John Bowe had taken his place. Johnson, a fair and reasonable man, still regrets the way it happened, calling it 'a commercial decision'.

Then Moffat again found money, this time from generous ANZ Bank sponsorship; Hansford was back with the boss in a white Sierra for the 1988 Bathurst 1000. To run it, Moffat had hired a Swiss genius called Ruedi Eggenberger who'd won at Bathurst the year before only to be disqualified. Ruedi came armed with a laptop computer, unusual for its time; an engine algorithm that defied understanding; lead driver Klaus Niedzwiedz; and a sudden inability to speak English, so he had no way of communicating with the local officials who had disqualified him the previous year.

A little more than halfway through the race, Niedzwiedz opened a full lap on the field. Moffat had enjoyed just one 29-lap stint, the last competitive kilometres he'd ever drive at Bathurst, then the car was handed to Hansford for a stint.

'It didn't feel right. Something was gnawing at me,' Moffat said. 'Organisers pulled a pace car on Gregg, so they could send out a clean-up van to pick up broken cars and debris. Gregg fell into line, third in the queue behind lapped cars. In a turbo-charged car, air temperature is critical. You need to gap the car in front to give yourself clear air.

'When the race went green, Gregg brought himself up to speed, but it wasn't as sweet as before. We all knew Gregg could have managed the safety car period better. Ruedi had the bonnet up, then he had the spark plugs out, but nothing will restart a car when its head gasket has blown.'

In the professional world, a mistake like that would be enough to demand dismissal. It's a mark of the respect that Moffat—and the entire motor-racing fraternity—had for Hansford that it didn't happen. He raced on with Moffat, deviating briefly to Glenn Seton's Sierra team.

In 1992 Allan Horsley, the long-term motorsport manager for Mazda who'd managed Allan Moffat's Mazda campaign, and was a firm believer in Hansford, hired him to head Mazda's production car assault on a new event—the James Hardie 12 Hour at Mount Panorama.

The event, first held in 1991, had been the brainstorm of Vince Tesoriero. Convinced that the Bathurst 1000 was becoming brand specific—a race between two marques, Ford and Holden—Tesoriero believed that there was room for an open formula that would showcase production cars on Australia's most testing track.

Horsley entered the race four times, the last time at Sydney's Motorsport Park when it moved from Bathurst. He won it on each occasion. Hansford, his anchor driver, contested three from 1992 to 1994; in succession he claimed a class third, a second and finally an outright first.

'He was the benchmark,' Horsley said. 'You'd look at his lap times, his braking marks, his time on the throttle and then you'd compare everyone else in the team to it.'

Neil Crompton, now the country's leading TV motorsport commentator and then a highly competent race driver with burning ambition, shared the Mazda 12 Hour win with Hansford. 'I was the number two in the car, but he treated me like number one,' Crompton said. 'He was always concerned for your comfort in the car. It was more important to him that you were set up right. Of course—Gregg could drive around problems.'

Larry Perkins—six-time Bathurst 1000 winner (three when he hired Hansford), national Formula Ford and Formula Two champion, European Formula Three champion, Australian Rallycross champion and Rothmans Formula 5000 International Series winner, and with eleven starts one of the most capped of Australia's seventeen Formula One competitors—found Hansford on the top of Skyline. 'I was driving a Lotus Esprit in the 1993 Bathurst 12 Hour and we'd put it on pole so I was at the front of the field,' Perkins remembered. 'I got stuck behind this Mazda for several laps and I was seriously impressed with his lines and his pace. He was right up there—not ten-tenths but pretty close, and he was picking the same braking and turning points and apexing at exactly the same spot every time. There was no wasted effort. He was being kind to the car and keeping up the pace.

'I decided to find out who he was. I was looking for a co-driver for my own effort in the Bathurst 1000 later in the year.'

Hansford had just passed an unintentional audition in front of one of the most astute race engineers and drivers on the Australian domestic circuit.

Six months later, Hansford and Perkins won the Bathurst 1000 in Perkins' Castrol VP Holden Commodore, just 10 seconds clear of Mark Skaife and Jim Richards in a similar car. It was one of the closest non-pace-car–affected finishes on record. The Perkins effort was so cash-strapped that Hansford had to bring his own fireproof race overalls to the race. 'When we won we both pulled on Castrol rain jackets to walk onto the podium so we'd look like we were in uniforms,' Perkins said.

In that 1993 race, Hansford match-raced both Jim Richards and Mark Skaife in the two stints in which they faced off and, conserving his car for both fuel use and brake wear, he gave away little to the two champions. It was a masterful performance from an essentially part-time driver. When Larry Perkins took the flag just 10.54 seconds ahead of Richards, their race was hailed as 'a triumph of pre-race planning, race-day tactics and sheer driving prowess'. It was Hansford's finest car race, and his name was indelibly in the record books as the only person to triumph at Bathurst on two and four wheels.

The following year he and Perkins finished third and he was booked again for 1995.

But that didn't happen. Nor would Hansford ever have a chance to defend his victory in the James Hardie 12 Hour.

Motorsport in Australia in the 1990s was in a state of great turmoil. There was a huge split forming between Supercars—the 5-litre V8s—and the smaller classes. Teams were crumbling; commercial alliances were either forming or splitting asunder.

Hansford was not a political player. He was a simple man, born to privilege, who lived to have fun. He conducted his business out of a briefcase, dropping in on friends for long amiable chats. There was no chicanery in Hansford's outlook.

But for someone so laid-back, his personal situation had taken a sharp turn. He'd split with Julie, mother of his two boys Ryan and Rhys, and had begun a new relationship with model Carolyn Donovan and they'd had a son, too, named Harrison. More than anything Gregg needed to be in a relationship—whether personally or on the track. He needed support. It had always been available to him in motorsport. In bikes, it was Neville Doyle; they'd travelled the world together, racing in Europe and the US. Then, in car racing, he'd had Allan Moffat, Dick Johnson, Colin Bond, Larry Perkins and—possibly most of all—Allan Horsley. They had been his rocks. He trusted them all.

So when, in late 1994, Hansford was approached to drive in a fledgling 2-litre touring-car series formulated in direct opposition to the Supercars, he sought out his mentors. Unanimously they said no. Two Litres was B-grade, they said, and he was a fully fledged member of the A-team. But Gregg was feeling his oats—he was only 42—and he went ahead anyway. He knew the car owner, Ross Palmer, a lovely, respectful Queenslander, and he knew the race engineer of the car he'd drive. The comfort zone was there.

On 5 March 1995, on the second lap of the very first round of the 2-litre series, Hansford aimed his front-wheel-drive Ford Mondeo into the fast first turn at Phillip Island. The car speared off into a tyre barrier before bouncing back onto the track and into the path of an oncoming car. It was a classic, tragic, T-bone crash. Later, evidence emerged that the fatal impact had occurred in the car's initial contact with the barrier. That brought some relief. It's too horrible to contemplate that Hansford's last moment might have been spent staring down a 200-kilometre-per-hour missile aimed at his door.

'I'd had dinner with him at the circuit the night before the race,' Allan Horsley said. 'He was typical Gregg—content in himself and excited about the things that mattered to him. He told me about Harrison taking his first steps and he confided that he was going to marry Carolyn.'

'I was with friends on Bribie Island,' his son Ryan, now a part-time racer, said. 'They got a phone call and we travelled home all the way to Nan's place at Bardon without anyone saying a word—and with the radio turned off. When we got there a crowd had gathered and I thought, "Gee, Dad must have won the race."'

Gregg Hansford's funeral in Brisbane was one of the largest in motorsport history—the entire board of Mazda flew in for it. (Only Peter Brock's funeral, eleven years later, was larger. It filled St Paul's Cathedral in Melbourne.)

As an outcome of the crash, the regulations for the new 2-litre touring cars were changed, demanding two warm-up laps instead of the traditional single sighting lap. Officials determined that a car that puts its power to the ground through its steer wheels needed more time to bring its rear tyres up to equal temperature.

In the National Motor Racing Museum at the bottom of Conrod Straight, there is a section dedicated to Gregg Hansford. Outside is the monument to Peter Brock.

2

In the Shadow of Brock

Peter Brock and Mount Panorama are ingrained equally in the collective national consciousness, way beyond the popularity of the sport they represent. Name a motorsport racetrack in Australia? Mount Panorama. Name a race driver? Brock. The equation is mathematical: combined, they are larger than the sum of their parts. Brock won the Bathurst 1000 and its predecessor a record nine times. It could have been ten. He made an error in his first-ever race at the Mountain and, arguably, it cost him a debut victory.

It was half a century ago that Peter Brock first came to Mount Panorama. He was lean, roughly hewn in looks and manner, a little dangerous—a wild man from the backblocks of Melbourne. There was nothing 'perfect' about Peter—not back then.

'Peter Perfect', the name by which he'd be known to a legion of fans, would come later, when his skill and determination coupled with his extraordinary success at Mount Panorama would see him crowned King of the Mountain. His most convincing victory, shared with Jim Richards in 1979, was by an unprecedented six laps.

It took a hugely powerful TV network executive to enshrine Brock and his Mountain in folklore. Even Brock could not have done it on his own.

Yet Brock was a legend long before he died. Like Michael Hutchence and Heath Ledger, he was darkly compelling, good and bad to know in equal parts. An early chequered flag has proved no impediment to the growth of his persona.

That Brock died in a high-speed race crash in an open-road rally has only added to the drama of his story. There's a depth to him that few of his genre can eclipse and it's given him longevity.

More than a decade after that crash, his statue stands proudly at the entrance to Mount Panorama—larger than life—a deliberate exaggeration.

Peter Brock never went unnoticed.

In the late 1960s, Brock was recently out of 'nashos', the national military service conscription lottery that picked young men at random according to their birth date. At best, national service put their lives on hold; at worst, it sentenced them to death by combat. Brock was full of resentment. Later, publicly, he removed the two years of compulsory national service from his stated age, as if it didn't exist.

And yet he'd not served in the Vietnam War, as 15,000 other conscripts had, and he'd not been one of the 200 conscripts killed in the war zone. Instead he'd been posted to the Australian Army's Puckapunyal training camp, only 100 kilometres from his home, and later to Kapooka, 340 further kilometres up the road, serving his time building a red-hot racing car based on a tiny Austin A30 saloon with a Holden straight-six motor rammed into its cramped engine bay. He did some of the work in the army's machine shops on the government's tab.

Nashos taught Brock to drink and smoke, chase girls and defy authority. He embraced each with obsessive determination. His lifestyle matched his race pace.

By the time he arrived at Mount Panorama he was already in the midst of his first divorce, aged 24, and he was an emerging star. His raw talent, his dark side—which unsettled some but attracted many—and his aggressive, giant-killing little Nashos-built A30 (just the right vehicle to allow him to thumb his nose at the accepted norms) made him a crowd favourite and people were paying to see him play. A NSW promoter had offered appearance money to bring him across the border from Victoria. Race teams, thin on the ground at the time, eyed him with interest.

Harry Firth, one of the giants of Australian motor racing, got to him first. He also picked up Colin Bond—the yin to Brock's yang—and bound them both to servitude in Holden's first national dealer team. To the public they were the chosen ones—the stars. But inside the team it was a different sort of conscription. Firth didn't pay well, if at all, and he forced Brock and Bond to accept conditions and indignities that would today be totally unacceptable. To give Firth his due, though, perhaps he saw it as tough love, a rite of passage, a knocking off of the rough edges. At least he let them race.

The Bathurst 500 on Mount Panorama, 5 October 1969, was to be Brock's first big hit-out.

The Mountain had already stamped its authority on Australian motor racing. Since its inauguration in 1938 it had earned renown as one of the world's most challenging and daunting racetracks. By Brock's time it had already showcased Australian world champions—Jack Brabham in cars, Kel Carruthers on bikes—and it had made legends out of open-wheeler drivers and racing motorcyclists. Two years before Brock turned up, Confederation of Australian Motor Sport (CAMS) Gold Star winner Kevin Bartlett had become the first-ever driver to lap above the magic 100-mile-per-hour (161-kilometre-per-hour) track average—and had been hailed as much for his bravery as his skill. Mount Panorama over-rewarded the overachievers, but the penalty for overstepping the boundary was severe. Bevan Gibson had died on Conrod Straight just six months before Brock's debut; had he lived, Gibson could easily have challenged Brock for Firth's attention.

There was not a lot in Brock's public persona then that made him appear respectful—not like later in his career, when he was enshrined by his obvious and genuine empathy with his fans. The young Brock was brash, cocky and confident—just another selfish, self-centred racing driver. Mount Panorama was there for his taking.

Until he saw it.

There is nothing like your first sighting of Mount Panorama. For a race driver bred on flat tracks, the sheer scale of the Mountain's contours cannot be envisaged or imagined by any other means. Even today's computer simulations, which many drivers use to learn a new track before they arrive, massively under-call the Mountain.

'Harry [Firth] had to take him for a drive around, show him how to race the Mountain, point out the hazards and where to brake and where to get on the gas,' Colin Bond said, 50 years later. 'He never did that for me.'

There was a tough independence in race drivers then. As Larry Perkins put it: 'If you were good enough, you'd go fast. If you weren't, then you'd go home.' No one was going to help you, not even your teammate. You were expected to work it out for yourself. Later, in the days when race cars grew computers and a driver's every lap and every corner were recorded for all to see, all that changed. Today the teams huddle around laptops to read traces that accurately plot corner speeds, braking points and pedal pressures, track position, slip angles, and a multitude of engine, transmission and suspension geometry inputs that lay bare the skill—or otherwise—of the driver. Teams make changes—to the car or the driver—and get faster according to an algorithm. 'Kids on computer games know more about setting up a car than I ever did,' Jim Richards, seven-time Bathurst 1000 winner, said. 'The closest I ever got to using telemetry is seeing that my teammate is faster at certain points of the track and then going out and trying to beat him.' Usually he did.

Fifty years ago, Brock just knew he needed to be fast. And Firth held the key.

Harry Firth—taciturn, tactical, and not necessarily to be taken at his word—was a Bathurst winner. He'd won in 1963, the inaugural Bathurst 500, in a Ford Cortina GT, and again in 1967 in the very first Ford Falcon GT. He'd built both for the Ford Motor Corporation. Before that, before the race moved to Mount Panorama, he'd won two of the three Armstrong 500s at Victoria's Phillip Island racetrack—one in a Mercedes-Benz and the other in a Ford Falcon.

So Firth knew the Mountain, and he knew long-distance racing. In 1969 he was appointed to run the Holden Dealer Team, the first time the factory had truly put its stamp on a motor-racing effort.

General Motors in the US had imposed an international ban on motor racing but Australian sales chief John Bagshaw used an intricate matrix of financial deception to fund a local team through dealer contribution. To succeed in the showroom, Holden needed to go racing. Bagshaw knew that every time Ford won, unopposed, it was a direct hit to Holden's bottom line. Any way you looked at it, it was a factory team he wanted and Firth, poached from rival Ford where he'd been a proven winner, was expected to deliver.

Taking Brock on an exploratory lap of the Mountain, as much as it went against the grain, was part of the deal. It's likely it was mandatory for both of them. Firth knew where the camber of the road could be the driver's friend; where to position the car under Big Tree, the reference point at the top of the Mountain that appears on no circuit maps and that only drivers know; how to drift the car in order to save brakes; how to graze the drainage grate at the fearsomely fast McPhillamy Park sweeper to position the car for the exit; and how to brake and change gears for Skyline so that you wouldn't launch off into space in the days before they inserted a gravel pit and a bigger fence.

Firth's tuition was invaluable to Brock and it was a favour Brock later passed on to a young Craig Lowndes on his Mount Panorama Supercars debut. 'We didn't drive the track,' recalled Lowndes, Brock's natural successor. 'Peter just sat me down and talked me around. I was way out of my depth. That talk gave me so much confidence.'

Firth had kept his powder dry when he entered the three works Holden Monaros for Mount Panorama in 1969: he had refused to nominate their drivers. It was the first time a works team hadn't come clean on its entry form. Mystery mattered to Firth. He made it clear, though, who wouldn't be there. Bruce McPhee, the veteran driver from the NSW Central Coast who'd won in 1968 in a privately entered Monaro, had been turned down for any further Holden support. Firth, the ultimate autocrat, needed to be a new broom, no matter how useful McPhee's knowledge may have been. McPhee had his own way of doing things and that didn't suit Firth. The fiercely independent McPhee switched camps to Ford.

Firth was known as 'The Fox'. He lived in a world of high security. He was also a strategist. He'd got it in his mind that he wanted two teams that were compatible and one that was a wildcard. So he chose two rally drivers (with race experience), two open-wheeler drivers (for their sheer speed) and one veteran paired with a rough newcomer.

At the preliminary Sandown Three Hour long-distance race, just three weeks before the Bathurst 500, Firth ran two Bathurst open-wheeler experts, Spencer Martin and Kevin Bartlett. It was the biggest hint you could get—the two drivers who were the fastest ever around Mount Panorama, and who knew every nuance of the circuit, would be in the works Holdens. Except Bartlett wasn't available for Bathurst; he was already committed to his open-wheeler patron Alec Mildren in an Alfa Romeo GTV. He was keeping the seat warm for Colin Bond.

Firth was uncertain about Bond. 'Harry knew me as a rally driver,' Bond recalled from his lakefront holiday shack just north of Sydney, his freshly caught mud crabs on the boil. 'It was Mike Kable who told him I could race as well as rally, and I got a phone call—first time I'd spoken to Harry—asking me to drive with Spencer at Sandown. I was committed to a rally in New Guinea'—Bond was driving for the Mitsubishi rally team—'so he got KB instead of CB.'

Firth had been surprised to learn Bond had won at Mount Panorama in his supercharged Lynx Peugeot open-wheeler, and that he had driven an underpowered Isuzu Bellett into a coincidental thirtieth place in two successive years in the Bathurst 500. 'The Bellett was a rocket down the mountain but going up it was like there were no corners at all,' Bond laughed. 'The Monaro changed that.'

General Motors engineer Tony Roberts, a noted rally driver who had been third at Mount Panorama the previous year in a private Monaro, would partner Bond.

Henk Woelders was one of the open-wheeler drivers. It was, to a degree, a political placement—he was the son of a Holden dealer and an employee of another. He would later dominate the Australian Formula 2 Championship. He was down to drive with Spencer Martin.

Martin spun off early in the Sandown race; his Monaro crashed backwards through a safety fence and caught fire when the hot exhaust pipe rammed its way through the fuel tank. He was trapped when the doors jammed shut and he leapt out through a window. The brakes were at fault. 'They went straight to the floor,' Martin told me. 'I managed to grab third gear and throw the car sideways [at 200 kilometres an hour], otherwise I would have gone head-on into the barrier. It was a full twenty years later that I was told mechanics had driven the race cars to the circuit on road brake pads and had neglected to change them to the harder competition pads for the race.'

To admit that at the time would have looked clumsy, especially with so many high-ranking Holden executives in the grandstand, so Martin wore the blame. 'They brought the car back to the pits and by then it had cooled down a bit and Harry put his foot on the brake and got a bit of pedal pressure.

'"There you are," Firth said. "It must have been your fault."

'I replied, "Harry, I must have put my foot on the clutch by mistake."'

It was a sarcastic response, but also an admission that in Firth's world, you had to give a little if you wanted to take. Martin kept his drive at Bathurst.

But with just days to go, he was out. He and his brother Gerry had a silly road crash in Sydney. They were going too fast, hooning, and the hard landing broke a vertebrae in Martin's back. 'I went to hospital without calling Harry. Then I took my first steps and knew I'd be no good.' The inevitable phone call to Firth—at the beginning of race week—received a cursory response:

'Just, "Okay, Cock".' (Firth used the word like others use 'mate'.) Then clunk. It was Martin's last association with the team.

Firth was now down a driver. 'I got the phone call on the Wednesday of the race week,' said open-wheeler driver Peter Macrow, who'd raced a works Toyota Corolla at Bathurst two years previously when the team was disqualified for cheating. 'Harry told me to get to Mount Panorama as fast as I could, so I chartered a Cessna. When I got there he threw me the keys to his road Monaro and told me to go for a speed to [nearby town] Blayney to learn the car.'

Veteran Des West was in too. He'd raced in every Mount Panorama long-distance event except for 1964; he'd come second in '68 in a privately entered Monaro but had been disqualified when the valves in his cylinder head were found to be oversized, providing a significant power advantage. He was a man after Firth's heart: old-school, Des was fond of a calming cigarette while racing. He'd light up heading up Mountain Straight and would try to take his last drag down Conrod. If he hadn't finished, he'd simply hold the cigarette down low as he sped past the pits.

Peter Brock's older brother Neil knows how Peter's call-up came about. 'He took the call from Firth at the newly opened Diamond Valley Speed Shop—the family business,' Neil said. 'Our parents [Geoff and Ruth] had funded the retail outlet and a wholesale spare parts operation, GB Accessories, as a foundation for Peter's racing career. It was somewhere for him to go from and come back to.'

Neil, recently awarded a Medal of the Order of Australia for service to his local community, and 'the only member of the family not interested in motor racing', is the Brock family's reliable historian. His dad Geoff, he said, was a racing fan and had been instrumental in taking his four boys—Neil (born 1943), Peter (1945), Lewis (1948) and Phillip (1950)—to local race meetings whenever they could, though only when football didn't interfere. The Brocks' first love was VFL, which morphed into AFL, and their loyalty lay with blue-collar club Collingwood—the Magpies, or just plain Pies. 'We'd all pile in the car and head for every Collingwood match and if there was room for anyone else they were most welcome, as long as their allegiance was right,' Neil said.

For a while all four boys shared one small room, sleeping in bunk beds. There were no posters of racing cars on their walls but plenty of footballers, like Ray Toomey, Bobby Rose, Lou Richards—Magpie heroes all of them.

The Brocks were a mighty tight family unit. They'd grown up in rural Hurstbridge, now a Melbourne suburb but back then an absolute backwater. They didn't connect to the electricity grid until 1956, when Peter was eleven, and town water didn't come until the early 1960s. Geoff made a good living running the local garage, which became a Holden sub-agency, and also by selling and installing standalone 32-volt electric power generators. 'We had one ourselves,' Neil said. 'It was tied to a bank of batteries, which could power up most household appliances and lights, but not all of them at once. Most nights you'd be calling out for someone to turn something off.' Because the family only had two rainwater tanks and supply was limited, the boys were allowed just one weekly hot bath, with the water boiled in the woodfired washing copper in the outhouse and carried in buckets to the bathtub inside their home. Access to the bath was strictly sequential. 'The last of the four got pretty dirty water,' Neil said. 'It made us competitive.'

The Brocks loved their Holdens. When the first 1948 Holden FX Series was delivered in town to the local postman, Geoff had the family out on the roadside to see it arrive. He called it a 'momentous occasion'.

Neil Brock is a sensible, measured man. A 50-year senior member of Victoria's Country Fire Authority, he takes his position as the elder Brock seriously, and is now the oldest member of a proud pioneer family that traces its roots in the Diamond Valley back to the Brock boys' great-great-grandfather Alexander, who was granted land selection there in 1866. It was on that land—named Kirk Clifton, for the Scottish village from where Alexander's father John had emigrated—that thirteen-year-old Peter Brock learned to drive in his homemade paddock-basher Austin 7. That car has become part of his legend.

'It's a bit complicated,' Neil says, referring not to the chronology of events but to the dynamics of his family. When Peter started racing his Austin A30 Holden, displaying obvious talent and ambition, Geoff and Ruth were right behind him. When he started winning—it's said he scored 102 wins in just 65 race meetings—his aspirations ramped right up. That's when Geoff and Ruth started the Speed Shop. 'It caused some concern in the family,' Neil recalled. 'I wasn't affected because I'd chosen my own path with the fire brigade, but our other brothers thought it was a bit one-sided—to their exception.'

And then came Firth's phone call.

'I really thought it was one of my mates trying to wind me up and I almost hung up there and then,' Peter told motoring journalist Wayne Webster, who would get truly close to Brock, writing his biography and racing with him in long-distance off-road events. It all happened in a rush. Brock borrowed a Holden—not a two-door Monaro but a four-door top-of-the-range Premier—and proceeded to thrash it around the back roads of Hurstbridge. His favourite test strip was Brocks Road (still there), which wound past his grandparents' farm.

With only days to go until the big race he went to Calder, a stop-and-go racetrack outside Melbourne, for an official test. But instead of winding out his race car, his job was to undertake specific mechanical evaluation, holding the big V8 in third and driving for lap after lap to discover how much punishment it could take at varying engine revolutions. The first time he got to drive the car properly was in practice at the Mountain.

Peter had been to Mount Panorama before. He and his teenaged mates had gone to the first Bathurst 500 and camped on the Mountain, and Peter had walked the track periphery, not the track proper, in support of the driver who was closest to being his hero. Sydney ace Brian 'Yogi' Muir had been hired to race a Holden EH S4 that year, partnered by Spencer Martin. The S4 was the absolute gun Holden of its time, purpose-built for Bathurst, and most eighteen-year-old enthusiasts, as Brock was at the time, would have killed for its rear boot badge. (Jimmied off the bodywork, the EH 179 badge with its chequered flag motif was the ultimate prize, especially worn as a belt buckle. There's no suggestion that Brock did that.)

Harry Firth won that year in the Cortina GT. An S4 came second, but Muir was way down. 'I put it on pole but it had dreadful axle tramp and it broke the rear axle mountings while Muir was at the wheel,' Spencer Martin recalled. Long stops left them thirty-eighth, nineteen laps off Firth.

Thirteen years later, when Brock—by then a national hero—first competed in the Le Mans 24 Hour race, he secured Muir, then living and racing in Europe, as his co-driver. It was a massive disappointment to Brock that when their BMW broke down early he found Muir packing his bags to go home. They were in a small caravan at the back of the pits, with Peter's ubiquitous kettle on the small gas burner. 'No, no,' Peter implored. 'We can fix this.' He worked for hours through the night to change the gearbox, knowing full well that he had no chance but damned if he'd give up his quest. Muir, by then a hardened professional in the European way, was at first reluctant but caught up in the Brock enthusiasm (that happened a lot), pitched in to help and they ploughed on, only to again break and retire. Muir went on to win the European Touring Car Championship but died in his early fifties—a heart attack on the way home from a race meeting at Silverstone in the UK.

Fresh-faced Colin Bond and Tony Roberts won the Bathurst 500 in 1969, 44 seconds ahead of Bruce McPhee and Barry Mulholland's Ford. Des West and Peter Brock were third, 37 seconds behind. They were the only crews to go the full 130-lap (804-kilometre) distance. Another Mount Panorama debutant, Allan Moffat, was fourth in the first of the works Ford Falcon GTHOs with co-driver Alan Hamilton.

Brock could have won it, but he blew his chance. He wasn't the lead driver in his car—that task fell to the experienced West, who started and finished. Brock got a couple of stints in the middle, a valuable learning curve; all he had to do was maintain race pace and hold it together. But he speared off down the escape road. There were no car-to-pit radios in those days, and West, watching with Firth, suspected brake failure.

Brakes were the weakest link. After Martin's off at Sandown, Firth had illegally drilled some holes in the bodywork to give the brakes extra cooling. Nothing too sophisticated—he'd used a cold chisel. He'd also brought in some trick brake pads from England, but didn't have enough to go around so he fitted locally made ones to the Macrow and Woelders car, confining them to slower, safer lap times that would net them an outright sixth. Brock and West were on the good pads, however, and in winning contention.

'West said to Firth: "Bring him in—the pads won't last any longer,"' Colin Bond recalled. It was an unscheduled stop—the last thing you ever want in a motor race—and the pad change took forever. When Firth saw the ones that came out of the car he was furious. There was still meat left on them—almost half their life was left, which was enough to get to the scheduled stop. 'Do you want me to put these back in?' Firth snarled, holding them up to Brock in the car. It was obvious he'd simply overdriven. The time lost in the pits was far greater than the finishing distance between the first- and third-placed Monaros. Brock had gifted the win to Colin Bond.

For many reasons the 1969 race has been hailed as the most significant long-distance event in the history of Mount Panorama—the start of the clash of the titans, Ford and Holden, and the moment at which automotive tribalism was born. In truth, Ford and Holden had gone toe-to-toe at the Mountain the year before when Holden hired private team owner David McKay to field a covert effort on their behalf. He'd very nearly won too, beaten only by privateer McPhee who'd found a brake mechanism improvement that would escape the attention of the scrutineers in charge of determining vehicle legality.

But 1969 would also go down in history as the year that Ford and Holden declared their intentions, when they applied the full weight of their marketing muscle to the battle for the souls of motor-racing enthusiasts and the support of their families for generations to come. And it was the year that two stars were born—Moffat for Ford and Brock for Holden. It was the two men, more than their machines, who propelled touring-car racing (later to be V8 Supercars) into its golden era, with Mount Panorama as its mother lode.

Within a short four years, the showroom stock class would eclipse all other forms of motor racing in Australia. Mount Panorama, which had built its awesome reputation on the back of titanic clashes between open-wheeled racing cars, massive sports cars and motorcycles, with sedan cars almost as an afterthought, would shut down all four-wheel motorsport except for the long-distance classic on the NSW October long weekend. The annual Easter meeting, shared between bikes and cars, would be left as the exclusive domain of the motorcycle racers. And Mount Panorama, along with Brock, would enter its glory years.

Mike Raymond, an amply proportioned, bespectacled speedway promoter with a sharp staccato voice and a rattle-gun delivery, helped cement the legend of Peter Brock. With Brock's nine great wins behind him but his career still active, Raymond crowned

Brock 'King of the Mountain'. Only Raymond, who is quietly writing his own memoirs and is loath to share, knows how much it cost to hijack the Midnight Oil song of the same name and turn it into a motor-racing anthem. Brock was surprised when the Raymond-produced promotional video was first broadcast shortly after the song's release in 1990 but he was by no means falsely modest. By then he'd been King of Moomba, Melbourne's iconic street festival, and he was accustomed to his name being used beyond the boundaries he set for himself.

'Humble isn't the word you'd use to describe Peter,' Bev Brock, by far the most durable of his partners and the one who maintains the legend, said. 'He was a perfectionist. At night in bed he'd talk about living up to what he saw as the exaggerations that surrounded him. "I'm a mere mortal, Bevo," he'd say.'

Raymond changed the face of motor racing in Australia and used one weekend in October, the Bathurst 1000, as the cornerstone of his campaign to elevate the sport into public entertainment. He'd learned that lesson well on the hard-packed dirt tracks of speedway. Mike and his younger brother Steve, later to become a highly awarded radio and television journalist, would go to the speedway at the old Sydney Showground to be thrilled by the bikes and the midget speedcars charging sideways around the tall wooden-planked, half-kilometre oval—the same oval where, once a year, the state's best and most expensive livestock would parade at the Royal Easter Show. A true speedway enthusiast always sat in the open stand above the pits because that's where you'd be showered with soil, and sometimes assaulted by clods of earth as hard as cricket balls flung up by the rear wheels. It was a sensory experience. You were so close you felt you could reach out and touch the competitors.

But the commentary in the early '60s was woeful, limited to announcements of results delivered in a monotone. The Raymond brothers thought they could do better and offered themselves to the promoter, the legendary John Sherwood, co-owner of Empire Speedways. He needed the Raymonds—they were a missing link in his package.

And they were fabulous. As a young newspaper journalist, I earned much-needed extra income covering the 'skids' each Saturday in the season, filing for all three Sunday paper editions from the bank of phones in the organiser's office under the grandstand. And I'd stand next to the Raymonds, in awe, in the middle of the arena—Mike the larger, Steve then the smaller—as sometimes one, sometimes both of them, pirouetted dizzily around 360 degrees, following and calling the action as it sped around them. They were by no means Laurel and Hardy, even though they looked a little like the comedy duo. They were deadly serious about the business of enlivening the crowd experience, and their audiences reacted enthusiastically. Their between-race patter and competitor interviews (not that there was much time between rapid-fire races) were as entertaining as the competition. They created personalities.

Mike took his immense promotional talent to Sydney's other ovals—Liverpool Speedway and then to Parramatta City Raceway. One became 'The Place of Pace', the other 'The Speedway by the Freeway', each defined by the memorable Raymond one-liners. With more chutzpah than anyone else could imagine, Mike persuaded the great US driver A.J. Foyt, four-time winner of the Indy 500, to come to Australia to race on a Saturday night. Ron Casey, the pugilistic former swimming coach who was Channel Nine's head of sport and host of the network's first *World of Sport* (before it became *Wide World of Sports*), secured Mike Raymond and me to host a weekly motorsport segment—Raymond on speedway and NASCAR, me on circuit racing. It was an uneven contest. Mike, quick-witted and promotionally savvy, would always find a way to brand me a 'toff' and score a point for the skids.

And then, suddenly, he came over to the other side. Channel Seven had been the host broadcaster of the Mount Panorama long-distance races since their beginnings. Even as early as 1963—the first 500—the broadcasts were not only drawing a substantial audience but were making the channel a heap of money. Geoff Healy, the network's long-serving and illustrious technical director, confirmed that by the mid-1980s the race was raising in excess of $1 million in advertising revenue on the Sunday alone. Raymond's job with Channel Seven, as commentator and later as network executive, was to protect and expand the investment.

Creating personalities would do that. Working with the sponsors, he went to the US—his source of speedway inspiration—and brought back 'Grand Marshals' (an expression unknown in Australian motorsport, which tugged its forelock to Britain). They were essentially high-profile ambassadors, like Bill France Jr from the family that invented speedway, and commentators like Chris Economaki, who defined in-your-face Indy coverage. Raymond named the Bathurst 1000 'The Great Race', and invented names for his drivers: soon-to-be-five-time champion Dick Johnson became 'Tricky Dicky'; Larry Perkins was 'The Cowangie Kid'; 1986 and 1990 winner Allan Grice, a fiery competitor, became 'Spicy Gricey'; Glenn Seton, the Supercar champion who never won the

Bathurst 1000, was 'The Baby-Faced Assassin'. And Peter Brock became 'Peter Perfect'.

The breakthrough came in 1979 when Healy, driven by Raymond's relentless pursuit of personality promotion, invented RaceCam. The in-car camera used a microwave radio transmitter to communicate with a helicopter, which struggled to keep up with the speed of the racing cars down Conrod Straight. The technology put viewers in the driver's seat, and totally transformed not only motorsport but all sports: within one season David Hill, executive producer of rival Channel Nine's World Series Cricket, had effectively used the same technology to power Stump Cam, the tiny camera that gave those at home a batsman's view of the crease.

'The idea came from my son,' Healy said. 'I was driving him to school and he said, "Let's video the drive," and he held our small video camera out the window. When we looked at the result, with its wide-angle lens it looked fast, really fast, and I started to think, "Maybe this will work for Mount Panorama."' It was a marriage of just-available technologies. Healy was able to put a live-to-air camera on a gimbal inside the cockpit, activated remotely by a joystick in an outside broadcast van, and combine the vision with driver commentary from the cockpit. Just a year before it couldn't have been done. In 1979 Channel Seven used RaceCam in just one car—a Toyota Celica owned and driven by Liverpool car dealer Peter Williamson. 'Willo's' commentary—'There's that rotten Volvo, holding everyone up'—was scintillating and in 1980 most of the top teams were clamouring to be on board.

Some weren't. English ace Tom Walkinshaw, who would ultimately own Brock's Holden Racing Team, was a stand-off.

Pragmatically he reasoned his business was to go motor racing without distraction and he was concerned—without reason, as it turned out—about the onboard camera's electronics interfering with his car's own battery power.

RaceCam created heroes. It helped that drivers wore open-faced helmets so that the camera could capture their lips moving and the TV audience could see their emotions. When Dick Johnson spun while talking to Mike Raymond, his every reaction was captured as it happened. 'Mike nearly died,' Johnson said. 'He was very aware of his responsibility when he was talking to us and he thought he'd caused me to lose concentration. In reality my rear spoiler broke in two and sent the car into a spin.'

When Glenn Seton's Ford failed just nine laps from an otherwise certain Bathurst 1000 win, RaceCam captured Seton's raw emotion in the car, stranded at the top of the circuit, while Channel Seven's coverage cut between Glenn and his father Barry, a former Bathurst winner, crying in the pits. When full-face helmets were introduced, 1976 winner Bob Morris was one of the first to experiment with a new voice-activated microphone concealed in his chin guard. For half the race commentators would cross to him without getting a response: Morris's voice couldn't rise above the mechanical noise in the car. Technicians left his mic open just in case, and then he was baulked by a slower car and he yelled, really loudly, an expletive, live to air. 'And that was the voice of Bob Morris,' commentator Garry Wilkinson quickly chimed in, 'telling a slower competitor to "back off".'

Peter Brock was never totally comfortable with RaceCam. He was, according to Mike Raymond, 'half scatterbrained'—unlike Dick Johnson, who had a rejoinder for every situation but claimed he didn't rehearse. Brock was better talent one-on-one over a cup of tea in his pit. Not many people can talk without compromising their lap times, and eventually voice-to-voice transmission was limited by the exact concerns Raymond had about interrupting a driver's concentration. The technology is still there but is reserved for non-competitive moments.

'RaceCam had so much impact,' Raymond said in an interview several years ago. 'No one knew Moffat and Brock all that well, but TV changed that.' Add Mount Panorama to that list. The best racetrack in Australia was still relatively shrouded in mystery until Raymond shouted, 'Be there!'—his best known call to action—and everyone came.

Part 2

Precious and Precarious

Anyone will tell you: Mount Panorama is the pinnacle of Australian motor racing, the fulcrum on which the sport pivots. But it wasn't always so. In its first fifteen years of existence, the Mountain could have fallen victim to any number of threats—from authorities, from the changing administration of motorsport, from competition mounted by an avaricious neighbouring council, from lack of funds and commitment by its own administration. And that's even before you take into account World War II.

3

A New Era

The first race meeting at Mount Panorama was one of the most ambitious that would ever be staged there. It was Easter 1938, and cars and motorcycles gathered at the Mountain for their first festival of speed. The Great Depression was lifting but World War II was fast approaching. There was a subtext of espionage and intrigue.

Alan Sinclair, by many accounts, was a spy.

The news spread through the pit area of that first Mount Panorama race meeting, and it's likely to have been true.

The young Englishman, a Cambridge graduate with a colourful past, had arrived in Adelaide during Christmas 1937 with four racing and sports cars in the hold of the SS *Orford* and immediately entered the South Australian Grand Prix. His supercharged Alta, not a pukka Formula One car but a converted sports-racer, was deemed so formidable it was made scratch vehicle in the handicap event, starting last in the handicap race while slower cars—the limit men—got underway sometimes many minutes in front. In practice for the race he'd lapped the Lobethal Street circuit in the Adelaide Hills at an average of 84 miles per hour (135 kilometres per hour). It was fast enough to win the Grand Prix if he could maintain that pace.

But within two laps, according to the Adelaide *Advertiser*, 'Sinclair's Alta was trailing a 200-yard smoke screen like a destroyer'. He was out.

It was of little matter for Sinclair: he was on a grander mission. A German motorcycle racing team had arrived in Australia at the same time and he was shadowing them. Wherever they went, he went.

In the paranoia of the pre-war period, with Hitler already on the march in Europe, the Germans were thought to be using their racing as a cover to establish pro-Nazi contacts in Australia. Lead rider Ewald Kluge, so good that he was soon to become an Isle of Man TT winner, openly wore the swastika on his helmet.

His team manager, Baron Klaus Detlof von Oertzen, was transferring substantial sums of money to Australian accounts, allegedly from the Nazi treasury, and he was taking photographs of sensitive defence facilities (such as they might have been). The German's presence in the Adelaide Hills, an enclave for German migrants to Australia, increased the vigilance of authorities and there was little opportunity for subterfuge. Obviously exposed but technically not breaking any laws, the Germans stayed in

Australia only two months—long enough for Kluge to win at Lobethal and again at Ballarat, and to set a new Australian speed record for 250-cc motorcycles on a road outside Canberra. They exited the country, perhaps a little hurriedly, before the Mount Panorama meeting.

Sinclair, happy-go-lucky and freed of his assignment, stayed on, entered the 1938 Australian Grand Prix—the first to be held at Mount Panorama—and partied hard.

He was welcomed by the Grand Prix organisers. International racing drivers were thin on the ground. The mayor of Adelaide had greeted him (along with Kluge) with a civic reception and therefore he was seen as an asset. Even if he hadn't won anything.

The spy rumour had legs, as it turned out. Less than two years later, in the midst of the Blitz, Sinclair—known as a playboy in Australia—was revealed as one of the major spooks in Britain's MI5 security service, secretively headquartered in St James's Street in bomb-ravaged London. According to those who met him, he was a total hard-arse.

No one had heard of Peter Whitehead.

He was a blow-in. The slightly built, shock-haired Englishman—cherubic and rosy cheeked in some photographs, gaunt, fine boned and with a hint of James Dean menace in others—walked into the NSW Light Car Club office in Sydney so late that entries for the 1938 Australian Grand Prix should have surely been officially closed. He asked, politely, if he might secure a place in the field.

'What car would you like to enter?' he was asked.

'I've brought my ERA R10B with me from England,' Whitehead replied.

The ERA—the letters stood for English Racing Automobiles—was nothing less than the fastest, most successful single-seat racing car in Great Britain. There were none in Australia; not even the wealthiest of enthusiasts could secure one.

Whitehead was the 23-year-old eldest son of one of England's most successful textile families, based in Bradford, West Yorkshire. Like Sinclair, he'd been dispatched to the colony on a mission. His was to learn more of the family business.

In the late 1930s, Australia was providing more than 50 per cent of Britain's total wool imports. With a war—perhaps a world war—looming, it was vital to secure supply, especially if military uniforms were to be made in great numbers. It was not immediately apparent that young Peter had grasped that message, though. He'd arrived at Sydney's Woolloomooloo docks with his racing car in the hold and with a travelling companion, Kenneth Maxwell, who was to fettle the car. If he was to spend a year in Australia, Peter reasoned, he'd damn well enjoy himself. He and Maxwell purchased an open Railton sports touring car, named for land speed record car designer Reid Railton and regarded as one of the great high-performance ragtops of the era; it was simply to act as transport and tow vehicle for his jet-black ERA. The pair had then set about researching all that was available for their pleasure—from speedway, to Australian speed record attempts, to Mount Panorama.

There was huge excitement about the first Australian Grand Prix at the Mountain. For months people had been building or buying cars to take to the tenth Grand Prix in Australia's history, and the first to be held on a circuit purpose-built for the event. It had been run previously on makeshift circuits created by closing public roads, and although Mount Panorama was technically a public road too, everybody knew the truth.

The motorcycle competitors were equally motivated. They'd created a Tourist Trophy race to be called the Australian 150th Celebrations TT, marking a century and a half since Captain Arthur Phillip had arrived in Sydney Harbour. For the bikes, after seven years of risking death at Vale, there was an amazing buzz about being on Mount Panorama. Sharing it with cars was no imposition; it just added to the strength of the occasion.

A shop on Sydney's magic mile of motorcycles, just down from the University of Sydney, became the epicentre of the excitement and a beacon for enthusiasts.

Leo Tobin, a star on the old Vale circuit with two successive wins in the Australian Senior TT, had acquired Jimmy Pringle's works Manx Norton to ride at Bathurst. Pringle was an Australian international. In 1933 he had been twelfth outright in the Senior race at the Isle of Man TT, with a lap average above 71 miles per hour (114 kilometres per hour). He would have been crowned rookie of the year if such a phrase had existed then. He was exalted in Australia.

But in 1938, perhaps suffering the first stages of the cancer that took his life early, he announced his retirement and sold his works bike to Tobin. The Norton was proudly displayed in the front window of Tobin's bike shop on Sydney's Parramatta Road. Each night a crowd gathered at the shop, Tobin delighted to talk up his chances.

MOUNT PANORAMA

There were two ways to go motor racing in Australia. You could build your own car or you could buy one from overseas. Generally the imports were past their use-by date—but not by much, so they were still useful tools. In a world of one-upmanship, it helped if a car had provenance. A pedigree might not make the car go faster but it had real cachet in the pits.

For the Mount Panorama race, John Sherwood—master promoter, one of the organisers and keen entrant in the Grand Prix—had imported an MG NE Magnette. And it wasn't just any MG: it had been driven by world land speed record-breaker George Eyston. That was Sherwood's style.

Victorian grazier Colin Dunne, a real talent, had secured the supercharged six-cylinder MG K3 once driven by Prince Bira of Siam. His Serene Highness Prince Birabongse Bhanudej Bhanubandh raced under the name Bira and would become one of the principal private customers of the ERA racing car company. The MG K3 was one of his earlier cars, bought when he was a teenager, and although it had passed through a couple of hands by the time Dunne acquired it, the Australian enhanced it by dressing it in Bira blue—the prince's national racing colours. It was an affectation that could have looked silly, but when he came second in the Adelaide prelude to Mount Panorama and claimed fastest lap, it took on the patina of a tribute.

Ambitious local Central West farmer Jim Fagan had decided to make a bid for the big time. The Europeans had adopted a new 3-litre turbocharged formula and he went chasing the very latest Maserati 8CTF, but only two had been built for works duties. So he dropped back to another K3 MG with pedigree—this one alleged to be the ex-Tim Birkin/Kaye Don car. The claim was perhaps a bit fanciful. Birkin, one of the 'Bentley boys' who'd won the Le Mans 24 Hour race, had died in 1933, the year the K3 was launched.

But the GP winner, everyone reckoned, would come not from those cars. More likely it would be one of the homemade 'specials'.

Their vast distance from the UK and the US had bred an innovative spirit in Australian racers. As some of the world's best cars that had been secured for local competition got slower with the years, they'd be stripped to their chassis to become specials. At the time there was nothing less valuable than a used racing car. You either converted them or scrapped them. Tom Peters, who'd raced his Type 37A Bugatti in the 1936 Grand Prix in South Australia and claimed the lap record before breaking down, entered the Bugatti fitted with a Ford V8 engine for the 1938 race. The passing of time has made that practice seem so wrong. The spindly French donor car, complete with its rasping four-cylinder engine, is today valued at auction in original condition at upwards of $1.35 million.

Young Frank Kleinig, who would go on to become the doyen of a family motor-racing dynasty, stripped his patron's MG Magna to its chassis, convinced the boss to import a 1.5-litre supercharged Miller engine from the US at a cost of £400 (more than $50,000 today). He then decided the innovative engine—eight cylinders in line, spinning up to an incredible 8000 rpm—would be too delicate for Mount Panorama, so at the last minute replaced it with a heavy eight-cylinder Hudson, the go-to performance engine of the time. It was incompatible and destroyed the handling of the lightweight car.

In this butchers' picnic, Peter Whitehead and his ERA shone like the crown jewels.

It was a true works car: purpose-built, front-engined, with an aluminium cylinder head and bespoke supercharger, and it ran through a pre-selector gearbox, which meant you had to choose the gear you wanted long before you took it. It called for intelligent driving, You sat on an ERA, not in it; your legs straddled the transmission tunnel and your back rested on the tail-mounted fuel tank filled with 35 gallons (159 litres) of volatile methanol. You didn't want to be in a rear-end shunt.

English Racing Automobiles had been established only in 1934 as a foil to the faster, more complex and vastly more expensive continental formula cars. The company had three partners, the best known of whom was Raymond Mays, who was later to morph ERA into the far more contemporary BRM Formula One team. The pre-war ERA, by its owners' decree, would remain a voiturette—a Formula Two car—with the base twin-cam engine available in three sizes: 1.1-litre, 1.5-litre and 2-litre. Early ERAs dominated the voiturette class and, in an act of great salesmanship, Mays took his works machine to Europe in 1935 to stir up the continentals in their championship series, snapping at the heels of the Formula One cars.

Wealthy patrons, ultra-high-net-worth individuals, queued up to buy the customer models. Prince Bira's cousin, also a Siamese prince, purchased one in the Siamese racing colours of blue and gold as a gift for Bira's twenty-first birthday. Pretty girls at his party formed an orderly line to sit in the car, which was exactly the plan. The cousins bought two ERAs and named them, with intentional irony, Remus and Romulus, a reference to the twin brothers of Roman mythology who founded the great empire of Rome and upon whom they modelled themselves. The cousins' grandfather, after all, had been the King of

Siam, said to be the character on which the musical *The King and I* was based. Later, they bought a third ERA they named Hanuman after the Hindu god of celibacy. The freewheeling princes had a sense of humour.

Whitehead ordered his car direct from the factory in 1936 as a 1.5-litre model, and it cost him £1 per cubic centimetre of engine capacity (£1500 was around twelve years of average earnings for a male worker in 1936; females earned half that amount). With racing partner Peter 'Skid' Walker, he'd come third in the Donington Grand Prix that same year, backing it up with a string of podiums across Great Britain. Walker was comparatively impecunious; Whitehead certainly was not. Attaching yourself to Whitehead's comet was a good career move. They'd go on to win the Le Mans 24 Hour race together, post-war, for Jaguar. His circle of motor-racing friends called Whitehead 'The Chancellor of the Exchequer'.

Whitehead had been racing for five years when he came to Australia. One of the cars Alan Sinclair brought to Adelaide was ex-Whitehead. As former Cambridge University men, they would be renewing their acquaintance on Mount Panorama.

Organisers took one look at Whitehead's car and his record and handicapped him severely. Staggered starts were the only way to run a 'fair' race. There was a massive speed differential between the fastest and slowest machines. At Mount Panorama today, the contemporary Supercars Top Ten Shootout invariably has a spread of less than 0.7 seconds between first and last places. Not so in 1938—you could measure the time difference between fastest and slowest with an hourglass. The only way to keep everyone motivated, and secure their entries, was to impose a handicap so that all entrants theoretically had an equal chance of winning. In a perfect world, the entire field would come together on the last lap and fight out the victory on the last corner. Beating the handicapper was something of a dark art.

For the Australian Grand Prix, over a very loose approximation of 150 miles (241 kilometres) Whitehead would give away 34 minutes to the limit man: South Australian Ron Uffindell in his 750-cc Austin 7 Special. Handicappers estimated the tiny Austin, which had been driven all the way across the Hay Plains to get to Mount Panorama, would be at least a minute a lap slower than Whitehead's works ERA. It would complete seven laps of the course before the works car would even be allowed to start. Uffindell was just one of those who hoped they'd thrown the handicappers a dummy.

The Bathurst City Council had done a grand job with the basics of Mount Panorama. But there was one detail still lacking: by Easter 1938, the circuit was still unsealed. At the grand opening of the track, in front of 72 motorcycle competitors, 38 grand prix drivers (some with riding mechanics) and a smattering of the rubbery estimate of 48,000 spectators who attended the inaugural meeting—18,000 payers at the bikes and 30,000 at the cars—Mayor Martin Griffin promised tarmac for 'next year'. New South Wales Secretary for Public Works Eric Spooner agreed. Surfacing would be completed by year's end.

To keep faith with its gazetted purpose as a scenic road, Mount Panorama was only closed for practice from 6 to 8 a.m., and only for six days before the event. Two afternoons were also reserved from 4 to 6 p.m. For the rest of the time the steamrollers were out, compressing the surface and allowing local traffic on the circuit. There'd been heavy rain in the previous fortnight and there were grave concerns about how the pressure of competition would affect the track. So many spectators had arrived early, camping around the Mountain haphazardly, that the local newspaper speculated on their ability to get in the way of the racing, perhaps causing drivers to slow. The issue of their safety, though, was not raised.

Twenty-year-old Queensland motorcycle state champion Les Sherrin became the first person to win a race at Mount Panorama. It wasn't easy. The masters of the old Vale track, Don Bain and Cec Weatherby, hounded him all the way over the 25 laps (154.3 kilometres) of the Junior TT. He took the lead for the first time on lap five, fought furiously with Bain, then fell back on lap fifteen when he made a pit stop for fuel. Even then, fuel strategy on the long mountain circuit played its part. Sherrin took back the lead when the others pitted just three laps from home.

There was precious little protection for riders. The run up from Griffin's Bend at the top of Mountain Straight to the steep uphill Cutting had at least been ploughed back on either side, but it was deceptive. Sherrin would almost have preferred to have trees define the path in the thick dust, rather than allowing himself to drift too close to the edge.

Legends were formed that day. Harry Hinton, who would become the most successful racer of his era at the circuit, won the sidecar race—the first of sixteen victories he'd claim at

Mount Panorama. Isle of Man TT competitor Cec Weatherby high-sided his sidecar in the downhill Esses, the first serious crash of the meeting. Red flags at the top of the Mountain delayed the start of the Senior TT.

From the start Art Senior, Vale TT winner and even then a veteran, shot to the lead, but Leo Tobin had an ace in his armoury. Concerned about the track condition—he'd assumed it would become broken up as the day progressed—he'd fitted heavy-duty knobbly tyres to the rear of his Pringle Norton. They were like motocross cases and they were an absolute winner, gripping the surface as other bikes slid. He stormed to the lead on lap two. When Tobin pitted for fuel halfway, 27-year-old Eric McPherson, riding the same BSA with which he'd contested the sidecar event, went through. McPherson would go on to become a post-war representative in the Isle of Man TT, and one of the giants of the sport. But on that day, faced with Tobin's furious assault, McPherson became just another casualty. When he pitted for fuel he dropped behind Tobin, then two laps later he crashed on the uphill right-hander at the top of Mountain Straight. Leo Tobin led home a clean sweep of Nortons in first, second and third. To round out the day, Tobin went out in the final race, a handicap, to set the outright motorcycle lap record—3 minutes 42 seconds, an average of 62.18 miles per hour (100.08 kilometres per hour).

Alan Sinclair was in trouble. While Peter Whitehead had practised well, clearly the fastest of the motor-racing contestants, Sinclair was not on the time sheets at all. He was, some said, on

A NEW ERA

the police charge sheets. Sinclair had discovered the six o'clock swill, the uniquely Australasian phenomenon that resulted from the laws forcing hotels and public houses to close their doors at 6 p.m., inciting a riot of drinking in the hour before. Introduced during World War I, early-closing legislation would not start to be repealed until the mid-1950s. Some reports said Sinclair had spent the night before the Grand Prix in the cells. Certainly he did not start in the race.

The Englishmen had secured lodgings in the elaborate three-storey Royal Hotel. With its wonderfully ornate iron-post-and-railing verandahs, the Royal had been the centre of Bathurst society since the 1840s and would soon become the hub of the main street madness that for years characterised Mount Panorama race meetings. Whitehead, Maxwell and Sinclair were just two days away from laying the foundations of an unfortunate tradition.

Whitehead had also had a stand-off with officials. He wanted, he'd said, to drive without a helmet or head protection. It was essential that he be able to clearly hear the exhaust of his engine. Given the raucous note of the supercharged ERA, it was an odd request, but they acquiesced. In a race in which the rules could be bent so that Barney Dentry was able to take his wife Bess along as riding mechanic in their Riley 9, the simple matter of a helmet was easily agreed on.

Of 38 entrants, 30 made it to the start line. The most notable non-starter, discounting Sinclair's Alta, was John Sherwood's MG. The ex-Eyston car had ingested great dollops of Mount Panorama dust and its crankshaft bearings had been damaged. He installed new ones of lesser quality; in a flat-out test on the open road in his racing car, they failed too. Sherwood hastily arranged to share the driving duties in the near-stock MG TA of Alan Crago.

When Ron Uffindell's pretty little aluminium-bodied Austin 7 was flagged away, it was almost a full lap before the next three cars, led by Alf Barrett's Morris Cowley, driven by Colin Anderson, were given the right to start. Whitehead sat in his ERA, a blanket wrapped around its engine against the cold. Parked to the side of the start/finish straight, he was able to watch cars whoosh by while others made pit stops. The race was unfolding in front of him and he'd not yet even begun. Four minutes in front of his start time, the two leading specials—Kleinig's ill-handling Hudson and Tom Peters' Bugatti Ford—took off side by side into Hell Corner, grazing the straining wire stump on the apex of the corner that had led to the motorcycle racers naming it Hell: 'Hit the stump and you were going straight to hell.'

There's a starting technique for the ERA. You can't dump the clutch because the pre-selector bands won't take the strain. Instead you hold the revs at between 4000 and 4500 rpm and let the rear wheels spin. For a racing driver, inducing time-wasting wheelspin is counter-intuitive, but it's better to modulate the throttle and control the wheelspin than risk burning out the bands. Whitehead did it right, launching the car at Hell Corner and automatically reaching down, a full foot (30 centimetres) from the steering wheel to a metal lever on the right side of the cockpit that pre-selects the next gear. There's a real skill in that too. On the bouncing, bumpy, corrugated track that Mount Panorama was fast becoming, Whitehead had to balance and

A NEW ERA

steer the car with his left hand while dropping his right way down near his knee.

The car loved to oversteer, hanging its tail out. It's a controlled art. For Whitehead it was a matter of inducing a little understeer first, pushing into the corner, and then using the throttle to create a counter-steering drift. He was a master, and the ERA was a willing accomplice. Together they were quite a team. Their beautiful, howling, four-wheel drift through Griffin's Bend at the top of Mountain Straight had spectators enthralled. It's dangerous on that corner, and nowadays no onlookers are allowed near it, but back then they lined the track on both sides.

It was going to be a close-run race. The specials in front of Whitehead were lapping only around 10 seconds slower than the ERA. In theory, Whitehead should have been able to catch them with only 2 minutes to go. He had to push. On lap nine he set the fastest lap of the race, 3 minutes 23 seconds (68.4 miles per hour/109.45 kilometres per hour). And still that pretty little Austin 7 was lapping like clockwork and leading. Uffindell wouldn't be passed until over halfway, on lap 22.

On lap nineteen Alan Crago flashed to the pits for a stop that would make a Supercar team proud. The MG took a tank of fuel, a new right rear tyre and a driver change, all in 21 seconds. With Sherwood at the wheel, all bluff and bravado, the MG passed the Austin 7 just three laps later and became the new leader. At the 100-mile (161-kilometre) mark, Sherwood stretched his advantage to 60 seconds. Whitehead was eleventh, 7 minutes 4 seconds behind. The handicapper's work was bearing fruit. The field—spread thin at the start—was starting to compress.

On lap 30 Les Burrows, a Bowral motor dealer in a Hudson Terraplane, unexpectedly became the new leader, 8 seconds ahead of Sherwood as they crossed the line. Burrows was performing better than his handicap. Whitehead, his hair streaming behind him down the main straight (later to be named Conrod) at 120 miles per hour (193 kilometres per hour), was sixth, 3 minutes 40 seconds behind. The ERA was geared for 145 miles per hour (233 kilometres per hour) but it would have been suicidal to stretch it out. The straight was too rough to attempt such lunacy—maybe later, if the Hudson continued to maintain its sub-handicap pace. Until then Whitehead had to hold his nerve.

It was punishing. Dust, stones and fumes sapped his strength. With five laps (just over 30 kilometres) remaining, a stone flew up and cracked Whitehead's tiny aero-screen—the only wind-break he had. Without a helmet, he was lucky the rock didn't take him out as well.

And then the Hudson started to slow; perhaps its engine was off-song, or its part-time racer was tiring. Just three laps remained and without the need for the big push he was planning, Whitehead passed the gallant Burrows and claimed victory, 1 minute 31 seconds ahead. Sherwood was third, sharing with Crago, 59 seconds behind the Hudson. Uffindell was eighth, 8 minutes 17 seconds back. Whitehead had come halfway around the world to win his first grand prix and it was time to celebrate. Or was it?

In what was to become another Bathurst tradition, lingering well into the 1970s when electronic timing was perfected, lap-scoring protests started to flow. Teams were incensed that their lap charts didn't tally with the official results. It also didn't help that their charts didn't tally with each other's.

The Light Car Club officials went into a huddle and made it all provisional. Even the prize presentation that night would need to be ratified.

With a beer in his hand and his yellow spotted tie somewhat loosened, Whitehead—ever the gentleman—praised the track, the officials and his fellow competitors, and said he looked forward to the asphalt. The track surface was becoming untenable, he said. The Bathurst City Council was delighted. The endorsement of the Grand Prix winner would hasten the track surfacing.

But, still, the lap-scoring debacle hit a sour note. Things quickly went downhill.

At the Walshaw Hall in downtown Bathurst that night, mayor Martin Griffin had just completed his celebratory speech and was about to present the Royal Automobile Club of Australia trophy to Peter Whitehead when the first vegetable—a large cauliflower—was thrown, hitting the mayor squarely on the head. That was followed by a shower of local produce. No one knew who incited it, but Griffin and the official party beat a hasty retreat.

Later that night, in their cups, the winner of the Australian Grand Prix and Sinclair, the driver who did not start, decided to enliven proceedings further. A bonfire in the main street outside the Royal Hotel seemed appropriate, fuelled by used racing tyres. Streaking (by Whitehead) was alleged but never proved. Charges were laid, but not against the Englishmen. Damage to property was quietly settled. It was a portent of things to come at Mount Panorama, but that was all in the future.

Less than 24 hours later, early Tuesday evening, the president of the Light Car Club of Australia, Melbourne-based Englishman George Martin, was driving his BMW 328 home from Mount Panorama. He'd debuted the streamlined 2-litre sports car in the Grand Prix and crossed the line as a low-ranked finisher. Now, as was the practice of the day, he was driving his race car home. Martin was the Australian representative of the Cunard-White Star Line shipping company, and he and Alan Sinclair had become friends. Sinclair had elected to return home to Melbourne with Martin and was following in a second car, accompanying Martin's wife. Fifty kilometres outside Wagga, near Holbrook, the open-top BMW hit a guidepost and flipped. When Mrs Martin and Sinclair arrived they found the car back on its wheels, the motor running, and George Martin dead at the wheel.

Peter Whitehead and Kenneth Maxwell spent 1938 in Australia, racing and winning at speedways and hill climbs (where a single car dashes over a measured distance, usually uphill) in New South Wales and Victoria. Whitehead won the Australian Hill Climb Championship at Rob Roy outside Melbourne but was thwarted all year long in his attempt to set a new Australian land speed record. He was hand-timed at more than 150 miles per hour (241 kilometres per hour) at the Canberra Speed Trials but his speed was disallowed because of a timing equipment failure.

Whitehead's story, too, would end in tragedy. He served as a tank commander in World War II, was seriously injured in a plane crash in 1948 that killed his female co-pilot, became Ferrari's first privateer customer, won the Le Mans 24 Hour in 1951 in a C-Type Jaguar, and returned to Australia in 1956 for the Australian Grand Prix at Albert Park in Melbourne, held during the Olympic Games. Driving his privately entered Ferrari, he claimed third behind the works Maseratis of Stirling Moss and Jean Behra.

Two years later Peter and his half-brother Graham were leading their class in the Tour de France Automobile when Graham plunged their Jaguar 30 metres off a bridge at Lassalle in southern France. Peter died instantly. Graham survived and continued racing for only two more years before retiring, still devastated. (The family textile mill that had funded it all operated for another 45 years until it finally closed under pressure of debt.)

The story of the ERA is far more positive. According to ERA historian Adam Ferrington, nineteen of the twenty ERA R10Bs ever built have survived to this day. One was destroyed in 1936 in a fatal crash in north-west France when the ERA's fragile rear fuel tank caught fire. Whitehead kept his ERA until 1952 and since then it has had only four owners. Noted historic racing enthusiast Nick Mason, drummer in mega-group Pink Floyd, had it for 25 years before he succumbed to an offer from Irish-born Californian finance industry man Paddins Dowling. Dowling returned the car to Australia to race in a historic meeting at Phillip Island, but it has never been back to Mount Panorama.

4

Preparing for War

War accelerates technology. It was as if the looming prospect of World War II hastened the desire of Mount Panorama competitors to find new and faster machinery to race before it was too late. All around them turmoil was erupting, and the Bathurst region was being turned over to the war effort. Mount Panorama hosted two race meetings in 1939, one after the war was declared. And then, as if to deny the conflict had already begun, there was another in early 1940. But by then many of the racers had already enlisted.

At 24, John Snow was a leading driver—and, because of his wealth, a major importer of racing cars.

PREPARING FOR WAR

Several of Snow's cars were being prepared at Mount Panorama on Good Friday 1939 when the tenth prime minister of Australia, Joseph Lyons, died of a massive heart attack at just 60 years old. He was the first prime minister to die while in office.

Few were more affected than the Snow family.

Sir Sydney Snow, John's father, knighted in 1936, was chairman of Lyons' United Australia Party. That weekend Sir Sydney was actively involved in finding a new prime minister to lead Australia into what, inevitably, would be war. With the Snow family's help, Robert Menzies was elected as Lyons' successor.

John Snow had entered the Bathurst race but was a last-minute shock withdrawal. There were two schools of thought— some said that he'd been dispatched overseas on urgent but unspecified business; while others claimed that he had been called to his father's side.

Snow had only recently returned from Europe. He'd gone just after the 1938 Australian Grand Prix, when the lesson of Peter Whitehead's victory had become glaringly obvious to the leading Australian competitors: the days of using redundant machinery, or building your own, were over. Nothing less than near-to-current European specification would do. And if one competitor was going to secure such a car, then all competitors had to do the same. The stakes, and the costs, had shot through the roof. Snow made a business out of it.

It helped to be backed by a wealthy family. The Snows owned a huge department store. Each year the young Snow had travelled to Europe to buy merchandise; this time he would also do the rounds of the racing-car factories. On his 1938 trip he returned with four cars, among them a 1935 2.9-litre twin supercharged Alfa Romeo P3 grand prix machine, the benchmark in European racing until the state-backed Mercedes-Benz and Auto Union teams turned up in the late 1930s. The P3 that Snow purchased had been campaigned by Enzo Ferrari's Scuderia Ferrari on behalf of the factory. Snow may have wanted it for himself, but with retail acumen he passed it on to Jack Saywell, another wealthy member of the Sydney motor-racing push. The car immediately attracted favouritism at Mount Panorama.

Saywell and Snow began a partnership in a specialist high-performance tuning business, Monza Service, in Bourke Street, East Sydney. They even imported a works mechanic, one of the Bentley boys—winners of the Le Mans 24 Hour race—to run it and care for their cars. It gave them a focused base, and most likely created tax relief. It was exactly the model Whitehead had adopted in the UK. Monza Service became the centre of wealthy sports and racing enthusiast activity in Sydney, even more so when it settled down after its first year of operation.

Alfa Romeos were in great favour.

John Snow brought back another Alfa for Sydney's Crouch family. Cecil Crouch had cheered his twenty-year-old son John to fifth in the 1938 Grand Prix in an MG TA. This Alfa wasn't a Formula car—not like Saywell's. Instead it was a sports racer, the spare car for Alfa's 1933 Le Mans 24 Hour assault. But it was still a huge step up. After the war, John—an old boy of Sydney's exclusive Sydney Church of England Grammar School (Shore)—would win the Australian Grand Prix, and father and son would become the Australian concessionaires for the spindly, British-built Cooper racing cars, playing a pivotal role in the career of Jack Brabham.

Alf Barrett, who would go on to be one of the best of the Victorians and regarded as 'The Maestro', used Peter Whitehead, not Snow, to secure a 1932 Alfa Romeo Monza Tipo 8C 3200. It may not have been the latest model but it had an excellent pedigree, and had lapped the banked Brooklands bowl outside London at an average of 129 miles per hour (207 kilometres per hour). Its specifications—180 horsepower (134 kW) through a closely spaced gearbox, coupled with fine handling—made it ideal for Australian conditions. He landed it in Australia at a cost of just under £1000 sterling.

In France, Snow bought a Type 135 Delahaye, the absolute best in long-distance sports rally cars. There was a backstory to that car. Snow was also on his honeymoon on that 1938 trip and he proposed to his new wife, Gwendoline, that they undertake a driving tour across Europe. It turned into a motorsport fest. Driving a Lancia Aprilia in a rally over the Pyrenees, going absolutely flat out at 90 miles per hour (144 kilometres per hour), Snow had been passed on both sides by the works Delahaye team doing at least a third of the speed again. He bought one of those exact works cars, raced it in the Antwerp Grand Prix and came fourth—watched by Gwendoline. Then he brought it back to Australia in time for the last competition event ever to be held at Mount Panorama on a gravel surface.

Since the turn of the century there'd always been a motorcycle or car club at Bathurst. The clubs' fortunes fluctuated with the local economy, but the construction of Mount Panorama fuelled their ambitions. The Light Car Club of Bathurst lobbied the City Council for use of at least part of the circuit without having to close the entire scenic road. Leave the big events to the big players—the Auto Cycle Union and the Light Car Club of NSW—proposed the Bathurst club, and let the local club run a hill climb and a sprint.

Hill climbs were hugely popular in the day, and in October 1938—with the tarmac ready to be laid—the Light Car Club of Bathurst ran its hill climb from the top of Mountain Straight up to McPhillamy Park, and a sprint race along Conrod Straight. They'd expected it to be a club event. Local enthusiast and later ace George Reed had entered his 1934 Ford Roadster, a hot-rodder's special, and he'd expected to go home with a trophy. Instead the big guns turned up. John Snow won the sprint in a dead heat with young Frank Kleinig in his Hudson special, and Kleinig just edged the Delahaye out in the hill climb.

A week later Mount Panorama reeked from the smell of hot laid tarmacadam, and the lap record would never be the same again.

There had never been such a graphic illustration of the difference between the 'haves' and the 'have-nots' in motor racing as there was in the late 1930s. The expenditure on new machinery by car competitors was breathtaking in its sheer magnitude. The purchase price, let alone the running costs, of Saywell's Alfa Romeo P3 would have been enough to buy the front half of the field in the Easter 1939 Australian Motorcycle Grand Prix.

Bernard 'Bat' Byrnes, soon to turn 24, wanted nothing more than to emulate his idol Arthur 'Bluey' Wilkinson. Bluey, who grew up in Bathurst, had aspired to not much more than the job he had as a butcher's boy until he stepped onto an old speedway bike in 1928, aged seventeen, and discovered he had talent. Ten years later he was world champion. Wilkinson's rise to fame had had a bit of luck in it. Bathurst had a quarter-mile dirt oval

Peter Whitehead slides his ERA R10B up through Griffin's Bend on his way to victory in the 1938 Australian Grand Prix, during the first race meeting on the 'scenic road'. (Chevron Library)

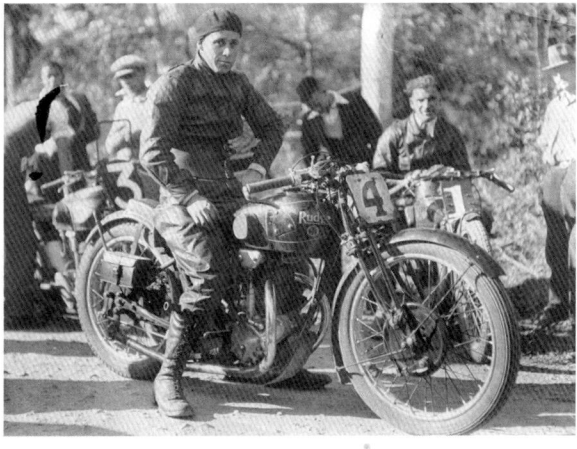

Twenty-year-old Queensland champion Les Sherrin won the first-ever race held at Mount Panorama, the 154-kilometre Australian 150th Celebrations Junior Tourist Trophy, in 1938. (Jim Scaysbrook)

The 'father of Mount Panorama', Mayor Martin Griffin (third from right), with motorcycle-racing legends Cec Weatherby (far left) and Don Bain (second from right), c. 1935. (Chevron Library)

Mount Panorama pit apron, 1938 style. Australian Grand Prix winner Peter Whitehead, his ERA in the foreground with blankets over its radiator, had to wait 34 minutes to start after limit man Ron Uffindell in his Austin 7. (Chevron Library)

Leo Tobin won the 1938 Australian 150th Celebrations Senior Tourist Trophy, the first Senior TT at Mount Panorama. His secret weapon was a heavy-duty knobbly rear tyre to better cope with Mount Panorama's unsealed surface. (Jim Scaysbrook)

Cec Weatherby leads the way from Reid Park to McPhillamy in 1938's Senior TT. The image is notable for the unsealed surface, the lack of safety fencing and the sparse spectator presence despite the claim of 18,000 attendees. (Jim Scaysbrook)

J.O. Sherwood, a driving force behind Mount Panorama, won the 1939 150-mile (241-kilometre) race in his MG NE, from American Paul Swedberg in John Snow's Delahaye. (Royal Automobile Club of Australia)

Ray White (right), president of the Auto Cycle Union of NSW—the governing body of two-wheel racing—congratulates Ron Miles, winner of the 1958 Junior TT. (Jim Scaysbrook)

J.O. Sherwood rounds what would later be named Murray's Corner—the sign helpfully indicating the direction of travel. (Primotipo)

Australian Grand Prix victor Lex Davison and wife, Diana, drove to Mount Panorama from Melbourne the day after their wedding in their Alfa Romeo sports-racer, for Lex's first race, in 1946. (Davison family)

In 1951, Doug Whiteford (Lago Talbot) hit Lex Davison (Alfa Romeo). The Lago's badge lodged in the back of the Alfa, and Davison, aggrieved, refused to return it. (National Motor Racing Museum)

Before the mid-1950s, Reg Hunt drove this homemade special, nicknamed 'The Flying Bedstead', built with engine man Phil Irving who went on to join Jack Brabham. (National Motor Racing Museum)

Bill Murray (MG, no. 21), for whom Murray's Corner was named, won the 1947 Australian Grand Prix at Mount Panorama in a car built by ace Sydney tuner Rex Marshall. (National Motor Racing Museum)

October 1958: eventual winner Lex Davison (Ferrari no. 12) stalks Stan Jones (Maserati no. 4) and Ted Gray (Tornado) in the Australian Grand Prix. (Chevron Library)

'Gelignite' Jack Murray earned his notoriety in the Round Australia Trials in the 1950s; here he is in his D-Type Jaguar in the Bathurst pits. (National Motor Racing Museum)

Three generations of Hintons rode at Mount Panorama from the first meeting in 1938 to the last in 2000, scoring 24 wins between them. Harry Snr (right) stands with Harry Jr (centre). (Jim Scaysbrook)

In 1967 Kevin Bartlett (leading) and Spencer Martin staged an epic duel in which Bartlett became the first person ever to crack the 100-mile-per-hour (161-kilometre-per-hour) lap average. It earned him 100 bottles of champagne. Martin also broke the three-figure barrier but was unrewarded. (Kevin Bartlett collection)

1969 world 250-cc motorcycle champion Kel Carruthers was undefeated on the revolutionary Honda Four at Mount Panorama between 1961 and 1965, launching his international career. (Jim Scaysbrook)

Arthur Blizzard OAM and his wife Jan carried Mount Panorama motorcycling into the modern era. They were as influential in motorcycle racing as Jack and Tottie Hinxman, and Ivan and Leonie Stibbard, were in car racing through the ARDC. (The Project Group)

Vince Tesoriero introduced professionalism and broad public appeal into motorcycle racing in the 1970s, aiming to make the sport as popular as surfing had been in the '60s. Later he inaugurated the Bathurst 12 Hour long-distance race. (The Project Group)

Journalist Mike Kable (centre) is flanked by three-time world champion Sir Jack Brabham (right) and six-time Bathurst 1000 winner Larry Perkins. (The Project Group)

Queenslander Sandy McCrae won the main sidecar event at Mount Panorama a record eight times in seventeen years. His first riding partner, Monty Perola, died in a road crash as pillion to McCrae. (Jim Scaysbrook)

Father-and-son sidecar team Stan and Steve Bayliss dominated racing in the 1970s on their 'kneelers'. They won and came second in the Unlimited three years in a row. (The Project Group)

Wheels off at 280 km/h: Ron Toombs lived, and died, at Mount Panorama. He won his first race there in 1961, retired in the mid-1970s and was killed in the Esses in his comeback ride. (The Project Group)

The day the motorcycle world changed: Warren Willing leads Gregg Hansford on Yamaha TZ700s in 1974, both airborne on Conrod's first hump. (The Project Group)

Fearless Ikujiro Takai knew no limits. Sent to Mount Panorama by the Yamaha factory, he won the Unlimited Race in 1976 and 1977, but it was Warren Willing who claimed the lap record—the first rider to break a 100-mile-per-hour average. (The Project Group)

Early GoPro: American stuntman Everett Creach devised this helmet-cam in 1974 for the movie *Sidecar Racers*, shot at Mount Panorama during the actual race meeting. (The Project Group)

1970 Australian Touring Car champion Norm Beechey brought this Chevy Nova to Mount Panorama in 1966. He dominated the race until a slipping clutch dropped him to second behind Pete Geoghegan. (Chevron Library)

The greatest touring car race of all time: Easter 1972, when Allan Moffat (Ford Mustang, no. 9) battled with Pete Geoghegan (Super Falcon) after Bob Jane (Chevrolet Camaro, here in second place) dropped out. Geoghegan took the win. (Bill Forsyth/Chevron Library)

In big powerful sports cars, Neil Allen (Elfin 400), leads Frank Matich (Matich SR4, with high-mounted wing), and 22-year-old Victorian Bevan Gibson (Elfin Repco) through the Esses, Easter 1969. (Ray Berghouse/Chevron Library)

Two laps later, Bevan Gibson's Elfin Repco flipped upside down on the second hump of Conrod Straight. It was an unsurvivable crash. (National Motor Racing Museum)

Sir Jack Brabham, by then three-time world champion, brought his Brabham BT31 to Mount Panorama in 1969, fitted with experimental aerodynamic wings. He dominated the Bathurst 100 that year. (Ray Berghouse/Chevron Library)

Colin Bond drove the last 'hot Holden' at Mount Panorama. In 1973, at the final Easter event for cars, he claimed three wins from three starts in the Repco V8 sports sedan known as 'The Beast'. (Bill Forsyth/Chevron Library)

Harry Firth crashed out of the 1962 Bathurst Six Hour when he rolled his Ford Falcon at Hell Corner. The next year he came back and won the first Bathurst 500 in a Ford Cortina GT. (Chevron Library)

In 1967 Firth hired young Sydney ace Fred Gibson and the Falcon GT pair scored the first V8 victory in Mount Panorama's Great Race. Fourth-placed Kevin Bartlett (Alfa Romeo, no. 61E) was faster through Murray's Corner. (Bill Forsyth/Chevron Library)

A PR shot of Bathurst long-distance winners. From left to right: Bob Morris (1976), Colin Bond (1969), Peter Brock (nine times, 1972–87), Allan Moffat (four times, 1970–77), John Goss (1974, 1985) and Bruce McPhee (1968). (The Project Group)

Bill Brown rolled two Ford Falcons at the top of the Mountain. He vivisected this car in 1971, two years after his first crash just 150 metres further down at Skyline. Note the absence of a safety fence on the opposite side of the track. (Bill Forsyth/Chevron Library)

James Hardie Industries chairman John Reid AO (left) took a personal interest in his company's race, perhaps investing far more than its commercial return. Tom Walkinshaw (right) won pole position for the 1985 race. (The Project Group)

The king of commentators, Will Hagon, holds Andrew Johnson's arm aloft after Johnson's 1980 win at the Australian Unlimited GP. Rob Moorehouse was killed in the same race. (The Project Group)

'Why are they booing me?' Prime Minister Bob Hawke asked 1983 Bathurst 1000 winner Peter Brock. 'They're not booing you—they're booing him,' Brock said, pointing to Allan Moffat. Brock and Larry Perkins (left) commandeered John Harvey's (right) car to win after their own broke down. (The Project Group)

speedway down by the showgrounds; Wilkinson was one of the best local battlers there, on his beaten-up old Rudge, but he was going nowhere. Then world champion Lionel Van Praag came to town on a promotional tour of country venues. He asked who the best local rider was. 'Bluey,' someone said, 'that red-headed bloke over there'—and Van Praag loaned Wilkinson one of his spare bikes. The race that followed was a classic, and Wilkinson beat the champ. He was on his way. He'd neatly bypassed road racing and stepped straight into the exciting, death-defying and potentially lucrative world of English speedway.

And back then the money really mattered. These were the Depression years and in the English league there was good money to be made by riding often and being quickest. Both came with big risks, but if you got it right, you could earn a decent living and look after your family. Twenty-three riders paid the ultimate price in the league in the 1930s but Wilkinson wasn't one of them. He was a winner and a hero with true grit. When he broke his collarbone the night before his 1938 world title race, he simply strapped it up and rode through the pain.

'Bat' Byrne (because he rode like a bat out of hell) was four years Wilkinson's junior and hadn't had the breaks. He felt trapped in his role as a could-have-been in road racing. All he wanted to do was get to England and crack a spot in the league, although with no money and no entree that was just a wild dream.

But Byrne was resourceful as well as ambitious. His outlook emulated modern-day race preparation; he and his tuner Charlie Ogden worked hard at visualising the 1939 race, which would be the first to be held on tarmac. They worked on gearing and brakes and tyre wear, and on judging how fast they'd have to push without breaking to stand a chance against the very best of the road circuit riders. They even thought about the one fuel stop that would be necessary to get them to the finish. Along with their mechanic Frank Hammond they devised a special quick-fill, gravity-feed fuel drum—perhaps the first ever made in Australia—in order to gain them a few precious seconds of advantage over their opposition.

Mount Panorama lived up to their expectations. Lap speeds increased exponentially. The previous year's outright lap record on dirt was a distant memory. The lightweight 250-cc bikes were averaging 5 seconds a lap faster than that over their entire race distance. The new tarmac was still treacherous. It offered amazing traction in places but was still rough in others. Riders needed to learn the track and pick their line through the emerging potholes. In the 25-lap, 154-kilometre Junior GP, the winner Eddie Wannick and challenger George Hannaford had both pulled a sensational 25 seconds out of the lap record. Pitching into the uphill cutting, Hannaford fell and caught his left hand in the drive-chain, necessitating the amputation of two fingers. Another rider took over his bike for the Senior GP.

For its entire history the combination of Mount Panorama and rain have created consternation. The circuit is so contoured and the elevation so great that it's possible to encounter different weather patterns on different parts of the circuit. You can be speeding down Conrod Straight in sunlight and, if you're game, look across to Mountain Straight and see rain falling. Your pit crew can signal all okay at the bottom of the Mountain and two minutes later you're sliding on a slick surface at the top.

Big drops of Bathurst rain began to fall as the field lined up for the Senior GP—and then they stopped. The experts sped away at the start. Byrnes had expected that. His job was to keep them in sight. Nine laps later Art Senior coasted to a halt. But Don Bain, the all-rounder who could ride every category on the card and win them all, was going strong. At the pit stop, the quick-fill tank worked and Byrnes gained several seconds. With the pressure on, Bain pushed too hard and his engine failed. Eric McPherson, Australia's Isle of Man representative, crashed but remounted. Byrnes pressed on, riding to plan. Six laps from home it started to rain. Many riders were forced to tear off their goggles and ride squinting through the shotgun pellets of rain. Two crashed. And then, after years of minor placings and could-have-beens, 'Bat' Byrnes was the Australian Grand Prix champion. He was surprised to learn that in the dry middle stint of the race he'd established a new outright circuit lap record of 3 minutes 14 seconds (71.12 miles per hour/114.53 kilometres per hour). That record would stand right up until 1948.

One of the cars John Snow brought back from the UK was a powerful Ulster MG NE Magnette. It was entered on the NSW Grand Prix card for Easter 1939 by someone unknown—T. Wood. Obviously it was a pseudonym but only Snow knew for sure the identity of the driver. It wasn't until practice that John Sherwood revealed himself. Sherwood was under some family pressure to stop racing, it was explained. Perhaps they thought it too dangerous. His father, C.O. Sherwood, had been a pillar of the automotive community. When, in 1909, a lobby of conservatives quite content with the status quo of horse-drawn carriages had vehemently complained that people were allowed to drive motorised vehicles without training, C.O.—on behalf of the New South Wales Government and the Royal Automobile Club of Australia—had become the state's first driver trainer. He held licence number one. There's a photograph of him in the hallowed halls of the Royal Automobile Club today, proudly at the wheel of his brand-new Australian Six.

At 32, John—like his father—was on several committees and was a major influence on the organisation of the 1939 Mount Panorama race meeting. He was a man of substance. But he had the racing bug and with some chicanery he'd entered Bathurst for one last fling before finally retiring to appease his family. As a consequence, perhaps unintended, he'd also outfoxed the handicappers. T. Wood was given a 25-minute advantage over the scratch car, predictably Saywell's Alfa Romeo P3. The previous year J.O. Sherwood had only 22 minutes separation from Peter Whitehead and came third. With some controversy, John Barraclough, a central member of the Sydney motor-racing push of wealthy young drivers, supported the theory that Snow and Sherwood had been deliberately obtuse. Snow, he said, had made promises to other buyers about the competitiveness of their cars and this 'mystery MG' upset the applecart.

Saywell was having a hard time getting the Alfa to settle on the new surface. The luscious red car was skipping and dancing on the long straights, an exciting sight for the alleged 40,000 spectators at Mount Panorama—surely an exaggeration—but not exactly the handling characteristics a racing driver most seeks. In the braking areas, especially heading into Pit Corner (now Murray's Corner), Saywell was not certain which wheel would lock up next. His improvement in lap times would not replicate the motorcycles'. By the end of the race he'd claimed a new lap record but it was 'only' 3 minutes 9 seconds—around 7 per cent better than Whitehead's best the previous year on the unsealed surface. Comparatively, Bat Byrnes had achieved a 13 per cent gain over Leo Tobin's record. If Saywell had been able to perform similarly he would have set the first sub-3-minute lap of the Mountain.

John Snow's Delahaye was to be driven by American speedway sensation Paul Swedberg, who was a major contender on the short circuits with his 1750-cc Offenhauser midget. Swedberg had already entered the tiny-wheeled speedcar for the Grand Prix, but with the Delahaye on offer, the Offy could wait in the pits. In Snow's hands the Delahaye could have been a match for Saywell's ill-handling Alfa but, understandably, Swedberg was ultra-conservative; he was almost 30 seconds off Saywell's best practice time and only 3 seconds clear of Sherwood's MG. The practice times were somewhat misleading. Bad weather had swept across Mount Panorama in Sunday's practice—so bad that one session had to be totally abandoned.

The handicapping was tough. In the race a tiny two-stroke German-made DKW left the start line first, heading for the fog that had enveloped the top of the mountain. Saywell had an excruciating 40-minute wait until it was his turn to go. There were 27 starters, one more than a Supercars field today. Frank Kleinig, with new and much bigger brakes on the Hudson MG, would start 5 minutes—well over a lap and a half—ahead of the Alfa. Yet he'd been only 3 seconds slower in practice.

Mount Panorama was bone-jarringly tough on a driver. As his starting time approached, Sherwood tightened the massive kidney belt he was wearing externally over his racing blue overalls to hold his core intact, and pulled on three pairs of socks to guard against the extreme heat that was being generated through his engine firewall. Starting with ten cars in front of him, Sherwood took the lead by less than one-third race distance.

Speed up the mountain was the determining factor at Mount Panorama. The MG was pulling just over the ton, 100 miles per hour (161 kilometres per hour), down the main straight but was far slower up Mountain Straight where it simply ran out of horsepower, whereas Saywell, with a big gulp of courage, could pull better than 130 miles per hour (209 kilometres per hour) in both directions. But Saywell spun twice on Hell Corner and finished in sixth.

Sherwood, going like a train, won by 1 minute 12 seconds—almost the length of the main straight—ahead of Swedberg in the borrowed Snow car. Sherwood went to raise his right arm in triumph and signal his new retirement, but he couldn't. The MG was so cramped and his body language on the big steering wheel had been so violent that he'd been hitting his elbow on the car's spinning rear wheel, and was bleeding and bruised.

In the pits Kleinig examined the crankcase of his Hudson special's engine. Officially it had 'run its bearings'. But his competitors knew it was more than that. He'd had a massive internal detonation, over-revving while he held the car flat out down the main straight. His conrods were bent and twisted inside the engine. From then on, the main run down the hill would be known as Conrod Straight.

On 3 September 1939, Prime Minister Robert Menzies announced that Australia was at war with Germany. 'In the

bitter months that are to come, calmness, resoluteness, confidence and hard work will be required as never before,' he said. 'Our staying power, and particularly the staying power of the mother country, will be best assisted by keeping our production going, by continuing our avocations and our business as freely as we can.' The Light Car Club of NSW took that as a firm direction to continue with its October race meeting at Mount Panorama. There would be no motorcycles. The Auto Cycle Union had signed on for one race meeting a year at Easter. The Light Car Club had decided that two were better than one.

John Snow, soon to be commissioned into the 2nd Armoured Car Regiment Division of the 2nd AIF, was back in the Delahaye. Curiously, he was seeded fourth in the field for the October race. In front of him was Alf Barrett's Alfa Romeo, Frank Kleinig in the Hudson and a newcomer, Rob Appleton, in a Bugatti-based Ford V8 special. The car had already had a chequered career. In its 'pur-sang' form it had been driven by Bill Thompson to win the 1930 and 1932 Australian Grands Prix at Phillip Island. But on the King's Birthday weekend in June 1938, the now-V8-engined hybrid had plunged into the crowd at the Penrith Speedway west of Sydney. Three spectators were killed and another nine injured. Its driver, Wally James, and the car's owner, Ron Mackellar, retired from the sport. Mackellar succumbed to alcoholism and died in 1941.

It was a time for racing cars with tragic histories. John Snow had acquired one too, and entered it in the October race for young John Barraclough. The Alvis Terraplane had originally been just an Alvis. It ran under the superstitious '13'—a number banned from most race programs—and it was called

'The Lucky Devil'. Its original driver was a racer born near Bathurst, Reginald Garlick, known as Phil. Garlick made his name on the short-lived and star-crossed Olympia Motor Speedway in Sydney's Maroubra. The concrete one-mile (1.6-kilometre) speed bowl, built in the sand dunes, was renowned almost from its inception as a killer track. In just two years, seven drivers and riders died there, four of them when they ran high on the bowl and launched over its metre-high vertical lip. Garlick was the last to do so. His wife, Nellie, listening to the live radio call of the race at their home in Rose Bay, heard it all. Garlick's grave in South Head General Cemetery is a bizarre monument to motor racing. His bust sits atop the gravestone, his head clad in a racing helmet and hands clutching a steering wheel.

Jack Saywell and the Alfa P3 did not contest the October race. There was a definite technique to running the temperamental Alfas and Saywell didn't have it. Alf Barrett had worked it out. His car came with an instruction manual. It outlined a conservative state of tune, one that was more likely to keep a car reliable when it was competing so far from home. It's a protocol most suppliers of high-performance competition cars maintain to this day. Saywell, on the other hand, had imported a mechanic and he tinkered with the valve timing. This combined with the number of times the Alfa had its drive wheels clear of the ground as it danced across Mount Panorama's rough surface, sending the revs up, had caused the engine to blow up. Even as war was being declared, Saywell—rightly lacking confidence in a local rebuild—crated up the engine and consigned it to the hold of an Italian freighter to go back to Italy for complete refurbishment. He never saw it again. It was alleged the freighter was one of the first civilian vessels to be torpedoed. The Saywell car would re-emerge post-war as another locally made hybrid special.

It snowed lightly at Mount Panorama on the morning of the October race, perhaps an omen for a man of the same name. By 1 p.m., when the limit man got away in bright sunshine, John Snow had 27 minutes to wait before he started. He was the most organised of racing drivers. Corner speed was not his goal. That, he reasoned, was where most mishaps occurred. He divided the Mount Panorama track into six sectors, each able to be attacked with judicious use of the accelerator and with minimal harsh steering or braking input. It's as if he'd taken instruction from the prime minister: calmness, resoluteness and confidence would win the race. The heat of the afternoon worked in his favour.

Tyre management is critical and in the heat tyres started to blow. Frank Kleinig, up to third and ready to challenge, delaminated his right rear tyre and pitted to change it. Scratch man Barrett's right rear tyre was worn through to the canvas, the yellow marker on the casing clearly showing. As he passed the pits his crew pointed frantically. Distracted by this, he missed his braking point and shot up the escape road at Hell Corner. Next time past, he ignored the pit and kept going. In the Esses—the worst possible place—the tyre blew. Heroically he held it together and rushed to the pit, his own body pummelled by pieces of disintegrating rubber. Young Barraclough escaped when a backmarker rolled in front of him into what would later be named Forrest's Elbow, the downhill left-hander onto

Conrod. He retired with steering damage. Snow cruised home to win, almost 2 minutes up on Kleinig. Alf Barrett skimmed 4 seconds off Saywell's Easter lap record—an indication of the fierce pace of the race.

Bathurst in Easter 1940 was suffering from a crippling drought. Fuel rationing was soon to be introduced, and a makeshift army camp was hurriedly being constructed at Kelso on the outskirts of the rural city. The first Australian troopship bound for the UK, the refitted Cunard-White Star Line RMS *Queen Mary*, was due to depart Sydney Harbour just six weeks after the last race meeting at Mount Panorama. The rallying cry of 'carry on' was becoming louder by the moment. A few of the racers arrived already wearing their military uniforms. Australia had introduced compulsory three-month military training for all single men who had turned 21 in 1939, but these conscripts could only serve in Australia or its territories. The majority of the military intake for overseas fighting was made up of volunteers who simply wanted to serve.

Some intended it as a great adventure. The Great War had taken four punishing years. Surely this one would be over much sooner, they thought—perhaps a year. It was a chance to see the world. Don Bain, motorcycle hero of Vale and now of Mount Panorama, had joined the RAAF, where his mechanical skill would be invaluable in keeping Australia's pilots aloft. In 1944 Bain would have under his command an eighteen-year-old leading aircraftman who'd joined up the moment he'd reached the minimum age. His name was Jack Brabham.

PREPARING FOR WAR

Although the entrant numbers, understandably, were down, Mayor Griffin, caught up in the wartime rhetoric, congratulated riders and drivers alike on their courage and enterprise. In the pits he looked with bemusement at the 4.5-litre Blower Bentley, the first Bentley to race at Mount Panorama. Hanging from its rear was a huge gas producer, fuelled by charcoal. The coal-fired car lasted just two laps but it made its statement. By war's end you'd see coal burners everywhere on the streets.

Bat Byrnes, still in Australia, was forlornly resigned to his motorcycle career aspirations being dashed by the war, but he held high hopes at least for his title defence. In the NSW Senior TT on Easter Saturday there were just 23 starters and within five laps both Leo Tobin and Art Senior were out with mechanical failure. Don Bain was more than a minute behind but closing fast. Byrnes took off just like his nickname demanded. By race end the veteran Bain had closed to within 22 seconds and their furious pace had lowered the race-winning time from 1939 by more than 7 minutes. Byrnes held on to win.

With two wins in succession, perhaps there was still a chance of getting to the UK. Byrnes was determined to seek out Bluey Wilkinson. But Wilkinson, riding through beachside Bondi in Sydney just a few months later with his wife Muriel as pillion, died under the wheels of a truck. Byrnes would go to the UK, but it would not be until two years after the war ended—too late for a 32-year-old to realise the true potential he'd had as a much younger man.

Paul Swedberg was booked to return to the US on SS *Mariposa* the week after the Bathurst meeting. This time he'd race his Offenhauser; with its tiny midget racing-car wheels slightly enlarged at the rear, a two-speed gearbox fitted, and a handbrake—the only brake—operating only on the rear axle, it was totally unsuitable for the towering Mount Panorama track. Swedberg would serve in the US Air Force when his country joined the war and he'd die in a racing car, practising, in 1946. Englishman Bill Reynolds had arrived in Australia in 1939 with a four-wheel-drive speedcar and had beaten Swedberg in one of the many 'world championships' at the Sydney Showground. For Mount Panorama he'd secured Alan Sinclair's Alta now fitted—predictably—with a Ford V8 engine. Reynolds obtained a special permit to enable him to drive the Alta, unregistered and without lights, all the way from Melbourne, where he'd bought it, to Bathurst.

Swedberg and Snow turned on the dice of the race. The tiny Offy was desperately lacking in brakes and, with the tall Swedberg poking high out of the cockpit, it was a mobile windbreak on the straight. But its power-to-weight ratio was enormous and it leapt up the mountain. The odd couple—American cheek and French chic—passed and repassed for several laps. It's possible their race was not entirely legitimate, but it was highly entertaining.

Alf Barrett, finally, won a Bathurst race. With the exclusive insignia of the British Racing Drivers' Club emblazoned on his overalls, he slammed through the field from his scratch start to finish 38 seconds ahead of Snow—about the same time, perhaps, that Snow lost in his sham-battle with the Offenhauser.

A small township made of corrugated iron sheds sprang up on a dusty, exposed plain at Kelso just east of the city, overlooked in the distance by Mount Panorama. It would be home for 5000 troops. The camp had originally been planned as a way station for the 1st Armoured Division but local farmers and graziers objected, citing irreparable damage to their paddocks and harm to their stock if tracked tanks were to be crossing their land. The army capitulated and assigned the facility to infantry training. The road to Vale and its link to the back side of Mount Panorama was perfect for teaching soldiers to drive trucks and jeeps. For almost six years the Mount Panorama circuit was fated to fall into disrepair, hastened by the pounding of heavy machinery over its fragile tarmac. It was, all things considered, a small price to pay for Bathurst's role in Australia's war effort.

5

Police and Politics

Australia had a population of 7.5 million at the end of World War II. Almost a million of them had served in the military during the war. Twenty-seven thousand had died. Motorsport suffered casualties commensurate with the national average. There were faces that would never be seen again. One was the three-time winner of the Australian Grand Prix, Bill Thompson, whose Catalina seaplane went down in the Pacific off the Marshall Islands in 1945. Psychologists speak of wartime survivors seeking dangerous sports as a substitute for military action.

The NSW police commissioner, William 'Big Bill' MacKay, did not want Mount Panorama to start up again at the end of the war. No way.

MacKay was the law in New South Wales, and in many respects was a law unto himself. In his term in office he'd outlasted no fewer than four state premiers—some said he'd hectored and beaten them into submission—and he had very definite opinions about what was right and what was wrong. Motor racing was intrinsically wrong, he believed, not because of its speed but because of its lack of safety precautions. People's lives were at risk every time they visited a motor race. Seen through the prism of today's perspective, it's hard not to agree with him; safety at the time was, at best, given lip service. 'I was six years old when my dad took me to Mount Panorama for the first time,' Brian Nightingale, one of the stalwarts of Bathurst motor racing, recalled. 'We were standing at the bottom of Conrod Straight on the outside of Murray's Corner. And John French in the FJ Holden was coming straight at us. The only thing between us and him was a wire fence. I jumped behind my dad—I'd never been so scared.'

Motor racing wasn't a big deal on Big Bill's agenda—more of a sidebar, really. His attention was consumed by the organised crime, political unrest and insurrection that threatened the very fabric of Australia.

In 1932, as a detective inspector, MacKay had been at Premier Jack Lang's side at the opening ceremony of the Sydney Harbour Bridge when Francis de Groot, a member of the New Guard political party, rode in on his horse and slashed his sword at the ceremonial ribbon. It was Big Bill—183 centimetres tall, with 100 kilograms of raging bulk—who wrestled de Groot to the ground. The scene remains one of the great images of political protest in Australian history.

Three years later, as the state's new police commissioner, MacKay brokered a peace treaty between the two queens of Sydney crime—Tilly Devine and Kate Leigh. It was the height of the Razor Gang wars, so called because the cut-throat razor was the weapon of choice of the rival gangs. They were fighting for control of the prostitution, liquor and drug trades at the height of the Prohibition era, and they'd turned the Kings Cross and Darlinghurst areas into a killing ground. MacKay summoned both women to his office—Devine, the queen of Woolloomooloo, and Leigh, the queen of Surry Hills. The violence and the drug dealing had to stop, he told them. In return he would not 'actively enforce' control of bootlegging or prostitution.

His reward for keeping law and order, no matter how compromised his position, was to be sent on a six-month fact-finding mission through the US, Great Britain and Germany. He returned full of praise for J. Edgar Hoover and the FBI, and for the discipline of Nazism and the efficiency of the German police. The German youth movement particularly impressed him as a means of 'subordinating the individual to the welfare of the nation'. In 1937 he started the first Police Boys' Club in New South Wales.

State and federal governments used MacKay's specially trained squad to infiltrate those applying opposing political doctrines. His officers produced much of the material that enabled the Communist Party to be declared an unlawful association in 1940.

You crossed Big Bill at your peril. When the Police Association of New South Wales complained about his methods, he posted all seventeen members of its committee to rural stations. And when the mood took him, he turned the police marching orchestra into a Scottish pipe band, dressed in the MacKay tartan in honour of his Glaswegian origins.

MacKay first served notice on motor racing in 1938. The NSW Light Car Club and Empire Speedways were to jointly promote the Sesquicentennial Grand Prix at Parramatta Park—a 3.2-kilometre public road through the trees. It was to be centrepiece of a grand celebration of Australia's 150th year of establishment and a huge boost to the thriving Parramatta retail community. Its star was to be Peter Whitehead. Major competitors had practised on the circuit under the watchful eye of police, who declared the circuit safe. There was huge excitement and promoters, including the ebullient John Sherwood, were expecting 50,000 spectators. They'd pre-sold many tickets and built a 1100-person grandstand at the start/finish line. But at 5.30 p.m. on the day before the race Big Bill banned it. The corners, thought safe by some, were a danger in his eyes. It's likely that with his busy schedule, he'd only just noticed. But a fresh application for the race to occur the following week with new fencing erected was rejected. MacKay seldom backed down. Mayor John Irwin, the owner of a Parramatta hardware store, demanded a public enquiry. It never occurred. Mount Panorama had been warned.

Bathurst's mayor Martin Griffin died suddenly in 1941, aged just 57. His successor, Alan Morse, was neither an orator nor a visionary but he was well connected, and it's likely that with the election of Bathurst-born Ben Chifley as prime minister in 1945, Mount Panorama had some degree of tacit immunity.

The repatriation of the entire area was a priority. The army camp at Kelso was quickly being turned into a gigantic migrant hostel and some money was able to be diverted to essential track repairs. The local car club, now reconstituted as the Amateur Drivers' Club, had been pre-emptive. Just four months after the ceasefire with Japan was signed, the club conducted the first post-war race meeting in Australia, a hill climb through the Esses, on New Year's Day 1946. It went off without incident, won by Frank Kleinig in his hand-built Hudson special.

The NSW Victory TT took place on the Mountain just fourteen weeks later. It was a hectic time in Australia's post-war recovery, with many things to do, but Big Bill thoughtfully sent a welcoming committee. As motorcyclists rode into Bathurst they were greeted by police—lots of them. Snap inspections occurred, fines were issued and fights broke out. Returned soldiers who'd just cheated death were not about to submit to the presumption of authority. It was a harbinger of the confrontations between authorities and Mount Panorama racegoers that would erupt for decades, and it attracted media attention. Among the melee, wealthy Sydney motorcycle shop owner Ron Kessing, a business partner of Don Bain, claimed the Senior TT on Bain's 500-cc Velocette, dubbed 'The Monster'. A fast-finishing Harry Hinton crossed in second, with the still-ambitious Bat Byrnes in third.

But in the last race of the meeting—the Unlimited Handicap, won by Jack Forrest—Mount Panorama suffered its first fatality. *The National Advocate* reported it sensationally, apparently straight from the police deposition sheet:

[Bernard] Henry O'Halloran (65) a patrolman, of Bentinck Street, was crossing the road near the end of the long straight

[Conrod] when Ray Edwin Fletcher (21), of Marrickville, came out of a dip in the road at 95 m.p.h. and smashed into him. O'Halloran was killed instantly and his dead body was thrown through the air into the crowd where it struck Pte Charles Hurst (24) of Russell St, inflicting severe leg and chest injuries . . . A spectator at the scene of the tragedy said that O'Halloran had only taken about two steps on to the track when he was struck.

The newspaper claimed, pre-emptively, that Fletcher also had died: on his way to hospital by ambulance. And a later coroner's report confirmed it: 'Dr Mulvey gave evidence of having made an examination of the body of Fletcher,' it said. 'Fletcher had a fracture of the cervical vertebrae which had caused sudden death.'

Somewhat melodramatically, *The National Advocate* reported Fletcher's bike was carrying the number 13.

Regrettably, it was not the only incident surrounding the races that year.

The *Advocate* reported that Peter Jenkins, on a BSA 250, suffered concussion and major facial lacerations when he slid into a barbed-wire fence. Another motorcycle in the pits caught fire and 'burned to the ground'.

And in the city of Bathurst, at the corner of William and Brilliant Streets, two motorcycles en route to Mount Panorama collided with a car carrying a family of seven. A babe in arms (there were no child restraints back then) was killed.

Under the circumstances it was a miracle that the permit for October's car race meeting was not pulled there and then. The meeting would go ahead, but 1947 would be a different matter.

On 2 October 1946 Alexander 'Lex' Nicholas Davison, governing director of Paragon Shoes and, at age 23, already a pillar of Melbourne business and society, married Diana Crick, 'several years younger'—and a motor-racing dynasty was begun. Three of their sons would race at the top end of the sport and, among their motor-racing grandchildren, one would twice win the Bathurst 1000.

They were wed in St Peter's Church in Toorak: gap-toothed Lex in tails, Diana slim and elegant in white silk, with a décolletage that was daring for its day. After spending their first night together in a Melbourne hotel, the next morning—beaming with joy—they climbed into a raw, totally open two-seat racing Alfa Romeo. It had been cut down from Lex's father's saloon and had 150,000 kilometres on the odometer, and they drove overland 1500 kilometres to Mount Panorama and back so Davison could use it to compete in his first motor race. He would go on to become a four-time winner of the Australian Grand Prix and the inaugural recipient of the CAMS Gold Star, the nation's premier motorsport award.

'Lex had a fractured relationship with his father,' Davison's son Chris, one of seven Davison children, recalled. Davison was an only child and his father treated him with scorn. The real fissure in their relationship occurred in World War II when A.A. (Alec) Davison, the family patriarch, used his considerable influence to have Lex removed from the 106th Anti Tank Regiment and returned to Melbourne to work in their shoe factory under the guise of 'essential industry'. Lex's later attempt to re-enlist was also thwarted by his father. It was not long after Alec Davison died of cancer in 1945 that Lex had the family Alfa 6C—coach-built in Australia, with an elegant four-door body—cut and shut into something entirely more sporting. 'It was cathartic for him,' Chris explained. The car Lex and Diana drove to Mount Panorama had a raucous unmuffled exhaust, an engine and transmission that screamed at high revolutions, open sides, and a suspension that attacked the senses.

Lex Davison's debut was discreet but auspicious. He'd entered only a support race, a six-lap handicap, not the NSW Grand Prix. It was a try-out to see if he had any ability at all. In practice he slipped off the road in the Esses and nudged a tree—embarrassingly, in front of his new bride. In the race he was one of the first away, 45 seconds ahead of the winner; he and his friend John Barraclough finished sixth, 5 minutes 30 seconds behind. But every time he went through Forrest's Elbow in the blood-red Alfa, he was cheered by recently released Italian prisoners of war who'd been incarcerated in the nearby Cowra POW camp and were now awaiting assimilation in the Kelso compound. Lex waved back. It was grand sport.

Mount Panorama was in horrible condition—potholed and corrugated and, at the urging of competitors concerned for their cars and their own bodies, the main race was limited to 100 miles (161 kilometres). In the Grand Prix, anything above 100 miles per hour on Conrod Straight was considered foolhardy. Jack Murray—later to be universally christened 'Gelignite Jack' because of his exploits in the REDeX trials with the explosive, ostensibly to clear trees—did 110 miles per hour (177 kilometres per hour), but Murray was brave. His good mate Alf Najar, son of Lebanese immigrants who'd arrived from Tripoli on SS *Orvieto* in 1926 and made good in the rag trade, was having his first crack at the Mount Panorama full circuit. Najar had brought his beautifully bodied red MG TB special to the hill climb in January to try it out. Alf, Jack and Bill MacLachlan, also in the Grand Prix, were pioneers of the sport of water ski racing on the Hawkesbury River outside Sydney, tuning their ski boats in Murray's Bondi garage and toning their bodies in Murray's gym. At Mount Panorama Najar was the pupil and Murray showed him around. Down Conrod, Najar over-revved the MG and ran its bearings. Rex Marshall's crew from Monza Service (Najar was in with the in-crowd) did an overnighter to get him ready for the race. And he won.

Handicapping can be a wonderful thing. Najar and John Nind, both on MGs, started side by side halfway through the field and raced the whole event long, too far ahead of the scratch starters to be caught. Then Najar spun at Forrest's Elbow, handing the race to Nind; a lap later Nind spun too, in the Esses, giving it back to Najar. Bill Murray, in major contention, crashed his Hudson into the sandbags on Pit Corner at the end of Conrod Straight, and Najar was clear to claim his debut Grand Prix victory. That night, at the barbecue in the pits, Najar took a piece of charcoal, walked over to the place where Murray had crashed and graffitied 'Murray's Corner' on the fence. The name endures to this day.

Commissioner MacKay acted swiftly and with an iron will. In late 1946 he called together the Mount Panorama stakeholders— the Bathurst City Council, the Auto Cycle Union, and the newly formed Australian Sporting Car Club (ASCC), an amalgamation of car clubs that had been constituted only the year before to give motorsport a stronger voice. MacKay's conference was much more one-sided than the one he had held with Tilly Devine and Kate Leigh. He was offering no compromises. He told them, bluntly, he would not grant any future applications for motor racing at Mount Panorama. The circuit, he said, was unsafe, and in more general terms motor racing served no useful purpose.

In January 1947 the stakeholders tested MacKay's resolve. They made a formal application to conduct car and motorcycle races over the Easter weekend. The application was rejected as they'd expected. Fully prepared for Plan B, they appealed the decision, and a hearing was scheduled at the Bathurst Court of Petty Sessions. They thought they'd be okay; an appeal heard on the doorstep of the Mountain, with all its commercial implications for the city, would have to bring a positive result. But MacKay outmanoeuvred them. On the grounds of the distance that needed to be travelled and limited time to prepare, police applied for and received an adjournment—until the day after the Easter long weekend. The Easter meeting was off.

The racers had been right however, about where to stage their appeal. On the back of a multitude of promises they made, the Bathurst magistrate in June that year granted a permit to race in October. Those promises included track widening; additional safety fencing across the top of the mountain, at Murray's Corner and, curiously, along Conrod Straight (what were people doing there anyway?); and the crucial commitment to restrict spectator access in places like the inside of Griffin's Bend. It was important, because the Australian Sporting Car Club had secured the rights to the Australian Grand Prix—the first to be held after the war. And that was a big deal.

MacKay was not pleased. Police assistance would be limited, he said (no bad thing, considering their hectoring the year before) and there was rumour that competitors would be charged for dangerous driving on public roads. It was a fanciful claim. Nonetheless notices in the programs for both the car and bike races implored everyone—racers and spectators alike—to take care. They would be under scrutiny.

Jack Forrest, born 150 kilometres up the road in Wellington, was seemingly without fear. He gained a reputation as a habitual crasher. In the opening practice for the 1947 NSW Motorcycle Grand Prix he slipped and slid his way down through the Esses towards the last corner before Conrod. It was known simply as the Elbow, and occasionally the Devil's Elbow, one of the three most exacting corners on the circuit. Hard under brakes, Forrest's 500-cc Norton crashed (they call it 'dropping the model') and he smashed his left elbow on the pavement, grazing it to the bone. Harry Hinton, two years off beginning his international career and full of mirth, immediately renamed the corner Forrest's Elbow. Forrest and Hinton were the best of mates. While Forrest was getting medical attention, Hinton saw to the Norton, bending its handlebars at an odd angle so that Forrest, with his elbow tightly wrapped and virtually immobilised, could reach the grip and clutch lever. The next day Forrest leapt away, ignored the pain, set the fastest lap of the race and would have won if his engine hadn't cut out. Eric McPherson, on the 350-cc Norton on which Harry Hinton had already won the Junior GP, claimed his first Senior GP. It was an extraordinary victory. Small bikes shouldn't win big bike races.

POLICE AND POLITICS

It was a weekend for small engines exceeding expectations on four wheels as well as two. Bill Murray had switched from his Hudson special to an MG TC bullet-proofed by Rex Marshall, the go-to engineer in Sydney. TCs, launched post-war, had already become the all-purpose production racing car of choice. You could drive a TC to a race meeting with its lights, guards and windscreen intact, then detach them and have an open-wheeler racing car. Pretty soon people were building special-bodied TCs that looked for all the world like real racing cars. Murray's didn't. It was essentially a road body minus its lights—nothing 'special' about it—but as the favourites dropped out around it, the spindly TC took the lead on the last lap and delivered Murray the twelfth Australian Grand Prix.

In third place Lex Davison, incredibly enthusiastic and back for his second year, was driving the largest car in the race—a monstrous and magnificent white 7.6-litre supercharged Mercedes-Benz 38/250, built way back in 1929. It has since become one of the world's most sought-after collectables. A similar one to Davison's fetched US$7.4 million (A$10.4 million) at auction in 2004 and prices have skyrocketed since then.

The Davisons had arrived for the Grand Prix with an entourage, driving the big Merc up from Melbourne to Sydney on the coast road, along with the MG TC that Lex had just given Diana for her twenty-first birthday. The driving was shared by Davison and his pit crew, among them World War II Spitfire fighter ace Peter Ward. The drive up was part of the adventure, almost as good as the race.

Things happened at breakneck speed in the Davison family. Diana, determined not to miss the fun, had flown to Sydney with their first son Anthony, born just weeks before. They built a special crib for the tiny luggage compartment in the MG and Diana drove the last leg over the mountains with the baby on board. Lex, meanwhile, had serviced the big Benz at Monza Motors and left for Bathurst in convoy with Bill Murray, the race's eventual winner. At the base of the Blue Mountains in Lapstone, Davison and Murray, travelling briskly, passed a police patrol. Davison signalled 'Let's go!' to Murray and they took off, outdistancing pursuit.

In the Grand Prix, Davison, a tyro in the previous year's race, created thunder on the Mountain, drifting the big car up through Griffin's Bend. With eight laps to go he needed only six to catch and pass Murray, but he couldn't make it on his remaining fuel load. Frustrated, he pulled into the pits for a splash and dash, filling the air with what his good friend John Barraclough—reporting that year for a motorsport magazine—described as 'dreadful language'. Davison came third outright and first in the over-1500-cc class. In the circumstances the meritorious second place of Charles 'Dick' Bland, a Bathurst local, hardly rated a mention.

On 22 January 1948, police commissioner MacKay was entertaining senior police colleagues at his Edgecliff home in Sydney's Eastern suburbs when he suddenly collapsed and died. Big Bill was 63.

There were some, shedding crocodile tears, who thought Mount Panorama—and, for that matter, motor racing in general—was off the hook. But it wasn't to be. Motor racing was attacking itself from within. The newly minted Australian

Sporting Car Club was suffering severe financial losses on its race meetings. It was in no position to contribute much to circuit improvements and there were race drivers in its ranks who were beginning to side with some of the issues raised by the late commissioner. Mount Panorama was dangerous. And there was also the question of money. In a stance remarkably similar to that echoed by Supercars teams half a century later, the drivers saw themselves as the public drawcards but they were getting none of the takings. Ultimately they'd form an action group—a breakaway—within the Club to press their case.

The controlling body of motorsport was moving towards a similar view on safety.

The Automobile Association of Australia (AAA) was in charge of the road service clubs—the NRMA, RACV and the like—and notionally it was also the administrator of motorsport, answering to the RAC in Great Britain. The AAA didn't want motor racing in its portfolio. It cost a lot to run a sport enjoyed by only a few. To an organisation with influence in high places, whose core business was roadside assistance, insurance and increasingly the promotion of road safety, motor racing was non-essential. It had to go. Oscar Zehnder, the secretary of the AAA, was doing his best to warn the sport of impending doom but no one was listening. They were having too good a time.

The ASCC's club rooms, on the first floor of a garage in Cleveland Street, Redfern, were the Friday night gathering place for enthusiasts. They'd troop across from Rex Marshall's Monza Service (known to them as Multigrip Motors). There was, among others, Adam 'Curley' Brydon, aka 'The Mouse'; engine tuner Tom 'The Prof' Jemison; 'The Phantom Chef' Barry Revell; and David McKay, 'Sir Malcolm', who'd soon win the Australian TT for cars at Mount Panorama and become Australia's first touring-car champion at the nearby Gnoo Blas circuit. There was increasingly a greater number of trials, hill climbs and sprints to be contested, not to mention the unofficial races—Kings Cross to Rose Bay was a Saturday night delight, and the long wide expanse of Newcastle Street joining New and Old South Head Roads was the perfect place for a timed sprint before a hurried departure. The Phantom Chef didn't enjoy wheel-to-wheel racing on public roads: he revelled in chasing fire engines. This was the MG TC crowd, not as monied as their Victorian opposition but confident in the handicapper.

John Barraclough, bon vivant and man about town, led home an MG rout in the 1948 NSW 100 at Mount Panorama. Six of the top seven placegetters were MGs, three of them TCs. 'Back-off Barraclough' was given his name by Paul Swedberg when Barraclough was his pusher at the pre-war speedway meetings. 'Back-off' came from money: 'Father had a sports Hupmobile', he said in his autobiography. '[As a child] I started it with the hand throttle open and there was shrapnel everywhere. Father was not pleased but fortunately he had two of them.' He lived a peripatetic existence, his immense charm carrying the day when funds ran short. He drove a lot of other people's cars, stayed in a lot of other people's homes and, it's said, entertained a lot of other people's wives and daughters.

Controversial overnight handicapping had disadvantaged the Melbourne contingent. Lex Davison, off scratch in his newly acquired works Alfa Romeo 2900B Monoposto, retired after recording a massive 144 miles per hour (231 kilometres per hour) down the still lethally bumpy Conrod; Squadron Leader Tony Gaze, Australia's tenth-most decorated flying ace, just back from the UK with a supercharged Alta, ran his bearings; and the Maestro, Alf Barrett, could manage only eighth in the Monza Alfa.

The motorcycles took the meeting far more seriously. A new head of promotion, former wireless announcer Wally Capper, had taken John Sherwood's chutzpah and added to it. He declared the race would run as the prestigious Australian TT—the first at Mount Panorama— and that prize money would be guaranteed at £1000 ($2000, around $20,000 today). He introduced clubman classes, essentially a low-cost amateur formula, to boost the fields; mindful of McPherson's Senior win on a Junior bike, he banned cross-entering of machines. History records that his only disappointment was that an entry he received from a newcomer on a Velocette 350 for the Junior Clubman race failed to turn up: Jack Brabham, who otherwise might have pursued a motorcycle career, had accepted a last-minute offer to race his speedway car in Adelaide the same weekend. Bikes in the Senior TT would cover 100 miles (161 kilometres)—the same distance as the cars. It was a long way on a motorcycle, but they still did it 10 minutes faster than the fragile cars. Winner Frank Mussett (Velocette 500) became the first bike rider to exceed 200 kilometres per hour down Conrod—127 miles per hour, just over 204 kilometres per hour—and he did it lap after lap as he outdistanced Harry Hinton and the veteran Leo Tobin. Jack Forrest, challenging for the lead, dropped it again, but no new corner was named for him.

In 1949 the car contingent's luck ran out. In the last session of practice 28-year-old Jack Johnson, one of the MG TC brigade, turned hard right under brakes at the end of Conrod and inverted. Handsome Jack Johnson was trapped in the car and although his injuries did not seem serious he died that afternoon, the first car-racing fatality on the Mountain. Compared to the Auto Cycle Union, the cash-strapped ASCC had not been having a good time. Wally Capper, cheekily, had applied to Bathurst City Council to race motorcycles on the cars' date as well; he wanted to accommodate his clubman races, which were oversubscribed and growing. The ASCC had to stump up more money, which it barely had, to guarantee its Easter weekend slot. Relationships between the Club and the Council were tearing apart. The Council convened a Mount Panorama Citizens' Committee to 'help' the ASCC run its meeting.

It's said that 30,000 spectators turned up to watch the Australian Motorcycle Grand Prix that year. The queue to the circuit gates stretched back to the city, and spectators were abandoning their bikes and climbing fences to get in. The Senior GP was won by Bat Byrnes on a Manx Norton that was thirteen years old.

The 'cars' ran neither a GP nor a TT, the two most revered titles, but, instead, an All Powers Handicap over 25 laps, in many respects a lesser event. The lure of Mount Panorama still drew a strong entry but the curse of unreliability dealt with many of them. Arthur Rizzo, son of Maltese immigrants who owned a pool hall at Sydney's beachside Maroubra, won in an immaculate self-built Riley, which he and his wife Valerie had driven to the circuit. Rizzo won 20 out of the first 25 races he entered. The Rizzo Riley had become the benchmark for backyard specials.

Just after the Australian Grand Prix at Queensland's Leyburn Street circuit in September, Oscar Zehnder decided it was time to act. He made a phone call to the Sydney driver who, at 31, had just fulfilled his lifelong ambition of winning the Grand Prix. John Crouch was the right sort of chap: well connected, urbane, soon to become the Australian distributor for Cooper racing cars and Austin Healey sports cars. It's said they met in the panelled elegance of the library in the Royal Automobile Club of Australia, above Circular Quay, where conversations between gentlemen are never recorded. Zehnder, in polite yet strong terms, forewarned Crouch that the AAA planned to dissolve any agreement to administer motor racing. Crouch reported back to Norman Pleasance, secretary of the ASCC, and Pleasance passed on the message to his counterparts in each state. It would be another three years before anything happened—and then it occurred in a rush. A perfect storm was building.

Harry Hinton, for all his brilliance, had not won a Senior race at Mount Panorama. He'd won the Sidecar TT at the inaugural meeting in 1938 and then racked up a spectacular list of other victories: the 1940 Lightweight TT; the 1947, 1948 and 1949 Junior TT and GPs; and the 1949 Lightweight, all backing up the 1937 Lightweight he'd won on the old Vale circuit. The Hinton family was as close as you come to motorcycle royalty, but they didn't act like it. When in Bathurst they stayed at the private home of Robert Taylor, just around the corner from the Tattersalls Hotel; at night, the true enthusiasts would go down there to see Harry, and later his sons, work on their bikes. There was no lighting, no workshop lead lights—just a torch.

Harry loved a chat, encouraged youngsters, and the younger Taylor boy would later race in the junior categories.

In 1950, Harry's wife Vienie wasn't at Bathurst. She was already on a ship heading for England and the Isle of Man TT. The plan was that Harry would race at Mount Panorama then jump on an aeroplane—quite an experience—and join the ship in Fremantle. So Vienie didn't get to see him win his first Mount Panorama Senior. Initially it looked for all the world like he couldn't.

The riders balloted for grid positions and Hinton started near last, dropping further back when his Norton wouldn't start. But his ride was masterful. He carved through the field, won by half a lap and then sprinted for the airport. It was the start of the Hinton age of dominance. He'd win the Senior again in 1951 and then the Unlimited in 1952 and '53 when it changed its title. In 1953 he rode the card, winning the 250, 350, 500 and the Unlimited.

According to the Sydney motorsport push, Doug Whiteford was quite unlike most of the other Victorians who came across the border to Mount Panorama. 'The Victorian racing driver is usually an amateur who employs a mechanic to maintain his car and the sport is his hobby,' David McKay said, a bit disingenuously in his autobiography *Behind the Wheel*. 'People like Lex Davison are not found in racing in other states. If they were, they would probably own horses and be members of the Australian Jockey Club.' Whiteford, already 33, was a garage proprietor, pretty much without humour, who worked extremely hard to build his own car: a Ford V8 special nicknamed 'Black Bess'. In January 1950, with the old car refreshed, he won the Australian Grand Prix in South Australia, and at Easter he brought it to Mount Panorama and won the NSW 100 from an increasingly quality field. In October he won again, but in the confusion of combined scratch and handicap racing (a field would face a mass start but then handicappers would determine victory by mathematical equation as the race progressed), he was awarded only the scratch win over local Bathurst farmer Warwick Pratley, driving a car built by local engineering genius and driver George Reed. Pratley won again in 1951. But the writing was on the wall. Motor racing, especially open-wheeler motor racing, was entering its golden age, and a locally built car would soon become unlikely to make the grade.

The administrators of motorsport and the promoters of Mount Panorama car racing were battling each other to determine which group was the most dysfunctional. On 13 October 1952, the board of the AAA met in Brisbane and resolved to discard motor racing with immediate effect. Because no one had paid much attention, what could have been a seamless transition had become a full-blown crisis.

Somewhat simultaneously, the ASCC, which was trying to be all things to all members, conceded that it no longer had a place at Mount Panorama. It cut its losses by taking up with two other suitors: the nearby Orange City Council, with its soon-to-be-opened rival circuit Gnoo Blas; and a highly ambitious English promoter of motor oil products.

Leading ASCC committee members, among them Curley Brydon and David McKay, had already walked out in disgust, citing major mismanagement, and they formed the kernel of a new organisation called the Australian Racing Drivers' Club (ARDC). At its inception in 1951 the ARDC had built a small racetrack at Mount Druitt, using a disused World War II airstrip owned by former ASCC member and defector Belf Jones. It wasn't hard to do; with a bulldozer and a few working bees, you could put together a racetrack good enough to run a 24-hour race, which they did three years later. The ARDC had intended to remain small, with membership limited to actual competitors, and the drivers and teams sharing in the hopefully positive revenue generated by the race meetings. Bathurst wasn't on the ARDC's radar, but when the prospect of taking over Mount Panorama arose, it opened its books to enthusiasts and was flooded with support.

The ASCC, meanwhile, continued to split apart. 'The clue was in the sponsorship of the 1951 Bathurst 100,' hypothesised David Johnson, now a senior statesman of the early racers, an active club official and three-time NSW State Rally champion. The race was supported by REDeX, an oil additives company with big ambitions. Its owner in Australia, recent English emigrant Reg Shepheard, had seized on motorsport as his promotional tool and wanted to run a round-Australia trial—the biggest automotive event ever held in the country. He needed an organisation to run it and he'd chosen the ASCC. They were too focused on Mount Panorama to do both things well, if at all, and Shepheard was the club's salvation. 'Reg was used to taking punts,' David Johnson said. 'In commercial terms he was a gambler. If he'd said, "Do it my way", he would have been very persuasive, and as it turns out his way was the right way for the club.'

By January 1953 the Australian motor-racing landscape had seen seismic change. The Confederation of Australian Motor Sport (CAMS) had been formed to take over from the AAA; the ASCC was running its first race meeting around the relatively flat, triangular Gnoo Blas course, and in August would run its first REDeX Round Australia Trial. Taking advantage of the turmoil, the Auto Cycle Union under Wally Capper had applied for—and been granted—Mount Panorama access on both Easter and October dates, so there would be no cars racing on the mountain that year. The ARDC resolved to turn Mount Panorama into a household name in Australia, and 1954 was the year they would start their campaign.

The battle between Mount Panorama and Gnoo Blas would rage for a decade. Separated by just 60 kilometres, the two tracks were divided by raw ambition and exacerbated by a bitter power struggle to control motorsport in Australia. The Orange City Council, on behalf of its Cherry Blossom Festival, had seized on the opportunity to draw the Australian Sporting Car Club away from Mount Panorama. It offered great incentive—building a brand-new track to the Club's exact specifications was the main one—and it also put up the prize money and paid the promotional fees. The Bathurst City Council, somewhat caught out, responded with an offer to the Australian Racing Drivers' Club, which included building a new control tower, and outfitting the circuit with electric power (run underground), water supply and toilets. Both councils knew the value of motorsport, it seemed, when it was about to slip through their grasp.

Dirty tricks were alleged, and in some cases on display for all to see. Gnoo Blas was confronted with a protest from a consortium of religious ministers claiming that racing at the circuit on Sunday and charging an entry fee was in contravention of the Sunday Observance Act. Yet no such caveat existed for Mount Panorama, another reason for Orange to cry foul. They suspected even the Church was against them. Organisers of the Bathurst race stayed clear, warning Orange not to embroil them or the dispute could escalate to encompass track safety. Date clashes were rife. It was not uncommon for competitors to go straight from a race meeting at Mount Panorama to compete at Gnoo Blas the next day, raising howls of protest from Gnoo Blas that they were getting the tired remnants of the Panorama meeting. And yet it was Gnoo Blas that secured the first Australian Touring Car Championship.

CAMS was in conflict with the ASCC about the way it ran the REDeX trials. That resulted in the formation of a NSW splinter group, the Council of Combined Motor Clubs. For a while it looked as if CAMS would fold. The ARDC, through its president Arthur Hayes, stayed as tight as it could with CAMS. There was only room for one governing body and CAMS was the stronger, he believed. It took the resolve of Hayes and the diplomacy of one of the rebels, Doug Stewart, a brilliant businessman, to broker a rapprochement. Much later Stewart would become the president of CAMS. The CAMS war deflected a lot of the ASCC's energy away from making the Orange circuit great.

Gnoo Blas's chances of survival were always limited by its location—on a genuine public road, not on a scenic drive—and by the lack of total support from the town's citizens, especially the business community. The track circumnavigated Orange's psychiatric hospital—the main straight was called 'Mental Straight', an inappropriate name by any standards—and hospital management could influence the organisation of the race meeting, positively or negatively, seemingly on a whim. In 1960 the Orange Cherry Blossom Festival folded for lack of support. Gnoo Blas was close behind. Its last race meeting was held on October 1961, just as Mount Panorama was considering hosting a long-distance touring-car race for the first time.

Part 3
The Golden Age

There was a time when motorcycles and open-wheeler racing cars, both stunning in their naked beauty and tenuous contact with the laws of gravity, ruled Mount Panorama. No amphitheatre circuit could match the sight, sound and speed of these breathtakingly fragile machines flashing across the Mountain, appearing briefly like wraiths between the trees and the low foliage that lined the track.

Even when the sedans turned up, at first little more than an amusement, Mount Panorama presented them in a way the burgeoning city circuits could not. While the Tin Tops filled every centimetre of the tight city tracks with muscle and bravado, the Mountain provided a different canvas. And the sedan drivers rose in stature because of the way they handled the challenge.

6

The Golden Age of Motorcycles

Motorcycle world champions honed their skills at Mount Panorama. 'If you couldn't do good at Bathurst you were wasting your time going to Europe,' said champion Kel Carruthers. But the more the circuit adapted to accept cars—first the ultra-high-speed open-wheelers and then the long-distance touring cars—the more unsuitable it became for the bikes. Ultimately the motorcycle racing had to stop.

Mick Doohan, five-time world champion and Australia's most successful motorcycle export, won the last ever Unlimited TT at Mount Panorama on his first attempt—and he won the long-distance Arai 500 endurance race at the same meeting. Kel Carruthers, Australia's 1969 world 250-cc champion and an engineer of great influence in global motorcycle sport, dominated GP and TT races at Mount Panorama for four consecutive years and loved the swooping, dipping challenge of the place. Wayne Gardner, 1987 world champion, raced in the Arai 500 just once, came sixth, and rated Mount Panorama as one of three circuits in the world that he would choose not to race on. 'The walls and the fences are too close to the track,' he said. 'Especially for the high speeds that you generate.'

It was difficult not to agree with him. In 1980, when Gardner competed in the inaugural Arai—81 laps, equating to 500 kilometres covered in just three hours—Mount Panorama was well on its way to becoming a concrete tunnel. It was a necessity for the safety of the cars that raced there and the spectators that watched them. By the time Doohan arrived in 1987 for a production bike race and then his outright assault a year later, sand traps were starting to be built to mitigate the sudden impact between machine and retaining wall. But they were being built with cars in mind, and what saved cars and drivers would destroy bikes and riders. Motorcycles, for so long the mainstay of the Mountain, were being marginalised. Despite the protestations of the Auto Cycle Union that the race meeting in 1989—the year after Doohan's win—would go ahead, it didn't.

When Kel Carruthers dominated at Mount Panorama, relentlessly from 1962 to 1965 in preparation for his international career, Mount Panorama was just that: panoramic—a glorious vista where Skyline for the riders was truly a leap into space; where the trees were at least in the periphery, not grazing their elbows; and where the fences weren't leaving concrete scars on their leathers. Carruthers is the ultimate survivor. When we spoke at the Californian home he shares with his wife Jan—they were childhood sweethearts—he was a father of three, grandfather of five and great-grandfather of two. In a brutal sport that could take life instantaneously, Carruthers seldom crashed but often won. 'Mount Panorama was by far the best track in Australia,' he told me. 'It qualified as one of the "old" Grand Prix circuits alongside the Sachsenring, Ulster, Spa and the Isle of Man.' They were all circuits on which Carruthers would race in pursuit of a world title—and the starting money that kept him solvent during his campaign.

It's startling how few riders have truly succeeded at the pinnacle of Mount Panorama racing. The remarkable Hinton family, Jack Ahearn, Kel Carruthers, Ron Toombs, Bill Horsman, Warren Willing, Ron Boulden, Andrew Johnson and Japan's Ikujiro Takai are all multiple winners—many of them successively. It's the same in the sidecar class, which to many is the most thrilling and certainly precarious of all categories. Twenty-six of those race victories have been shared by just five family names.

Motorcycle racing works on a class system defined both by the engine size of the bike and the experience and skill of the rider. It was possible to ride everything from a 50-cc bike, screaming its head off down Conrod Straight—Victorian Barry Smith, a sometime Mount Panorama competitor, snagged a third in the world championship in that class—through to 1100-cc superbikes. A rider could be a beginner but not a novice—Mount Panorama was no place to have your first race—although some snuck through. It was possible to ride in a production category or on a full works-prepared Grand Prix bike. The top fields could be limited to a relatively few professionals, but in the beginners' categories the organisers would unleash grids of more than 100 well-intentioned amateurs, stretching back around Murray's Corner with a separate flag waver to start their race.

Among the madness would be three or four motorcycle-mounted non-competing travelling marshals. Usually former racers, their job was to insert themselves in the field so they could be quickly on the scene of a crash, all the while staying out of the way of the competition. All were volunteers and there was great cachet in being chosen. Most took their role seriously; some, by today's standards, did not. It was collegiate, a bonding experience. John Shanks, a racer in the 1950s and now retired to Bathurst, tells the story of his indoctrination into the 'Green Shed'.

'It was centrally located in the pits and it was the office and invitation-only entertaining area of ACU [Auto Cycle Union] race director Harry Bartrop,' Shanks recalled. 'Harry always asked us in for a beer, but he was, naturally, irate with his marshals if they were caught drinking beer at the side of the track. So we poured our beer into lemonade cans.' Bartrop was a former racer himself—third in the 1933 Junior GP at the Vale circuit—and a great organiser in his prime, but he had long since delegated responsibility. He delighted in the trappings of the job, particularly the powerful motorcycle and sidecar outfit at his disposal for high-speed 'track-clearing' laps between races. His party trick was to get the outfit on two wheels, lifting the sidecar wheel high in the air. He was relieved of his post when he rolled the bike at Forrest's Elbow with the mayor of Bathurst's secretary, Wendy, in the 'chair'.

And yet motorcycling made no apology for actions like that. It was working to rules it had made and which its wise old men regarded as universally acceptable. It took the intervention of husband-and-wife team Arthur and Jan Blizzard to clean it up. Both were stalwarts of the old-time club scene but they were aware of the vulnerability of the sport if that approach continued. Arthur, awarded an Order of Australia Medal for his efforts before his early death from cancer, and Jan, still awaiting her deserved recognition, travelled the world to race meetings, made friends in very high places, and transformed Mount Panorama motorcycle racing into an international force, all while working from the enclosed verandah of their home in Sydney's southern suburb of Loftus where they also ran their family plastering business. There is longevity in motorcycle administration. Twenty years after Arthur's death, approaching her eighties, Jan—who once was in the same swimming squad as Dawn Fraser and if not for Fraser's brilliance might have been an Olympic contender—had just announced her intention to retire as secretary of the St George Motorcycle Club.

Kel Carruthers first rode at Mount Panorama as a small boy. His father Jack was a top mechanic and sidecar competitor at the speedway, and he went to Mount Panorama to work on the successful Black Shadow Vincents, including those of Australian TT winner Tony McAlpine. 'We were in the pits, camping at the end of Conrod Straight and they put me on a Vincent and I rode it, solo, right around the circuit. I was wearing a pair of shorts, sandshoes, no helmet,' Kel remembered. He can't recall how old he was, but he'd played hooky from his church soccer club to join his dad. He was substantially younger than fourteen, which was his age when he left school to join Jack in the family motorcycle business.

Jack had a lucrative contract with the army servicing Harley-Davidsons, and he arranged for Kel to get a pre-licence-age dispensation to test the bikes on the road. Nuggety Jack had a big reputation. He was well respected, probably the number one Vincent man, and people came to him for technical direction. 'I knew all the big names long before I started racing—Harry Hinton, Eric McPherson,' said Kel. 'And when I started racing my "race buddies" were all eight to ten years older than me.'

Kel Carruthers first raced at Mount Panorama in 1955. He had just turned seventeen, and he won the 250-cc Junior B-grade race first time out on his self-built BSA Bantam—a flag-to-flag victory. On the strength of the Mount Panorama win he was promoted to A-grade at his next meeting. 'Dad had a lot of bits and pieces lying around the workshop and he advised me rather than helped me: how to balance flywheels, how to weld, that sort of stuff.' Kel was an only child. His mum, Lil, would go to the races and arrange for someone to take Kel's bikes to club events when Jack couldn't go. It seemed they were always on the road. 'Mum handled the paperwork side of racing,' Kel said. It was a big lesson. When he got to Europe half a decade later with Jan, her management of entry forms, carnets and especially the collection of starting money was the difference between fiscal success and failure. Racing, for the Carruthers, was always a family affair.

The 1955 NSW TT was Harry Hinton's last ride. The 44-year-old veteran had decided to call it a day. He'd had fifteen race wins at Bathurst across every category, including sidecars, on the Vale and Mount Panorama circuits, and suffered the physical aftermath of two major crashes, one on the Isle of Man, the other at Mount Panorama. The injuries nagged him incessantly. His sons Harry Jr, Eric and Rob were poised to take over, and later Eric's sons Tony and Peter would carry the family banner into battle as well. Hinton Sr was blind in one eye. He'd lost it in a motorcycle road accident when he was 21; the handlebar tore into his face and ripped the eye from its socket. But he seemed to have no blind side. Racers snuck up on him at their considerable risk.

In 1953 Mount Panorama had run its first 'international' motorcycle race meeting, setting up a very real rivalry between Hinton Sr and New Zealand counterpart Rod Coleman. Hinton dominated that year but in 1954, practising for the rematch, he suffered the second of his two major career crashes. Coming over Skyline he locked up and cartwheeled all the way down to the Dipper, breaking three ribs and his collarbone. Coleman won the Senior TT so 1955 would not only be Harry's swan song but also a chance to make good.

Hinton won both the Junior and Senior TTs at a romp. He trailed Coleman for four laps in the Junior then unleashed his works Norton down Conrod and held the New Zealander off into the braking area at Murray's. With the late afternoon sun already blinding the riders in the Senior event as they charged up Pit Straight, Coleman again took an early lead. Behind him father and son—Harry and Eric—diced for three laps, no holds barred, before Eric yielded. It took nine of the race's twelve laps (74 kilometres) for Hinton to get on the tail of Coleman's AJS. They crested the last hump on Conrod nose to tail and then Hinton pulled out of the slipstream and braked later into Murray's than he had ever done before. On the very limit of adhesion he went past, both riders missing the corner's apex, and by the time they got to Hell Corner, facing directly into the sun, Hinton was an indistinct backlit shadow in Coleman's vision and he couldn't retaliate.

On the victory podium Harry, Bathurst's two-wheeled maestro, stood proudly with third-placed Eric. A baton had been passed. Eric won the Senior in his own right three years later but in 1959 Hinton's eldest boy, Harry Jr, died as the result of a race crash at Imola in Italy. The Hintons raced on through two generations but, as Eric said, 'I never truly raced at ten-tenths again'.

The motorcycle industry was changing in the 1960s. The big British brands that had dominated pre-war and immediate post-war demand were no longer providing the total transport solution to an increasingly wealthy Australian population. They coveted a quarter-acre block and a two-bedroom fibro home, with a Holden not a Harley in the garage. When Marlon Brando's cult movie *The Wild One* came out in 1953, motorcycling ceased to be a transport solution and became a lifestyle statement.

The Japanese thought they had the answer. Soichiro Honda had a dream, and that's the name he gave his motorcycle. The Honda Dream was lightweight and clean, with an electric starter and turn indicators. By the mid-1960s Honda's NSW distributor Bennett & Wood had launched a massive advertising campaign—'You Meet the Nicest People on a Honda'—in a bid to reboot the image of motorcycling.

But in the early '60s, Bennett & Wood didn't even know whether the Honda would work. They imported one and sent it to Jack Carruthers to reverse-engineer it. 'We pulled it apart and inspected every bit of it,' Kel Carruthers said. 'And it was very good.' The Carruthers developed a close relationship with Honda. Another Sydney rider, Tom Phillis—four years older than Kel—had become part of Honda's fledgling grand prix team and would win the world 125-cc championship. Carruthers was asked to showcase the brand locally. He was given custody of one of the very first four-cylinder in-line 250-cc Honda grand prix bikes. It was like being gifted Norman Von Nida's golf clubs. Except, says Carruthers, 'It was an evil-handling motorcycle. The engine and the gearbox were nice, but the front brake was the same as on a production bike and it steered terribly. The first time I rode it at Mount Panorama it was "niggling" all the way across Reid Park and McPhillamy. I figured the more upright I could keep it, the more stable it would become.' It was the start of what became known as the 'Carruthers style' of riding—the body held within the bike and the centre of gravity as low as possible. 'Everyone started riding like that, but I was the first,' he laughed.

Kel and Jack performed miracles on the works bike, gradually transforming it into the machine they wanted. Between 1961 and 1965 Kel won the Lightweight (250-cc) TT or GP at Mount Panorama every time. He won the Junior (350-cc) race four times and cleaned up the Unlimited four times in a row on his Norton. In his penultimate year at the Mountain he rode a Norton Atlas in the production bike race and won that too.

All these years later Carruthers is still peeved by the suggestion that his Honda was the 'ex-Tom Phillis' machine. 'We lent our bike to him when he came back to Australia after winning the world championship,' he said, very much for the record. In 1961 Geoff Sykes, the secretary of Sydney's Warwick Farm Raceway grand prix circuit—a track built by the Australian Jockey Club only for cars—shut down every engine in the pits and sent Phillis for two laps on Kel's Honda Four. There was no commentary, no noise from the crowd, just the howl of the Honda as it worked its way up and down through its gears. Motorcycle enthusiasts were newly minted that day.

In June 1962 Tom Phillis died on the Isle of Man on the second lap of the Junior TT.

The burning hunger of top riders to test themselves overseas drove an evolution in Australian motorcycling. As soon as they had become race winners on the Mountain they began looking for the first ship to the UK and the Continent. Jack Ahearn, a tall, well-built, archetypically tough Aussie dominated Mount Panorama after Harry Hinton retired. Norton-mounted, Ahearn won four Senior TTs and GPs on the Mountain in six years, ceding only to Eric Hinton and to the accident-prone Jack Forrest in 1954.

Forrest won just the once; it was an amazing day. In a supporting race he blew up his bike and crashed on his own oil at McPhillamy Park; in another race he hit a rabbit, injuring his ankle so badly he couldn't push-start his bike without help. But in driving rain he went on to claim his only Bathurst

TT title. Forrest was travelling with Ahearn when Ahearn came second in the premier division of the 1964 world championship. Ahearn claimed he'd only remove the medal from his neck when another Australian did better. He had to wait until 1987 for Wayne Gardner, another rider who had the hunger, to win the title.

Mount Panorama's next dominant racer in the sequence, Ron Toombs, was the first who was content to stay onshore. He was a pre-war baby in a post-war bubble, too old to be a contemporary of those with whom he'd race later in his career, but too young—and, to a degree, too disconnected—to be part of the winners' circle when he entered the sport. He had no family history of motorsport. His mother had died when he was an infant. His dad had wanted him to play soccer.

Ron and his girlfriend (and soon to be his wife) Mavis first went to Mount Panorama as spectators. They stayed with friends in weekend rental houses at Katoomba so they could delight in early dawn rides to Mount Panorama to watch the bikes and the cars, grand-prixing their way back to their Blue Mountains base every night with races on the road that were as fast as those they saw on the track. But from early in his career Ron had a good friend and ace engine tuner, Tony Henderson, who defined a whole new way of going racing. Tony built them; Ron rode them. Racers think fast. Mechanics think slow.

The Henderson Matchless G50, now resplendent in Mount Panorama's National Motor Racing Museum, was the bike that ate Bathurst.

It won from 1966 to 1970, except in 1969 when, inexplicably, its engine seized. Toombs was the last of the true motorcycle sportsmen—well, he was among the last of them, at least. South

Australian Bill Horsman, who won two Seniors at the end of the Toombs era, was another. 'He was a lovely boy,' race organiser Jan Blizzard recalled. 'He'd drive over in his old ute, sleep in it, and would always be there to help everyone.' Bill was one of Jan's favourites. It helped to be on her good side.

The 1968 Australian Unlimited Motorcycle Grand Prix, starring Toombs and Horsman, plus Ahearn who was back from the Continent, was the end of the age of innocence. It could have come straight out of Hollywood. It was only a ten-lapper (61.7 kilometres) and Toombs had already won the Senior race from Ahearn and Horsman. In the process he'd set a new outright lap record of 2 minutes 45 seconds (83.67 miles per hour/134.66 kilometres per hour), a full second faster than Kel Carruthers had left it three years before. They'd carved relentlessly at each other throughout, and as they celebrated that race, the huge crowd buzzed in anticipation of the Unlimited, the last showdown of the day.

For the first nine laps it looked like a fizzer. Toombs got away first from Horsman with Ahearn on the newly disc-braked Norton dropping slightly back, and they stayed like that.

But on the last lap Toombs, in the lead, arrived at Forrest's Elbow, didn't see oil on the track and gently fell. Horsman arrived to find him down, went to pass and then stopped . . . and waited . . . while Toombs remounted and sent him on his way. Toombs, head down in a tuck, honestly expected Horsman to range up alongside him on Conrod but he didn't. Horsman's Norton had run out of fuel. Toombs paused at Murray's Corner, looked over his shoulder and saw nothing but daylight. He drifted up over the finishing line—it was almost impossible not to—to take the win. Then Horsman arrived, waggling his bike side to side to sluice petrol from the tank. But when he gassed it up, it spluttered and he fell off on the exit of Murray's Corner. Now it was Ahearn's turn. He'd seen none of the previous action but he stopped for Horsman, who picked up his Norton and started pushing. Ahearn was going nowhere, shepherding Horsman, until rider Geoff Lucas came into view. Ahearn's only sensible option was to sprint to the flag to take second; Lucas was third, and an exhausted Horsman fourth. Some, rightly, applauded the sportsmanship; others, perhaps those of the new era, decried it, saying it denigrated a national title.

In the 1970s Ron Toombs, almost twenty years older than Gregg Hansford and Murray Sayle, joined them in Team Kawasaki, fought hard for a win in the 1972 Singapore Grand Prix before his bike broke, rode on the fearsome almost-300-kilometre-per-hour Daytona Bowl before his bike broke again, and retired injured at age 43 after a race crash at a track in Sydney. Then, on Easter Sunday 1979, four years out of the saddle, he succumbed to temptation and borrowed a Yamaha TZ350 for a comeback at Mount Panorama. His funeral, shortly after, was one of the most poignant the sport has known.

In 1974 Arthur and Jan Blizzard—with great assistance from young promoter Vince Tesoriero, money from the tobacco industry and the not-so-coincidental launch of a new breed of rocket-ship-fast machines—lifted motorcycle racing at

Mount Panorama to brand-new heights of public awareness that would not be experienced again until the MotoGP World Championship found its way to Australia. Gregg Hansford and Warren Willing became stars, and they brought in their wake a whole galaxy of young hopefuls. For three years they fought out the Chesterfield Australian Grand Prix. Willing won it twice, his first in a nailbiter with Hansford, and his second gifted to him by Hansford, now on Kawasaki, who crashed in practice and broke bones in both hands. In the third year, the Hansford–Willing clash was again stymied by a broken gear lever for Hansford and a slipping clutch for Willing. In practice Willing created sensation beyond the race win—he completed the first 100-mile-per-hour (161-kilometre-per-hour) lap of Mount Panorama.

Organisers imported a revolving door of internationals to challenge the locals. In that third year, 1976, one succeeded. Team Kawasaki brought works rider Masahiro Wada; Yamaha countered with the pint-sized Ikujiro Takai. It seemed a strange, almost disrespectful thing to do, an admission that the locals might not, really, be good enough. The fact remained, however, that Willing wasn't a works rider, and that the Australian motorcycle market and those who watched motorcycle racing globally were both so important that factory participation was deemed essential.

Takai, just 160 centimetres tall, was known in Japan as 'The Little Giant'. He was neither graceful nor strong. He perched on his Yamaha like an apprentice jockey not afraid of a fall, relying on heels, knees and an unwavering faith in the laws of gravity to keep him upright. A sudden rainstorm in the last two laps saved him from a last-ditch charge back through the field by Willing, who was second, in front of Wada. With Willing and Hansford both overseas the following year he was unchallenged. Takai would die just four years later while testing a new machine.

In the third year of factory participation, 1978, the Japanese factory replaced Takai with their senior statesman Hideo Kanaya. He was a grand prix winner, third to his Yamaha teammate Giacomo Agostini in the 500-cc world title and now on the downward slope of his career. Yamaha fitted Kanaya's Yamaha with a massive fuel tank, enough to complete the full 30-lap (185-kilometre) distance without a stop. It was typical slide-rule engineering—all thought for the hypothetical, no consideration of the practical. The engineers were concentrating only on the machine, not on the rider who had to deal with the inertia of all that fuel weight for so long without a break. The little Japanese rider was totally exhausted when they lifted him off his bike, a winner, 1 minute ahead of Murray Sayle. The star act, the one the crowd had come to see, was back in ninth. Mike Hailwood, 'Mike the Bike', winner of nine world championships in three categories, had been persuaded out of retirement in New Zealand by racer, writer and enthusiast Jim Scaysbrook. It was asking too much for Hailwood to perform at the top of his game, but you never knew. Machine troubles on his Yamaha 750 restricted his movements but delighted the crowd. Hailwood, too, would die four years later, in a road accident.

In parallel with car racing, massive interest was shifting to production racing. Just as the Bathurst 1000 had consumed motor racing's open-wheeler categories, so production and improved production bike racing were what the public wanted to see. Tesoriero called them 'Superbikes'; the phrase stuck. The Arai 500, a long-distance improved production bike race named for the Japanese helmet maker, was born, and everything else—all those major events that had defined Mount Panorama—had just a little bit of the limelight taken from them. It was as if the main event had been relegated to a support category.

Pity the young Ron Boulden with his precocious talent. He was the racer born with a silver spoon in his mouth, derided and envied in equal parts. He wasn't like Hansford, who'd eased his way quietly into the sport. Young Ron arrived with his parents, particularly his mum Moyna, at his side, the best of equipment and the best of mentoring from racers as credentialled as Jack Ahearn and with bike preparation by Warren Willing. From 1979 to 1982 he won either the Senior or the Unlimited race at Mount Panorama, doing it in fine style, but copped derision from his contemporaries who said he lorded it over them. But it wasn't so.

Motorcycle writer Brian Cowan, who had lost his arm to a motorcycle accident out at Castlereagh Dragway, went in search of the truth. He found Boulden to be a young man so besotted with the sport that at age thirteen he'd worked in the local bike shop after school, seldom took a day off even in later years when he'd crashed his bike, and who was so serious about doing well that he'd simply forgotten to have fun. The fact that his parents bought the bike shop was just a result of belonging to a lucky-DNA club. In the Mount Panorama pits you were much better off being Andrew Johnson, the wild man from Victoria who delighted in blowing up letterboxes with stolen explosives and racing up Arthurs Seat, south of Melbourne, with his mates, or big-talking Kiwi Graeme Crosby, 'Croz', who could 'pop a mono' on his Kawasaki over Skyline and hold it all the way down to the Dipper without losing time. They were loved by the crowd.

And yet in 1979 Ron Boulden, still a teenager, out-thought Croz to win the Australian Unlimited Grand Prix. He knew he couldn't outride him; Croz was the best. But with the words of Jack Ahearn prominent in his head, Boulden stayed close the whole race, establishing a pattern in order to fool Crosby into believing that's all he had, then pulled 250 additional engine revs down Conrod on the last lap and won by a whisker.

Johnson was to be the last multiple winner of the Grand Prix at Bathurst, in 1983 and 1984.

Storm clouds of the very best sort were brewing. There was the possibility that the world motorcycle championship would come to Australia. A promoter, Bob Barnard, was doing the rounds, talking it up, looking for money. The Victorian Government offered financial support—a heap—and Barnard spent a heap more upgrading Phillip Island, not Bathurst. The circuits were equally distant from a major population centre, but Mount Panorama had become so car-specific that it was never going to be suitable for a world motorcycle championship.

In the last four years of its life under Auto Cycle Union promotion, from 1985 to 1988, the premier grand prix race at Mount Panorama was won in turn by Tony Hinton, grandson of Harry and therefore very appropriate; Honda's Malcolm Campbell; Yamaha's Michael Dowson; and, finally, by the man who even today is acclaimed as the greatest motorcycle talent of all time, better than Rossi or Márquez, Agostini or Hailwood: Mick Doohan. The first World Motorcycle Grand Prix in Australia was held in 1989, the year after Mount Panorama closed to motorcycles. It was won by Wayne Gardner.

Yamaha won the Arai 500 four times, Honda won three times, and a homemade masterpiece of a machine powered by a Suzuki engine and ridden by an astrophysicist won twice. To be fair, there was a 1979 Arai three-hour race won by Tony Hatton on a Honda that evens the score between the two major makes. But from 1980 until its finale in 1988 the Arai 500, taking a little more than three hours, was the pinnacle event for long-distance bike racing in the southern hemisphere—perhaps even in the world. It was open to production and improved bikes and also to prototypes as a means of drawing the best of the world's long-distance machines to the circuit.

Mount Panorama wasn't kind to the prototypes. It took several years for them to finish, let alone win. Organisers ran the first two 500s in the afternoon, deliberately pointing the bikes directly into the setting sun and declaring a lights-on period of twilight towards the end of the race to add to the drama. The 1980 winner Michael Cole finished with a torch taped to the front of his Honda to comply with the regulations—in fact several different torches as the batteries kept running flat. He could afford the pit stop. He was three laps ahead of the field.

The risk of crashes increased with the long distance and the risk of fatigue. Dennis Neill, the most awesomely aggressive stock bike rider of his era, didn't wait for either. Just five laps (30 kilometres) into the 1981 race his Honda pawed the air as it crested the hump on Mountain Straight and the wheel fell out of its forks. Neill and the Honda tumbled and twisted into the nearby orchard from a starting point of some 240 kilometres per hour, the rider fortunate to escape with head injuries and a broken arm.

The bike that set the Arai alight was the prototype McIntosh Suzuki of Rodger Freeth. He won twice, in 1982 and 1985. New Zealand builder Ken McIntosh, with the help of Freeth—the only astrophysicist in the race—constructed a bike that went around corners quicker than almost anything. Fitted with a near-standard engine for reliability, it was up to 10 kilometres per hour slower down Conrod, but fearless Freeth slammed it across the top of the Mountain so ferociously that the cumulative lap time was quicker.

Freeth was a speed freak. He rode GP bikes and production bikes, set a New Zealand land speed record—more than 300 kilometres per hour in a Porsche on a strip of road not meant for that sort of thing—and co-drove with New Zealand rally ace and three-time Asia Pacific Rally champion Peter 'Possum' Bourne. In 1993, Freeth died as a result of a crash in the World Rally Championship in Western Australia. Bourne, who would also later die in a crash in preparation for a rally, wore the numberplate 'ROJ' on his rally cars in tribute.

The honour roll of Arai 500 winners is impressive: Rob Phillis, who became Australia's most successful export to the Superbike World Championship; Kevin Magee, GP competitor and winner, now a GP commentator; and Andrew Johnson, Rod Cox, Greg Pretty and Michael Cole. And in its last year young Mick Doohan was drafted into the Yamaha team to assist an injured Michael Dowson, who was recovering from a broken wrist. They shared the ride and finished a lap ahead of the field.

Later that meeting, in the Australian Unlimited Grand Prix, Doohan was on a Yamaha 750, Dowson on a 1000. In horrible, wet conditions, Doohan was in a class of his own. He raced Rob Phillis on the Kawasaki, losing ground on the straight but passing him lap after lap across the top of the Mountain, pulling monstrous power slides with ease. Phillis ultimately sat back and watched in awe, finishing five seconds behind.

Sidecar riders live on a different planet. The 1974 Mount Panorama Easter meeting—the biggest ever held—was also the setting for a low-cost, B-grade Hollywood movie called *Sidecar Racers*. Everyone else may have been watching the Hansford–Willing clash, but the three-wheelers were all agog about their starring role in Universal Studios' production, intended to be the studio's sequel to its cult movie *American Graffiti*. It fell far short of the mark. With great risk, some riders—including Australian GP champion Stan Bayliss—strapped massive 35-millimetre movie cameras onto their outfits and their bodies to provide a unique perspective. For all its bulk, a sidecar is a delicately balanced machine and an immovable mass like a camera made riding on Mount Panorama even more precarious. The movie had a good cast—Australians Wendy Hughes and John Meillon, and Americans Peter Graves and Ben Murphy—but the stuntmen were the true stars. Their job was to emulate the real sidecar racers. And that was nearly impossible.

Sidecar racing is a hugely entertaining, highly acrobatic, risk-laden division of motor racing, which has always struggled to find a home. It has variously been associated with world championship

MotoGP, World Superbikes and even car races—neither fish nor fowl. It is also a victim of its own ambitious and largely unregulated development. In 1938, when Harry Hinton won the inaugural Mount Panorama Australian 150th Celebrations TT, he simply hooked up a solo BSA 500 to a wheeled platform that lacked strength and rigidity. Fifty years later, when three-time Mount Panorama winner and multiple Australian champion Stan Bayliss had his last race, he was in a cycle car—effectively a cut-down motor vehicle—powered by a Mini Cooper S engine driving the front steer wheels, and a single rear wheel trailing behind. In between there have been any number of configurations, limited only by the racers' imagination.

Hinton's rig was the most precarious. With great dexterity his passenger, Les Slaughter, leapt around the frame, using his weight to balance the outfit in corners, to assist in braking and to give the rear wheel more traction in acceleration. His body was, for the most part, outside the extremities of the superstructure. Through Hell Corner he would perch like an 18-foot-skiff sailor on a trapeze, his legs and arms locked rigid, his toes digging into the very edge of the platform and his hands clutching a railing while his bottom—the extremity of his body—skimmed the fence post on the apex.

The 1938 race was the closest on the card. Hinton and Slaughter won by less than a second; both they and the second-placed bike passed the earlier leader on the last corner of the last lap. Hinton then unbolted the platform and handed the BSA back to his great friend and rival Eric McPherson for the Senior Solo TT. McPherson was leading, too, but crashed mid-race. Bayliss's cycle car, now owned by his son Steve—also a champion—has been banned in international competition.

It's too safe, unspectacular and fast, requiring none of the gymnastics that have the crowds lining the fences.

Mount Panorama organisers invariably ran the sidecars as the last race of the day. The outfits, a term for a combination of motorcycle and sidecar, tend to drop oil and it was safer for the solos if the 'chairs' went last. A Mount Panorama top-of-the-hill crowd, exhausted by a day of weather and libation, would rise from their stupor and cram the fences for the sidecars. If the solos were the World Boxing Council—poised, professional and Olympian—the sidecars were the World Wrestling Entertainment: wild, seemingly unstructured and definitely guaranteed to thrill.

Sandy McCrae, a short, bespectacled Queenslander with a stutter, was the giant of Mount Panorama sidecar racing. He won the main event eight times over seventeen years. Possibly he could have won more but his sidecar passenger, Monty Perola, was killed in a road crash; he was riding pillion behind McCrae. McCrae took some time off to heal.

He came back as an innovator. His McCrae Special put both rider and passenger much lower in the frame. Getting the centre of gravity as low as possible was vitally important for balance and traction. The 'chair' became an integral part of the outfit, providing greater rigidity, but it altered the trapeze positions for the passenger. Instead of their bottom now being at the extremity it was their head, skimming the ground, way outside the sidecar's wheel as they worked to keep it flat on the ground.

'You won't find too many old sidecar riders these days without knee problems,' joked Steve Bayliss; he and his father Stan have six Mount Panorama wins between them. 'By the time I came into the sport we were kneeling with the engine tucked between our arms and under our chest.' The so-called Kneeler posed unique challenges at Mount Panorama. The safety fences were getting taller for the cars, so outfit riders, close to the ground, couldn't see over or around them. Steve once lost his passenger, Graeme Keyes, over the front of the outfit as they came to the Dipper. 'It was a front exit platform and he missed his handhold and went under the bike. I just managed to grab him and held on while he reached out and hauled himself back on board.' They scrambled through the corner and rode on. For more than a decade the Bayliss family was the one to beat.

Steve first came to Bathurst as a kid in the family's converted bus. They stayed not at the circuit but in the brickyard near the gaol—it provided warmth—with Steve sleeping across a shelf above the cabin. Stan left Steve's training to others. In 1972, in the Junior Sidecar TT, old Stan disappeared into the distance, daring Steve to follow. Instead, Steve became involved in a huge dual with Sandy McCrae, passing and repassing, and learning at every turn. Down Conrod for the last time, Steve had the wood on McCrae until the braking area, when the veteran simply outfoxed him and went on to take second. Bayliss Sr, who'd been moving away by 3 seconds a lap, was already over the line.

Throughout the 1970s Steve and Stan each won the Bathurst main event three times; for three years it was one from the other. 'The one I most enjoyed was when my leathers came undone the first time up Mountain Straight,' Steve said. Bayliss is not small—1.9 metres and 90 kilograms—and at 230 kilometres per hour his passenger, Graeme McGregor, was having some difficulty getting the burst zipper done up. 'We pulled up on the way up to the Cutting and I zipped up as the field went through.

When we took off in last place, we rode the race of our lives and carved a massive amount off the lap record to win.' Stan Bayliss was second.

In 1984, 28-year-old New Zealander Margaret Halliday swung for her boyfriend Doug Chivas Jr—the son of the car racer who was occasional driving partner of Peter Brock and one of the first committee members of the Australian Racing Drivers' Club—and created a world first that was hyped by the Mount Panorama organisers. They won the Australian Sidecar Grand Prix, setting a new lap record at an average speed of just on 150 kilometres per hour. When they checked the record books, they realised Margaret had become the first woman ever to win a grand prix, anywhere in the world.

The golden age of motorcycle racing at Mount Panorama ended in 1988. It was simply too expensive, and the reduction in crowd support too great, for it to be sustainable. The Auto Cycle Union left the Mountain in frustration.

Three years later the bikes came back. Vincent Tesoriero ran them as a feature alongside his Bathurst 12 Hour races but a double fatality brought his well-meant effort to an end. In 2000 Greg Eaton, a former Channel Seven executive who had overseen the network's sales activities in the Bathurst 1000, invested his 'net worth, around $1.6 million' in the last ever stand-alone motorcycle race meeting. It ended in acrimony. According to Jan Blizzard, a major scam involving up to 6000 counterfeit tickets was discovered. Eaton was accused of skimming the gate, an allegation he strongly denied. 'It took four years to resolve it,' he told me from Kuala Lumpur. 'I didn't go bankrupt but I had to liquidate my company. No one won.' Eaton now owns a successful TV event production company servicing motorsport across Southeast Asia.

7

The Golden Age of Cars

For 35 years Mount Panorama was the home of open-wheel motor racing. It hosted 40 race meetings, four Australian Grands Prix and ten national titles. Before it became the place of The Great Race—the Bathurst 1000—it had been the venue for some of the greatest and bravest open-wheeler racing the country had seen. Australia's greatest world champion, Jack Brabham, had not only raced there but had been on its organising committee. When a racer went overseas, looking for a car to buy for Australia, its specifications were written around Mount Panorama.

It was the most beautiful racing car Australia had ever seen. A Lago Talbot, in French racing blue, with its swooping exhaust pipes low along the rounded left-hand sill, an external airbox on the right that looked like a piece of avant-garde art, and a tan leather seat bolstered on both sides as if it was an armchair. The driver looked forward around a huge four-spoke steering wheel, peering over the cowling to line up the triple-laced front wheels—and on every visual plane saw only curves. It was as if the Talbot had been styled by Gaudí: it was said to have been the winner of the 1949 French Grand Prix in the delicate hands of Louis Chiron.

Stan Jones, beefy and as wide as he was tall—and the father of young Alan, who would go on to become world Formula One champion—had a look at this thing of beauty, the car they said would herald the demise of homegrown specials. And he called on Charlie Dean, who had been developing a local project car. It was called Maybach, and it was made from metal cut from the belly tanks of a Kittyhawk aircraft at the Commonwealth Aircraft Corporation, and powered by a six-cylinder motor salvaged from a German World War II half-track armoured personnel carrier.

Dean and Jones had already come to an understanding. Dean had been experimenting with the Maybach since 1946 but his interest was academic. Jones, he knew, could drive the wheels off it. Dean was to become one of the most influential people in the business of motorsport. He folded his own engineering company, Replex, into larger company Repco (Reconditioned Engine Parts Company) after the war and soon became their head of research and development. He stocked the place with motor-racing engineering talent, turned it into a skunkworks and used Maybach as his test mule. In the 1960s, along with CEO Sir Charles 'Dave' McGrath, he would commit the public company's funds to backing Jack Brabham's quest for the world championship in a car of Brabham's own making. Through the success of the Repco Brabham engine, the Repco name would become famous around the world. Charlie became Charles, wearing a suit and polished shoes; people thought of him as a corporate heavy. But deep down he was still Charlie, a mate of Jack's, in a grease-stained boilersuit.

In 1952 the two cars, Maybach and Talbot, met at Mount Panorama, with Stan Jones on board the Maybach up against Australian Grand Prix winner Doug Whiteford, now the owner of the Lago Talbot. It was the Australian Grand Prix.

The handicappers made Doug Whiteford the sole scratch man and allocated an advantage of 1 minute 16 seconds to Jones—over 38 laps (235 kilometres), a neat 2 seconds a lap. Jones had a handicap of his own. His special Pirelli four-ply racing tyres had failed to arrive and he was forced to start his fearsome Maybach on six-ply road tyres. Six-ply tyres heated up more quickly, retained heat longer and tended to blow out more readily. Down Conrod a driver could watch them expand as the heat pushed them to bursting point. A wise man may have perceived that as a signal to be conservative, but Jones took off in tyre-smoking fury at the start. Perhaps his strategy was to get so far ahead that he could afford a tyre stop. Whiteford tucked in behind, able to pass down Conrod but not able to hold the lead up Mountain Straight.

Gearing was everything. At Mount Panorama it was sensible to always gear a car for the climb up the mountain, not for the run down. They were lapping 3 seconds off Whiteford's record but the pace was still too hot for Jones's road tyres. Seven laps in he tore to the pits. It took 90 seconds to change the wheels—no wheel nuts back then; they used massive 'knock off' centre spline wing hubs that Charlie Dean belted with a copper hammer to loosen. It was to be the first of six stops, with Jones ferociously clawing his way back each time only to halt again. Doug Whiteford won his second of three Australian Grands Prix by 4 minutes 20 seconds from Jones. His first had been at Nuriootpa in the Barossa Valley driving Black Bess in 1950, and his last would be at the inaugural Albert Park meeting in Melbourne in 1953.

Whiteford drove two Lago Talbots in his career. The second is now owned by Australian Le Mans 24 Hour winner Vern Schuppan, who also competed in the Bathurst 1000. Schuppan drives the beautiful old car very hard in historic races: 'It feels like a big go-kart,' he said, standing next to the car in its air-conditioned garage, surrounded by other remarkable classic cars and motorcycles. 'You have to use proper body language to drive it, leaning out the side to sight the front wheels in order to hit the corner apex.' Schuppan is totally at ease with his seven-figure purchase, although 'the brake is to the right of the accelerator and it is a very long pedal'. Better not to get them confused.

The 1952 Australian Grand Prix was the last arranged by the Australian Sporting Car Club. For cars, the Mountain was closed in 1953. The Australian Racing Drivers' Club would reopen it for business in 1954. That year, Jones immediately took 7 seconds off the lap record. It was to be a tumultuous year for him. He won the New Zealand Grand Prix, the first time an Australian had won an 'international' grand prix, and he destroyed the Maybach in a fearsome crash on the makeshift Southport Road circuit in his home grand prix. Charlie Dean built him another.

It was truly the golden age of open-wheelers. John Crouch had secured the franchise for the rear-engined, English-built Cooper. Lex Davison called the spindly lightweights 'mechanical mice'—and in 1953 young speedway driver Jack Brabham and his father Tom had bought one from a deceased estate after the intended owner committed suicide. Brabham beat Stan Jones at Mount Panorama on handicap.

Keen observers at the Mountain had watched the form of a young Englishman in an ungainly car of his own design. Reg Hunt had arrived in Australia from Manchester in 1949. He brought with him his family and a crate full of welded frames and mechanical parts: 'They wouldn't let me import a whole car without tax so I brought it in as bits,' 96-year-old Reg told me, in his immaculate Melbourne penthouse overlooking some of his many property developments. Reg is the last of the top-line competitors of his era and his perspective is enlightening. 'I called Stan Jones "Tubby" and I knew how to rattle him: just stay on his tail and push him and sooner or later he'd overdo it. The way to tell was that the back of his neck would go red. You could see it change colour.'

Hunt's family was steeped in racing. His grandfather, George Cowley, was 65 when he took a third place in an Isle of Man TT race, and all four of George's daughters raced. Hunt's aunt Dot was a British speedway champion. His dad Bert and his mum Ethyl met at the speedway and they had young Reg on his first bike, a dirt-track Douglas, by the time he was nine. He had his first race when he was fourteen, raced at the Isle of

Man at sixteen, and arrived in Australia as part of the country's post-war immigration program at 26 to start a new life.

As soon as the local racing fraternity saw Hunt's box of bits built up, they christened it 'The Flying Bedstead'. The Cooper car company in the UK was making a lot of money out of building fragile 500-cc racing cars. They were the training ground for drivers like Stirling Moss. Hunt built on that concept. His Bedstead was lower, wider and handled better. If he'd stayed in the UK he might have put the Cooper family out of business.

At his first race meeting, Hunt met Australian engineer Phil Irving. Irving was already famous. With Phil Vincent, of the motorcycle company of the same name, he'd designed and built the awe-inspiring Black Shadow HRD Vincent. Together Irving and Hunt developed the Bedstead until it was a little rocket ship: 'He was the only man I ever knew who could smoke a cigarette down to the butt and never spill the ash,' Hunt said of Irving, holding his hand a full cigarette-length in front of his face. 'One day he arrived at my new home and got it wrong and there was ash all over the new carpet. So he stamped on it with his foot.'

There's an immutable law in motor racing: 'A good little car will never beat a good big car.' This played out at Mount Panorama more than anywhere else; the climb up the Mountain favours the powerful. In 1954 Hunt went back to the UK for a season's racing and returned with a works Maserati. And not just any Maserati. It was the 6C, predecessor to the legendary 250F, which was by far the most sought-after race car of the 1950s. Only a season before, Hunt's car had won the Italian Grand Prix driven by Juan Manuel Fangio. Hunt had his good big car and it was the best that had ever been brought to Australia.

Stan Jones was at the top of his game and he lived life large. He owned Superior Motors in Melbourne, with several branches, was selling a heap of cars and not saving a penny. His son Alan says he was the most generous man he'd ever known—they'd go to race meetings and he'd take not only a full complement of mechanics but their wives and families as well. When he had it, he spent it. Charlie Dean was building him a new Maybach but, unsure if it would arrive on time for Mount Panorama's Easter 1955 meeting, Stan brought a Cooper Bristol along as well. Dean arrived just as the track was opened for racing, the car still unpainted. But two cars and one driver? Simple—Stan gave the other drive to his mechanic Ern Seeliger. They called Ern 'The Baron' and his workshop at the back of Baker Street, Richmond, was where you'd find all the top Melbourne cars being tuned. The Baron's needs were simple. If he tuned your car, sooner or later he'd want to race it.

Hunt's Maserati took a bit of getting used to. It was configured in the European way. The gearshift was between his legs and the throttle was in the middle, with the brake pedal to the right. Skyline at Mount Panorama was not the place to stab the wrong one. Not that Hunt would do that. Of all the guns of the time he was the one regarded as the most cool and clinical. He was also pretty much unbeatable. In the three-lap (18.5-kilometre) sprint opener Hunt shot away, passing Lex Davison—the perennial fast starter—up Mountain Straight. Jones, in the brand-new car, was sideways a lot of the time. Seeliger, behind him in the Cooper, watched it all calmly and came home third.

When confronted with a choice, sometimes you make the wrong one. Jones was concerned about the new Maybach's handling so he swapped cars for the 26-lap main race (160 kilometres). He took over the Cooper and found himself in and out of the pits. Hunt cruised to victory while Seeliger, in the new Maybach, and Davison in his HWM Jaguar staged a huge battle for second and third place. Seeliger prevailed and Jones could only wonder what would have happened if he'd been at the wheel.

He'd never know. Not at Mount Panorama anyway.

Australia hosted the Olympic Games in 1956, and the Australian Grand Prix, held concurrently at Albert Park in December, was the focus of motorsport attention. Hunt had bought a new Maserati, a full-blown 250F; Jones ordered one too. Davison secured a 3-litre Ferrari.

It would be a watershed year for Hunt.

As much as he had been enjoying his motor racing, there was business to be conducted as well. His resolve to retire was confirmed when he was beaten at Mount Panorama on Easter Monday by Lex Davison, a driver he did not regard as a true rival.

Hunt liked Davison, though. 'He was a very pleasant man. He and Diana used to come to my home for dinner,' Hunt told me, leaning back in his couch and straightening the seam of his immaculate grey trousers, still held up by the braces that had been his trademark for more than three-quarters of a century. But as a racing driver? The smile said it all. 'Pleasant' is a Hunt euphemism for 'beatable'. Bib Stillwell was 'pleasant'; so was Bill Patterson. But Stan Jones definitely wasn't. Neither was Jack Brabham: 'Brabham would run you off the road.'

So how was it, then, that Davison beat Hunt at that Easter race meeting? The Bathurst 100 was a true handicap and the fast cars started at the rear of the field: Hunt from scratch, Davison 42 seconds in front of him. The two drivers destroyed the lap record, Davison totally at ease with his new Ferrari—more so, it seemed, than with anything he'd driven before. The pair took five seconds out of the record. Hunt claimed it by a whisker, but Davison won the race by a minute; he'd actually moved clear of Hunt.

It was a shock for Hunt. He was building a huge business— with his car dealerships and his property, it was becoming an empire. Perhaps there wasn't room for racing as well. 'It was at Mount Panorama that I thought of giving it away,' Hunt confessed. 'I'd been racing all my life and I'd had a gutful.' It was an extraordinarily strong statement from a near-centenarian all those years later, so I asked once more and his answer was just as forceful. He never raced at Mount Panorama again.

At the Australian Grand Prix, in December, Hunt finished fourth, the best of the locals after a wheel-to-wheel dice with Jones.

Hunt stepped from the car and never raced again. His beautiful home displays some trophies—not many—and his proudest one seems to be the small inscribed clock that identifies him as Holden's top-selling dealer for twenty consecutive years. He'd retired from racing at 33, at the top of his game, and gone on to the next phase in his spectacular life. 'That's the way to do it,' he beamed.

When Ted Gray took pole position in the 1958 Australian Grand Prix at Mount Panorama, legendary Australian sailor Lou Abrahams, later to be twice winner of the Sydney to Hobart Yacht Race, was as nervous as a first-time dinghy sailor in a strong breeze. Gray was driving the Tornado and Abrahams had built it. Tornado was the last of the great front-engined homemade special racing cars, and—incredibly—the race favourite. From day one the Tornado project had used Gray as its driver. Wangaratta-born Gray wasn't young. Twenty years before, he'd raced Peter Whitehead on the speedway. He'd destroyed Tornado 1 in a horrific end-for-end roll over at the bottom of Conrod Straight in 1955 and he was still suffering the residual effects of multiple fractures.

Tornado was a bitzer. It had an imported V8 Corvette engine, Holden suspension, Peugeot steering and Lancia axles. Its brakes were originally from a P51 Mustang fighter plane but they'd been replaced by the latest locally designed PBR units (PBR was a company started in Melbourne in 1927 by brothers George and Jack Paton and a division of Repco). Even the imported Maseratis and Ferraris were using those brakes. ('The Maserati mechanics took them home with them after '56 and copied the design over there,' Reg Hunt told me.)

In practice, Tornado's steering wheel came off in Gray's hands at the top of the Mountain. He spent a couple of moments, he told his crew, working out how to put it back on and only then thought about stepping on the brakes instead.

Stan Jones was chasing his still-elusive first Australian Grand Prix victory and in the 30-lap (185-kilometre) race he stormed to the lead at Hell Corner. At the end of lap one, just 1.1 seconds covered Jones's Maserati, Gray, and Davison's Ferrari. They were nose to tail and the rest of the field was already 7 seconds behind. Davison went past Gray up Mountain Straight but Gray pulled out and passed them both down Conrod and set about stretching a tiny lead on every corner. At one-third distance Gray's lead was out to 10 seconds; he was so far ahead he couldn't see the battling cars in his mirrors. When a driver is leading a race they start to imagine problems. Gray was increasingly sure he had a rear suspension issue and he started to ease off. At two-thirds distance he saw both red cars looming behind him and his nerve cracked. He swerved into the pits—there was no pit wall—and caught his crew by surprise. They refuelled his car—which he didn't need—and sent him off in pursuit, Gray pointing at his rear suspension, which they hadn't checked. Two laps later he brushed the fence at the top of the mountain and two laps later he retired with broken suspension. Jones was on his way to his first GP win. And then he too retired, his engine broken. Lucky Lex Davison, the man they said had the knack of being in the right place at the right time, took his third GP victory—and his second win at Mount Panorama.

It would be the last Australian Grand Prix at Mount Panorama. The races were allocated by rotation and new circuits were being built with great ambition. Warwick Farm in Sydney and Sandown in Melbourne would lay claim to the big-money international races—the so-called Tasman series—which would attract world champions to Australia annually. The ARDC was essentially a club with a club mentality and it couldn't compete.

In October 1960, Jack Brabham was a two-time world champion. He returned to Mount Panorama to win the 26-lap Craven A International, hastily convened in his honour, moving away from a battalion of rear-engined Cooper Climaxes. It was a revolution. A front-engined formula car would never win at the Mountain again. Brabham had left for the UK after winning the 1955 Australian Grand Prix at Port Wakefield in his Cooper Bristol from Hunt and Whiteford in their big forward-engine cars.

There were those among his contemporaries who said Brabham was good but nothing super special. Whiteford, they said, was superior. But it was Brabham who'd taken the risk. He'd sold everything and gone to the UK; convinced John Cooper to give him an opportunity; worked unceasingly to help design and build the cars, then transport them to race meetings and spanner them. Then, almost as an afterthought, he drove them to victory. In the process he'd turned into a hard man—not that he hadn't been already. He'd use the edge of the track to sling-shot stones at the car behind, and his tiny Cooper could become 10 metres wide if you tried to pass him. Off the track you dealt with him cautiously. A deal needed to be ironclad.

His rationale in the 1960s for starting his own team, Jack told me just before his death, wasn't just to win the world title in his own name. It was also to secure a bigger share of the spoils. 'I'd come to Australia to race in the European off-season and my job was to sell the car to an Australian and take a big paper bag of money back to John Cooper. I figured I wanted to own that bag.'

We sat knee to knee that day in 2014, shouting at each other—Jack was deaf from years of racing—and it was one of the great privileges of my career to be with him. I'd first met him at the

1960 Mount Panorama meeting, my first motor race. There wasn't much overseas TV coverage then. On Sunday afternoons Channel Nine had a short black-and-white motorsport segment hosted by Terry Byrne, who perched on a wooden stool and played snippets of Visnews footage, mainly of Jack. It was a must-see. My dad took me to the Mountain on the October long weekend and there he was: Black Jack. 'They didn't call me that because of my dark hair, my five o'clock shadow or my attitude,' Jack said drily, all those years later. 'John Cooper gave me the name because I came from Australia—blackfella country.'

In that last interview Jack hosed down a long-held belief that he'd not chosen to go to the UK but that he'd been forced out by the Confederation of Australian Motor Sport. It was, he said, only partially true. Advertising on cars was banned as being too commercial but Jack needed REDeX's money to buy his first Cooper. 'In return we called it the REDeX Special and put the name down the side of the car. I figured, like in speedway, sponsors would be welcome. At my first race meeting a CAMS official stood in front of my car and wouldn't let it go out.' Brabham and his team taped over the sign but the tape peeled off early in the race. 'Legend has it that CAMS' attitude to sponsorship was the trigger that caused me to head for Europe. That's stretching the point a bit. More likely if REDeX had withdrawn its sponsorship it would have been the trigger that stopped me motor racing. CAMS didn't understand that. You could say I raced that year in spite of CAMS.' Brabham won just as he pleased at Mount Panorama that October and set a new lap record. Then he sold his car to Bib Stillwell.

Coopers carried three drivers to victory in the next three years at Mount Panorama: Bill Patterson, a successful motor dealer who looked absolutely nothing like a racing driver; Bib Stillwell, a successful motor dealer who wore his overalls like Harry Highpants and went on to become world president of Learjet; and Lex Davison, who looked like a racing driver, acted like one and tragically died in his racing car.

Bib Stillwell's victory was made more memorable when he chased a Mount Panorama resident down Conrod during a practice session. The home owner drove out of his front gate and turned right at Murray's Corner to go to Bathurst just as Stillwell arrived to turn left up Pit Straight.

David McKay, who had first raced at Mount Panorama in an MG TC in 1951, formed his own race team, Scuderia Veloce. He became the motoring editor of Sir Frank Packer's *Telegraph* newspapers and was hugely influential in the development of the sport—and he employed people who could win. It wasn't that he wasn't capable himself. There was simply a changing of the guard.

Other drivers would become patrons too. Alec Mildren, an Australian Gold Star champion who'd first raced at Mount Panorama in 1950 in an MG TB, fostered Kevin Bartlett and Max Stewart, both of whom would also become Gold Star champions. Lex Davison formed Ecurie Australie and took on young Toorak neighbour Rocky Tresise; in a tragic coincidence of monstrous proportions, Tresise would die in his racing car the week after Davison died in his. David McKay had made his race team into a professional haven for drivers who needed management. He'd also taken on Spencer Martin, an impecunious Holden driver, and turned him into an indentured labourer, in return letting him drive some of the most desirable cars in the world. McKay and Martin eventually went their separate ways. 'I was working around the clock, day and night, on the race cars and some road cars as well,' Martin recalled. 'In 1966 we were at Surfers Paradise and I was looking forward to at least a day off but one of the race cars was blowing smoke so David told me to take it home that night—to Sydney—and fix it. He was paying me £100 a week. It was a basic wage.'

Martin gave notice. He turned to Melbourne tyre dealer, race driver and team owner Bob Jane. 'Bob asked me how much David was paying me and, like a fool, I told him. He doubled it but I should have got five times as much.' There were two sides to the story: 'I was surprised and disappointed,' McKay later wrote. 'I had expected too much and been too hard on the young man. I treated him as I would have a son and no doubt the "son" thought he'd had a lucky escape.' McKay said he'd had Martin lined up for a potential drive in Formula One. He had the contacts.

Frank Matich, a superbly talented engineer and driver in the Brabham mould, found his patron in wealthy enthusiast Laurie O'Neil. O'Neil once passed me at night on the Bells Line of Road, en route to Mount Panorama, his big 6.3-litre Mercedes-Benz bellowing through the high passes and using all the road. When we got to the motel we were both staying in, he was pseudo-solicitous. 'Are you okay?' he smirked. 'It's just that it's taken you so long to get here I thought you had a problem.' O'Neil wrote Matich open cheques and Matich won the 1964 Mount Panorama race in his Brabham Climax, beating Spencer Martin in McKay's similar car.

The Geoghegan brothers, Leo and Ian ('Pete'), had a different strategy. Under the direction of their father Tom, who'd raced early at Mount Panorama, they liked to own their hardware and have it sponsored. It made for precarious cash flow; Sydney driver Barry Collerson claimed he had to call on CAMS to retrieve his Lago Talbot—the ex-Doug Whiteford car—that he'd left with the Geoghegans as a deposit on a new race car when it became obvious to him there were money problems. Leo won the Mount Panorama open-wheeler race in 1971.

Jack Brabham returned to Mount Panorama in 1969 for the last Bathurst 100. It was the first over that distance (161 kilometres) in almost a decade and it would be the end for serious open-wheelers on the mountain. Brabham was by then a three-time world champion and the only driver—ever—to win a world Formula One title in a car of his own making. Not of his own design, though: Ron Tauranac, whose brother Austin raced their tiny Ralt at Mount Panorama in 1951, could take the credit for that.

It was a miserable, rotten race. Victorian up-and-comer Bevan Gibson had died in the previous event, and his teammate John Harvey, who'd been seriously injured himself the year before when his Brabham slammed into the trees across the top of the Mountain, was in no mood to challenge. Aerodynamic wings first appeared that year—even though there was little science to them. Some drivers, like Harvey and Neil Allen, had two of them, mounted high on stalks above their cars. Leo Geoghegan had one, and front trim tabs as well. Brabham had one at the rear, comparatively low and with no trim tabs to hold the nose down. Speeds on Conrod decreased by as much as 10 miles per hour (16 kilometres per hour) as downforce took its toll and slowed the cars in a straight line. But the wings obviously worked over the top of the mountain—Brabham set a new lap record and cruised home ahead of Harvey.

In 1970 Jack Brabham, soon to be Sir Jack, retired from open-wheeler racing. There'd been a spate of deaths. Bruce McLaren died testing at Goodwood; Piers Courage was killed in the Dutch Grand Prix at Zandvoort, and in practice for the same event Brabham had rolled his car, over and over, and he'd been trapped inside it, upside down, with fuel leaking. Brabham's father was at Zandvoort and he sided with Jack's first wife, Betty, in urging him to retire.

'I reckon I stopped too soon,' he told me all those years later, his frustration that he'd pulled the pin at 'only' 43 still palpable. 'Who knows what would have happened to the Brabham team if I'd continued?'

Mount Panorama attracted beautiful cars. The Old Red Lady was one of them. She was a Ferrari 250 LM, a closed GT built for long-distance racing in 1964. Only 32 were made and David McKay secured one for his Scuderia Veloce. He used its purchase to secure the NSW Ferrari franchise and it became his company's flagship. In 1965 Jochen Rindt won the Le Mans 24 Hour race in a 250 LM, already past its prime, pushing it to what he hoped would be destruction because he had a hot date in Paris, but the Ferrari would not break and kept him occupied right up to the chequered flag.

Spencer Martin fell in love twice the day McKay's 250 LM arrived. The car came off the passenger liner *Galileo* and was transported to David's home in leafy Burns Road, Wahroonga. They fired it up, popping and growling, all twelve cylinders of it, and a head appeared over the fence to see what the fuss was about. Vicky became Spencer's wife and mother of their three children. McKay's car would win the Surfers Paradise 12 Hour and 6 Hour long-distance race three successive times, the first time driven by Jackie Stewart before he became world champion.

The problem with Mount Panorama was that there was no logical category in which to drive the LM, no distance event where she could stretch her legs. But she had to go there. Mount Panorama and the LM were made for each other. Spencer Martin drove her in Easter 1965 and finished second to Pete Geoghegan's nimble Lotus 23. But that was irrelevant. The wail from its four pea-shooter exhausts sent shivers up the spine; down Conrod, Martin recorded a top speed of just over 169 miles per hour (about 272 kilometres per hour), the fastest anyone had ever been on the Mountain. The sight of the car, hunched down over its swooping Scaglietti-built body, accelerating up Mountain Straight in the late afternoon with the sun glinting off its Rosso Chiaro duco, was like a piece of modern art brought to life.

McKay also brought a Ferrari P4 to Australia—a much more visceral beast—and in 1968 it won at Mount Panorama in the hands of the mercurial Bill Brown, while Pete Geoghegan brought the Old Red Lady home second. The P4, an open two-seat racing car made for the USA's Can-Am series and one of Ferrari's less successful ventures, made a hasty exit from Australia, marginally ahead of the taxation department; its new owner, Australian Formula One driver Paul Hawkins, was killed shortly afterwards in another of his cars in a race at Oulton Park.

It's possible for a man to have a love affair with a car. The Old Red Lady stayed with McKay through divorces from his first two wives and his separation from Spencer Martin. He declined an offer that came with certain menace from a Sydney underworld figure who was later found dead of a gunshot wound in the cabin of his own car, and in 1978, when she'd not been raced for almost a decade, McKay crashed the car at Sandown, broke his leg, and embarked on a complete rebuild. 'I wrote David a letter after the crash, saying, "We can fix the Old Red Lady but not you,"' Spencer Martin recalled, and with the silence broken after eleven years, they reunited. The 250 LM was beautifully restored, won Concours d'Elegance competitions, and twenty years after its arrival in Australia was sold to Ralph Lauren to anchor his burgeoning car collection. Martin by then had a quarter-share in the Old Red Lady and was in many respects her custodian. 'Lauren paid $500,000, which was about $100,000 more than the market rate at the time,' Martin said. 'But he knew what he was doing. He was a collector of note and if he paid half a million dollars, that set the price for all other LMs.' Ferrari 250 LMs change hands very rarely. The last to be sold, in 2015 in the Ferrari 'bubble economy', fetched US$17.6 million (A$24.1 million) at Sotheby's without the provenance of Lauren's car, which still proudly bears its Scuderia Veloce rondel.

The Australian Tourist Trophy was created in 1956 so Stirling Moss had a national title of note to win in the support event for the Australian Grand Prix that year. Moss and Jean Behra had brought out two magnificent Maserati 300S sports cars to supplement their 250F Formula One machines. Moss was already a three-time winner of the RAC TT—the world's oldest continuous motorsport trophy, first given in 1905 on the Isle of Man (for cars)—by the time he came to Australia; he'd won twice in a C-Type Jaguar and once in the thundering Mercedes-Benz 300 SLR. He won the Australian TT in 1956 in the Maserati, along with the Grand Prix in the Formula One car, and the newly minted CAMS was left wondering what to do next with the race. In 1958 the TT was given to Mount Panorama—perhaps its natural home. The circuit's sweeping corners and long straights had something in common with the Isle of Man course.

To be credible, the TT really needed to have a strong field. In 1958, Doug Whiteford had Moss's 300S. David McKay had not long returned from the Kangaroo Stable to Europe tour, an assault on the Continent by a small group of Australians, among them Lex Davison and the veteran Tom Sulman. McKay brought back with him one of the relatively new Aston Martin DB3s, sold it to Bathurst chemist Warren Blomfield and then bought another updated model. Jack Murray (only recently christened 'Gelignite') had a D-Type Jaguar; South Australian Derek Jolly had secured one of the lightning-fast Lotus XVs; and Frank Matich, just starting to make a name for himself, was in a C-Type, like Stirling Moss had used.

The crowd loved the TT. The sight of Jaguar nose to tail with Maserati, closely followed by Aston Martin, was for all the world like today's Bathurst 12 Hour. They were doing just on 150 miles per hour (241 kilometres per hour) down Conrod, and they were relevant. It was actually possible to cheer for a brand name. Those brands may not have been affordable for the masses but that was part of the appeal. They were aspirational.

The big-bodied sports cars attracted windage and there was need for care. At the bottom of the straight Whiteford's Maserati was suddenly caught by a wind gust. Whiteford passed slower cars while spinning backwards, steering for the escape road, but he collected one of the heavy wooden-paling retaining fences instead. McKay became the first domestic winner of his national TT.

Three years later the TT returned to Mount Panorama. Bib Stillwell, getting wealthier by the moment from his interests in the Melbourne motor industry, arrived with a beautiful deep-green Cooper Monaco. It was a Formula One car with a bulging two-seat body. But as interesting as the Monaco was, it wasn't something the spectators could relate to. Stillwell led home Frank Matich, now driving a D-Type Jaguar, and Bob Jane, a lap behind in a Maserati 300S.

CAMS abandoned the TT six years later after it was won by Frank Matich's self-named SR3, a pure racing car. A good idea had been lost. Mount Panorama organisers were increasingly looking to touring cars as their way of connecting with their audience.

8

The Tin Tops

Six-time Bathurst 1000 winner Larry Perkins stumps people when he asks: 'When was the first motor race?' His answer is: 'When they built the second car.' In 1950 Australians bought 138,960 new motor vehicles (they buy 1.1 million per year today). They were rationed according to need. Those who could provide proof of hardship or needed a car to travel long distances had priority. It would be another ten years before annual availability crested 200,000. And yet from the time the first Holden rolled off the production line on 29 November 1948, people wanted to race them.

Twelve-year-old Bill Buckle travelled to Mount Panorama with his father, mother Elsie and sister Anne in the family's Triumph Dolomite, 'the most advanced sedan of its time', to watch Peter Whitehead win the 1938 Australian Grand Prix. They went to the top of the Mountain. Bill was used to motor racing. His father, William (W.G.), had competed since Bill was three—on grass hill climbs, in reliability trials and in special speed tests along the esplanade at Bondi Beach. But Bill's senses had never been assaulted as they were at Mount Panorama: 'I can hear to this day the back wheels of the racing cars spinning on the gravel.'

Thirteen years later Bill was racing at the Mountain, but not spinning his wheels. He was in a front-wheel-drive Light Fifteen Citroën Traction Avant, about to become one of the pioneers of touring-car racing.

From day one it was always more than just a bit of a lark. 'Win on Sunday, sell on Monday' may have been a far-fetched proposition back then, but it had an element of reality.

The first closed-car race was held at Mount Panorama in October 1950. It was no big deal—a sidebar, really, to the open-wheeler and sports cars. But right from the start it got the attention of the car makers. Those great mates-about-town Jack Murray and Bill 'Wild Bill' MacLachlan persuaded the Ford distributor to lend them a couple of V8 Ford Pilots. The 1949 Australian Grand Prix winner, John Crouch, was given a blue Peugeot 203 by its concessionaire, and Tom Geoghegan, a taxi proprietor from Liverpool (and father of Leo and 'Pete') was in a Jowett Javelin. But Victorian Peter Damman steered a green 3-litre six-cylinder Citroën to victory, even surviving a last-lap spin. That event was the progenitor of every touring-car race ever held at the Mountain.

The Buckles were well connected in the motor industry. W.G. had established Buckle Motors in 1927 on the original magic mile of motors—Sydney's William Street, where the rolling chassis that arrived at the wharves at nearby Woolloomooloo were finished and quickly sold. W.G. was the chairman of the NSW Chamber of Automotive Industries, the peak industry body for the state, and a business confidante of the immensely successful Maurice Shmith, whose son David had a stove-hot series of Austin-Healeys that he raced. Between them, the Shmiths and the Buckles owned the strip.

But W.G. had been gassed in France in the Great War and he died shortly after World War II of oesophageal cancer. W.G.'s trusted service manager Bill Lowrie took over the running of the business, becoming the custodian of the family's considerable investment. He gave Bill the sort of education his father would have wanted. Bill was sent to Adelaide to learn to assemble cars at the Dodge factory; the Buckles held the franchise for Dodge in New South Wales. Lowrie gave him a little bit of leeway to occasionally race an MG TA and when, with Bill's urging, the business acquired the state franchise for Citroën, Bill's talent at the wheel became a business asset. Here was Bill Buckle, the young man whose name was on the showroom door, racing the product—and winning.

In his first race at Mount Panorama, Easter 1951, he slotted into second place in both the handicap and scratch closed-car races; in October he claimed third outright and the next year he won. He'd had an early incentive that first year on the Mountain. 'I walked into the Royal Hotel'—where all the drivers stayed when they were in Bathurst—'and Lex Davison was at the next table. "Did you see that stupid young bastard in the

Citroën?" he was saying. "That guy is bloody mad.'" So Buckle sought out Bill Murray, who'd won the 1947 Australian Grand Prix, and arranged for lessons. 'It frightened me half to death!' Buckle recalled being shown the quick way from Skyline down to Forrest's Elbow in his front-wheel-drive car, hanging on in the passenger seat—no seatbelts. The lesson eventually made him a race winner.

In 1953, Mount Panorama's gap year for cars, Buckle took off to the UK to work for the Citroën factory at Slough, and when he came back he had a big idea. He persuaded the Buckles board of directors to let him build a lightweight sports car out of fibreglass. The open-mouthed Buckle GT was, according to Buckle, 'not a commercial success', even though the suspension—designed by Jack Brabham's partner Ron Tauranac—allowed it to crest Skyline at 100 miles per hour (161 kilometres per hour), Buckle says. But it was a fine racing car. Some of the people he'd raced with, and beaten, in closed-car races bought them, notably the acclaimed Sydney photographer Clive Kane who paid £1780 for it, and rated it better than an Austin-Healey. Buckle built Goggomobil models, too—more than 700 of the tiny two-stroke runabouts, at his own factory. Then, when David Shmith secured the Toyota franchise for New South Wales—the first granted outside Japan—Buckles became one of its first and most successful dealers. Buckle was one of the factory's initial intake of racing drivers in the early Mount Panorama long-distance races. The same concept applied. His name, on the side of the race car, was the same as the one on the dealership door.

A Holden first raced and won at Mount Panorama in 1955. Jack Myers, bespectacled, tousle-haired, untidy, unfashionable—today you'd call him a nerd—raced a range of formula racing cars and died in one of them, a twin-motorcycle-engined special, in 1962 at Katoomba's Catalina Park. But in '55, along with engine builder Merv Waggott, he turned an FJ Holden—the car every Australian wanted to own and which commanded almost 50 per cent of total car sales—into a racing sedan. The pair almost doubled the car's power from 45 to 85 kW (60–113 horsepower) and made it capable of a tank-slapping 105 miles per hour (168 kilometres per hour) down Conrod. This concerned Barry Gurdon. The sometimes grumpy Austin/Morris dealer from Bathurst, described by his daughter as 'a difficult man', had laid claim to what they were now calling 'sedan-car racing' in his supercharged Austin A50. He didn't need competition from a Holden.

Myers and Gurdon both had a big stake in Mount Panorama. Jack was vice-president of the Australian Racing Drivers' Club and Barry had been instrumental in convincing the ARDC to come to Mount Panorama. He'd won concessions at Bathurst City Council to make it possible for the ARDC to make the commitment. The ARDC's list of demands was large and Gurdon ensured they got the lot. Gurdon's contribution is forever under-called. Without his intervention it is very possible the Mountain would have languished.

In their first hit-out, at Easter 1955, Gurdon just held out Myers. But in October Myers took the ascendancy. Being beaten by a Holden was more than Gurdon could stand. Holden versus Austin was a big thing in Bathurst—long before Ford came on the scene. Gurdon took his A50 back to the workshop and the next year emerged with a larger, faster A90. He'd bored it out to 3 litres, supercharged it, even fitted disc brakes. Gurdon won that Easter but it would be the last time.

Leo Geoghegan was just twenty, and he arrived at Mount Panorama with his touring car on a trailer. That's not the way it was done. Jack Myers would drive his perfectly plain cream FJ all the way from Sydney's Kingsford to Mount Panorama, watching the gauges and never letting the car get close to its full performance potential of an 18.4-second standing quarter. Now here was young Leo with an all-black racing sedan. Geoghegan tore through the field to win the first NSW Road Racing Championship for Sedan Cars, with Gurdon a mightily disappointed third. Gurdon protested and it took twelve months of deliberations before the handicappers admitted they'd got it wrong and handed the trophy to the confusingly named Bob Holden in a Peugeot 203. Gurdon was still third.

'I was watching all this from up in Queensland and I thought, "I can beat those blokes,"' said John French, who would go on to win Mount Panorama's Great Race in 1981. 'You can win as many things as you like but unless you win Bathurst you're not famous.' A sedan car was the default option for people who wanted to go motor racing but barely had the money to do it. French was just scraping by. He'd drive his two-tone green FJ Holden as a sales rep, Monday to Thursday, then overnight he'd take out its standard motor, install a hotted-up racing motor, spend the weekend speeding around Queensland's motorsport venues, then reinstall the original unit for work the next week. It was cheaper, by far, than owning a standalone race car. The early touring cars were anything but standard. French's car was fitted with a four-speed Jaguar gearbox—cost: £50. It was heavier than the MGA four-speed that Leo Geoghegan used, but Geoghegan's had cost £110.

French relied on the kindness of friends. The go-fast cylinder head was made by Repco and cost £75. French couldn't afford it but he was given one by his friend Wally Anderson on the understanding he'd pay when he had the money. Queensland open-wheeler racer Glyn Scott—later to die in a crash at Queensland's Lakeside Raceway—found the new limited slip differential he'd bought for his open-wheeler wouldn't fit. But for £70 ('pay me when you can') it passed to French, who filed it down until it fit his Holden.

'I thought I'd tow my car to Mount Panorama—it's a long way to drive from Brisbane—but the FJ ute I used as a tow car was useless over the Blue Mountains,' French recalled. 'We had to take the race car off the trailer just to get over.' The Geoghegans would never have suffered that indignity. They set the benchmark for a professionalism that was starting to emerge. 'It was their life,' French said. 'It wasn't my complete life. I was always part time.'

French beat Leo Geoghegan at Mount Panorama but 'only with the help of the handicappers'. He was by far the most spectacular of the FJ drivers and that, later, secured him works drives in the Mount Panorama long-distance races with British Leyland, Alfa Romeo and Ford, with whom he won as Dick Johnson's co-driver. He probably had more fun than anyone else on the grid. 'I always took a sandwich along in the long-distance events, just in case I got hungry. I was a ham-and-tomato man. Kept them in the centre console. They came loose when I was driving, solo, for Ford in 1971—they were all over the floor,' he said to me. 'There was tomato everywhere!'

Jaguar arrived at Mount Panorama far too soon for Holden. In the UK, David McKay bought a 3.4-litre Jaguar on behalf of his oil company sponsor—christened 'The Grey Pussy' (Jaguars, after all, were cats). Frank 'Lofty' England, Jaguar's racing manager, specified it with a lower compression ratio to suit Australia's 'inferior fuel'. The car arrived while McKay was in the UK, and his first wife Betty drove it to the airport to pick him up on his return. Then they drove it to Mount Panorama, packed with the family's luggage and accompanied by their infant daughter Josephine. 'I had a few exploratory laps and marvelled at its speed down Conrod Straight—125 miles per hour [201 kilometres per hour] in overdrive was almost lazy. There was no noise from the engine, very little wind noise over the sleek compact body and the comfort of the luxuriously appointed interior seemed a little out of place on the race track,' he wrote.

McKay pulled out of the first race in 1958 when the power steering began to lock up: 'With Skyline corner coming up, which is like driving over a blind drop at 80 miles per hour [128 kilometres per hour] I decided this was no time to be driving with a possible steering fault. I backed off and coasted back to the pits.' In the next race however, 'I had a very comfortable and pleasant drive to win the touring-car race. Poor Leo Geoghegan's Holden expired with a broken crankshaft after chasing the Jaguar. John French hung on grimly in second place.'

The days of the hotted-up Holdens were coming to an end—they were too modified to be representative of road-going touring cars. CAMS declared new rules for touring cars and heralded the beginning of the Australian Touring Car Championship. In 1960, McKay became the inaugural champion, just up the road at the Gnoo Blas circuit in Orange. It was a Jaguar 1–2–3 rout.

The Australian GT Championship became the default category for the Holdens but their future also was limited. At Mount Panorama in 1960, Leo Geoghegan gave his 'slip-streamed' black FJ to younger brother Pete and took his Lotus Elite to victory in the first GT Championship. Pete came home third, with Porsches second and third.

French sold his Holden to wealthy and flamboyant Sydney car dealer Ron Hodgson, who'd already bought a Jaguar but declared he needed a second car. With the money, French paid off his debts to people who'd loaned him parts, and with the £1000 remaining built an aggressive homemade special called Centaur in partnership with Wally Anderson; with it, he won the 1962 Australian GT Championship. His old Holden was stolen from Hodgson's workshop and likely became the organ donor for a snarling pack of Friday-night racers.

Big Norm Beechey is the greatest showman Australian motorsport has ever produced. Nothing he did was ever half-hearted.

The first time Norm saw Mount Panorama he said it 'scared the shit out of me'. On just his second practice lap he became the first touring-car driver to exceed 150 miles per hour (241 kilometres per hour) down Conrod Straight, and he got lift-off. 'The front wheels left the ground and I was airborne,' Beechey said. 'Pete Geoghegan was beside me and he just looked across and went, "Whoa..."'

It was 1966 and the Australian Touring Car Championship, which had transformed motor racing in Australia, had come to Mount Panorama for the first time. People were watching open-wheelers less and touring cars more. The Jaguars had dominated the early 1960s. They won the first four Australian Touring Car titles in succession, but in 1962 Beechey, the one-man Barnum & Bailey of the sport, bought a monstrous Chevrolet Impala, a pillarless four-door hardtop, and the Jaguars had nowhere to hide. Norm Beechey was the father of V8 Supercars racing before the phrase was even invented. He went where he was paid to go—either by his sponsors or by the promoters—and Jack Hinxman, the boss of the ARDC, paid him 'beautifully' to race against Pete Geoghegan's black Jaguar at the wooden-walled Catalina Park at Katoomba. The Impala seemed to just fit within the fences 'I looked into the pits and there was no one there. They were all at the fence watching me,' Norm laughed. 'Pete's dad, old Tom, was waving a furled umbrella at him, telling him to go faster, but there was no way around the Impala.' The Impala, now restored in Beechey's home garage, remains the pivotal car in touring-car history, even if it never won the title.

Touring-car racing was on a growth curve. Geoghegan cast aside the Jaguar and secured a four-cylinder Ford Cortina GT. He raced it at Mount Panorama in 1964 and won the NSW Touring Car Championship before heading to Lakeside in Queensland to claim the national title. But it wasn't the car for either Mount Panorama or the championship. People had been excited by the Impala. The Cortina, no matter how enthusiastically driven, with its inside front wheel perpetually waggling in the air, was never going to cut it.

In the US, Ford released the Mustang. Bob Jane brought one to Mount Panorama in Easter 1965 and won on debut. Geoghegan's Cortina was third. The Cortina looked for all the world like a small black shadow cast by the white Mustang. Beechey bought a Mustang, too, and won the Australian Touring Car title. And suddenly everyone had one.

Beechey, the perpetual promoter, needed something to cut through. He secured a box-like Chevy Nova. 'It had almost a hundred horsepower [74 kW] more than the Mustang and when I went past Pete Geoghegan up Mountain Straight it looked like he'd missed a gear.' But the Nova used drum brakes 'about the size you'd find in a Holden' and when he arrived at the bottom of Conrod in the three-lap preliminary he was a good 20 kilometres per hour too fast at the turn-in. With Beechey crossed up and never, ever giving up, the Nova glanced off the outside fence. In the Touring Car Championship, the winner-take-all main event, Beechey's strategy was dead simple: 'Get to the front and stay there.' Beechey liked racing Geoghegan—they trusted each other. Not so against Allan Moffat and Bob Jane. 'Get them behind you and you'd wait for a collision. It was villainous.'

The '66 title turned out to be a man-on-man race—Pete Geoghegan versus Beechey. The big blue Nova drew ahead from the start and opened at least a second a lap. Geoghegan could do nothing until halfway, when clutch slip caused the Nova to fail and it fell back to the white Mustang. Geoghegan passed Beechey on the outside of McPhillamy Park, a sight to behold, and he won the second of his five titles.

It was four years before Beechey returned to Mount Panorama and when he did, he won. Beechey was the master of the Victorian tracks, the Geoghegans likewise in New South Wales: 'They used to tell me they got paid very well to come to Victoria to be thrashed by me.' Beechey saw Mount Panorama as neutral ground, 'the most challenging track in Australia', and it suited his style. 'It was a good track to show off your extra skill,' he quipped.

Automotive tribalism was born at Mount Panorama. Followers were either Blue or Red—Ford or Holden. CAMS had two touring-car series running simultaneously. One was for locally made production cars, Ford Falcon versus Holden Monaro. The other comprised the Australian Touring Car Championship, and it had never been won by an Australian car. The tribes were restless. They wanted a hero.

Beechey built a Holden—the most magnificent Holden ever constructed. It was a beacon for motorsport enthusiasts across the nation. The Championship had become a series and Mount Panorama was round two. In a series there is prudence in hanging back, scoring points. But that didn't suit the touring-car boys. Just as the motorcycles and open-wheelers had celebrated their golden age at Mount Panorama, this was theirs.

In practice for the 1970 race, Beechey did 151 miles per hour (243 kilometres per hour), with his car firing on only seven cylinders, down Conrod, and he would start from the third row of the tight-packed grid. It was a twenty-lap, 123-kilometre race and Beechey didn't waste a metre of it. From the flag he charged up on the grass to take second behind Pete Geoghegan's Mustang into Hell Corner. At the hump, he was first. But on the other side of the mountain Geoghegan repassed into Forrest's Elbow and then Allan Moffat's Mustang slipstreamed through on Conrod. Bob Jane was all over Beechey. They passed and repassed until Jane spun at Forrest's Elbow. 'I did not force him into error,' Beechey still claims. 'He lost control all by himself.' Moffat was black-flagged for dropping oil, but when he pulled to the pits the underside of the car was dry. He restarted, set equal fastest lap and then retired, disgusted with what seemed obvious interference by the officials. With two laps to go Geoghegan fell back on Beechey; his tyres were gone. Tyre conservation was a relatively new skill. Beechey took the win—the first for his yellow Monaro. Halfway through the year he won the Championship, the first for an Australian car.

Beechey's Australian Touring Car Championship victory in a Monaro enraged and incentivised Ford. If Holden could win a championship with a Monaro, Ford wanted to win one with a Falcon. Huge salesroom kudos hinged on the result. Ford's competitions department was galvanised to build two Super Falcons—one for Pete Geoghegan, the other for Allan Moffat. American Al Turner, Ford's Australian competition chief, saw no problem: effectively, he'd build up a Mustang within a Falcon body. It seemed simple but it wasn't. Allan Moffat, renowned as one of the best Ford test drivers in the world—he'd spent considerable time with the Ford Kar Kraft outfit in the US—couldn't get it to work.

Moffat was conflicted. He was engrossed in making his Ford Mustang Trans-Am a championship winner. (It never was, despite 101 race victories.) Ford said Moffat was intractable: he wouldn't give up his Mustang. But it wasn't so. 'We all wanted the Super Falcon project to succeed. Ford sold Falcons in Australia, not Mustangs,' Moffat told me. The Super Falcon was extremely powerful but it handled woefully and nothing seemed to make it better. The Ford stand-off with Moffat was becoming increasingly embarrassing. Ford gave the car to John French to drive in one round of the championship. He brought it home fourth after a race-long battle with Geoghegan; Ford told Moffat that surely French's result proved their point. 'It didn't,' Moffat said. 'The car was not a winner and French had overdriven it like a crazy man. You just couldn't risk your life like that.'

Pete Geoghegan moved to solve the impasse. For a lot of money, he said, he'd make the Super Falcon a winner. It just wouldn't happen at Ford's workshop and it would involve no one other than the Geoghegan team. Ford agreed. Geoghegan sought out John Joyce, one of a handful of Australians who had designed racing cars to world standards—in fact, his cars had led the world. Joyce worked at Lotus alongside the flawed genius Colin Chapman, and returned to Australia to start Bowin Designs. He designed and built 56 cars at his workshop at Brookvale in Sydney, and they won four Formula Ford championships and the Australian Gold Star. Joyce built Ford a new Falcon shell, with new pick-ups for all its suspension components—this time in the right places—and got the car's balance right.

Geoghegan went to Mount Panorama in the Super Falcon in 1972 to face off with Moffat in the Mustang.

There were others there too, but it didn't matter. Beechey stopped on lap four with a broken gearbox. Jane led for one lap, dropped back and pulled to a halt at the side of the track. Moffat was in the lead, Geoghegan directly behind. The Falcon had more brute strength up the mountain, the Mustang more speed down it. The lead changed several times each lap, but in those pre-transponder days, no one knew how many.

'And then a mist started to cover my windscreen,' Moffat said. 'Pete was pumping out oil all over the front of me. It was impossible to see. I turned on the windscreen wipers. That was a mistake. It just smeared the screen and made vision worse.

'I made the decision that the only way to catch Pete was to put my head out of the window. And the only way to do that was to take off my seatbelts and perch on the side of my bucket seat.' Moffat and Geoghegan were averaging 150 kilometres per hour, approaching 240 kilometres per hour up Mountain Straight and 260 down Conrod. 'It was the most dangerous, worst considered thing I've ever done in my racing career,' he said. Observers on Conrod said that Moffat's rear wheels were lifting off the bitumen over the second hump. They said the car was flying so far and landing so hard that there were deep scrape marks under the car and on the road. 'I broke the lap record like that and by the end of the last lap I was alongside him.' But Moffat was on the wrong line out of the final corner and Geoghegan took victory by 0.6 seconds.

Although he was a works Ford driver and so was Geoghegan, Moffat fired in a protest on the Super Falcon's oil. It was an indiscreet thing to do. By the time officials got to the Falcon it had been wiped clean. Stewards decided that as Moffat had set a new record on the penultimate lap the oil could not have been so bad. Protest dismissed. Bob Jane won the championship series that year—Mount Panorama was his only failure to finish—and

Moffat and Geoghegan went on to happily partner each other to win the following year's Bathurst 1000.

They called it 'The Beast'. Harry Firth built up an old six-cylinder Torana XU-1 used in rallies into a car powered by a Formula 5000 V8 engine. It was an unintentional homage to every hotted-up Holden that had competed at Mount Panorama two decades before. At the Easter motor-race meeting at Mount Panorama, 1973, Firth had Colin Bond drive it in all three events for which it complied. 'It wasn't much of a car,' Bond recalled.

'Sports sedans were just starting to become really popular and there was a lot of prize money on offer,' Bond said. These sedans had purpose-built chassis with incredibly powerful motors. 'But Harry said there was no money to enter the category. So he built this instead.' Bond thinks it was a bit of an exercise. Holden was soon to launch a V8-powered Torana—the SLR 5000—'and maybe they wanted to try out a few bits in this car'.

The open-trumpeted Repco V8 sat alongside the driver, a little forward of where the passenger seat would be, so loud that the driver was deafened (Bond, like so many former racers, now wears a hearing aid), and the four-speed gearbox was behind so Bond had to reach backwards to change gears. 'Its suspension was pretty standard and so were the brakes,' he said. But the power—The Beast easily topped 160 miles per hour (257 kilometres per hour), moving all over the road, and Bond was grateful he had no competition to make his job even harder. It was difficult enough just driving the car without having to employ race craft.

The Easter '73 meeting was a watershed for Mount Panorama.

Motor racing was going through yet another metamorphosis. The rules for touring-car racing had changed in favour of production cars, and the Geoghegan–Moffat clash the previous year would be the last time a round of the Australian Touring Car Championship was contested at Mount Panorama.

Mount Panorama was losing out to the amphitheatre circuits outside Sydney, like Oran Park and even the ARDC's own Amaroo Park. People could go there for just a day, not a weekend, see most of the action from one vantage spot and enjoy back-to-back racing—sometimes sixteen races on one card. It was difficult for Bathurst to compete in the instant-gratification stakes.

The Easter 1973 race meeting was particularly dissatisfying for the organising club. They'd not had a championship event on the card; that felt disrespectful to the great circuit and everything it stood for. It had been just like a big club meeting.

A committee, convened shortly afterwards, resolved to tell Bathurst City Council that the ARDC would concentrate on the promotion of its long-distance race, which was putting the city of Bathurst on the map in a way not even the Australian Grands Prix for open-wheeler racing cars had done. It recommended that the Easter date become the sole domain of the Auto Cycle Union.

Colin Bond, one of the most decorated drivers of his generation, took the chequered flag for the last closed-car race held at Mount Panorama in its first golden age. The Beast may not have been much, but it had carved itself a small place in the history of the mountain.

In one respect the long-distance event had hijacked motor racing at Mount Panorama. 'I say to the Supercars organisers even now that they should hold a sprint round of their championship at Mount Panorama months before the 1000,' Bond said. 'The teams would learn a lot and it would be great entertainment.'

Part 4

The Races That Stop a Nation

In automotive terms, the Bathurst 1000 rivals the Melbourne Cup as the race that stops the nation. Even if you don't follow the sport for the rest of the year, you'll want to know who won Bathurst. Now there's a new race on the Mountain—the Bathurst 12 Hour. The 1000 is run for Supercars (upper case), a term devised by local promoters to describe the formulaic 5-litre touring cars that contest what used to be the Australian Touring Car Championship. The 12 Hour is run for supercars (lower case), race versions of the high-performance production vehicles that populate the upper echelons of the global automotive market. The Bathurst 1000 is uniquely Australian. The Bathurst 12 Hour uses a unique Australian circuit as a platform for world competition.

9

A Wild Ride

It's easy to divide the Mount Panorama long-distance race into two distinct periods—pre- and post-Supercars. In the beginning, the 500-mile (804-kilometre) then 1000-kilometre Mount Panorama spectacle was conceived as a true test of showroom stock cars. It was never quite that. Liberal interpretation of the rules—cheating—prevented it from ever being a reliability trial. Which was just as well, because who wanted to watch cars staggering to the finish?

Barry Gurdon flung his supercharged Austin A90 down through the Esses. He was doing race pace, with passengers on board, no helmets, no seatbelts and no road closure. Gurdon, prominent member of both the Australian Racing Drivers' Club and the Bathurst Light Car Club, was determined he was going to secure the Armstrong 500 long-distance race for Mount Panorama. He had the decision makers trapped in his tiny Austin and the support of Bathurst City Council; the police, presumably, were on urgent business somewhere else in the city.

It was early 1963 and after three years at Victoria's Phillip Island the production car race was looking for a new home.

Phillip Island was the only Australian track that came close to matching the challenge of the Mountain, but the Island's track surface was breaking up badly and, incredibly, the bridge from the mainland was not capable of bearing the weight of the road-building equipment needed to repair it. (Later they built a new bridge.)

The Bathurst Light Car Club arranged for the senior management of Armstrong York, the shock absorber company that had conceived the race to promote and prove its products, to see Mount Panorama. They shot a film (no video back then) and hooked the company on travelling to Mount Panorama for an inspection. The sponsors weren't expecting the tour they got. 'My father got a cheap thrill from frightening people,' smiled Gurdon's daughter, Peta Gurdon-O'Meara, a former mayor of Bathurst who played a major part in protecting the track from reclassification under local government legislation.

The shock absorber people could see pluses and minuses. They'd set up the race in 1960 as much to influence Melbourne's car makers—of which there were many—as to promote to the public. Mount Panorama was a long way from the factories. On the other hand, the ARDC had a strong organisational record, the circuit had a reputation as a car breaker, and TV coverage was on offer.

In 1962 the ARDC turned its October date over to a six-hour race for production and sports cars. It was a dry run for the Armstrong. Jack Hinxman, the ARDC's secretary, was a no-nonsense ex-policeman who was big on planning and adherence to timelines. The Six Hour ran like clockwork. Forty-nine cars started and 41 finished. Brothers Leo and Pete Geoghegan won in a Daimler SP250 V8 sports car—the sort of car that British chaps drove to polo on the green—four laps clear of a Triumph TR4. The only significant non-finisher was Harry Firth's Ford Falcon. The Falcon's rear brakes seized going into Hell Corner and the car inverted; without a roll cage, its roof was flattened to the door sills. 'I wore a seatbelt with a dual cross over on each shoulder,' Firth said. 'That saved me, but it took a while to get the belt undone and find a way out, all the time with petrol leaking.' Firth managed to make his escape through a small gap in the rear window,

Firth and Bob Jane had won at Phillip Island the year before in a Mercedes-Benz and just three weeks after Firth's roll, the pair gave Ford their first major race win at the last 500 held on the Island.

Firth rolled there too, in practice. The crew built up the winning car for him overnight.

History paints Firth as rough, tough and invincible. He wasn't. He'd rolled a Falcon in a rally only weeks before those two race crashes and he was shaken. 'His brother Norm brought the car back to Melbourne for the rebuild,' Firth's long-time mechanic Ian Tate recalled. Firth stayed at the Island to rebuild his nerve.

The Armstrong 500 came to Mount Panorama in 1963.

It has since had ten naming-rights sponsors, a change of distance, unceasing modifications to its rules, and 63 drivers have had their names engraved on its trophy over 56 years. Seventeen of them are multiple winners. Such is the nature of the race, rewarding those who get it right, that those seventeen drivers have figured in 45 of the victories. Less than 2 per cent of the total race field has been female; the best outright result by a female driver has been sixth, awarded on countback after a crash in which the driver, Christine Gibson, was involved. The crash stopped the race; Gibson was exonerated.

The race has endured acts of treachery, avarice, ambition and massive confusion. It has created heroes and one of them—Peter Brock—is enshrined as its King of the Mountain. Brock is credited with nine victories at Mount Panorama—two of them controversial when he inserted himself in a team car after his own failed—but he latterly claimed ten because he was part of the winning team in the second of the Bathurst 24 Hour races held at Easter. The statisticians deny the claim. It wasn't the Bathurst 1000.

For its first decade, the Bathurst long-distance race was over 500 miles (804 kilometres). In 1973 it changed to 1000 kilometres. The reasoning was simple. In 1974 Australia was to abandon British imperial measurement and introduce the metric system—another colonial tie broken. 'You can't have a race called the Bathurst 804,' said Ivan Stibbard, Hinxman's deputy, who would take over the role in 1981. So they upped it to 1000 kilometres. There was another rationale, too: the winning time in the first 500 had been 7 hours 46 minutes. A decade later the winner completed the same distance in just on 6 hours neat.

The race wasn't taking long enough. TV networks had a lot of commercials to air and the viewing public—at the circuit and, increasingly, at home—deserved a full day's entertainment. The first race over the longer distance took 7 hours 20 minutes. In 2018, the 1000 was completed in 6 hours 1 minute 44 seconds—just 90 seconds more than the record for the 804-kilometre 500 race.

Armstrong's race was for strictly stock-standard, off-the-showroom-floor, affordable cars. And they had to be assembled in Australia. No imports. Even Firth and Jane's Mercedes-Benz in 1961 was built locally from a semi-knocked-down pack. (Back then Australia had a motor industry. In the early 1960s it was building more cars than Japan.) There was a £2000 upper limit on competing cars. A Holden or a Ford cost less than £1200 and a Mini Cooper was under £1000.

To creative engineers and ambitious car companies, the rules presented both challenge and opportunity. Rules demanded they register at least 100 vehicles. For the first Mount Panorama race, Holden pushed through a limited run of its EH S4, the boxy cult car with special racing drum brakes. At the last moment Ford weighed in with a high-performance disc-braked Cortina GT. It wasn't easy to buy either at a dealership; in Holden's case it was nigh on impossible.

Fifty-seven cars started the first race, and all but twelve finished. A lot of time was spent in the pits and yet winners-by-a-lap, Firth and Jane, completed their 500 miles in 28 minutes less than they'd taken in the Falcon at Phillip Island, and 13 minutes less than their race record in the Mercedes. For all its vertical gain and undulations, Mount Panorama was by far the fastest circuit.

Channel Seven had just four cameras at the race, and they were able to cover only the bottom of the track. On the last corner of the last lap they captured the drama in the baby-car class as the battle between Barry Ferguson's VW Beetle and Lindsay Little's Morris 850 ended when the Mini rolled. It popped back on its wheels to stagger across the line, second. That incident, more even than the race win, was water-cooler conversation the next day. It cemented the role of television in the creation of the legend of Mount Panorama.

Ford won six of the 500-mile races, Holden three and Mini Cooper S one. At the end of each race the placegetters in each class, plus the next highest finisher, would be corralled in an overnight parc fermé. The next morning, in the early dawn, they would be driven under police escort with sirens wailing to Barry Gurdon's garage in the middle of Bathurst for post-event scrutineering to determine if results would stand. It was a battle of wits and bluff.

'I don't want any car in the race that I can't sit in the back seat of,' Hinxman claimed. He mustn't have tried the tiny back seat of the 1966-dominating Minis. To save weight, many of the Minis had no springs under their tightly stretched seat covers. Nor did they have undercoat over their lightweight bodies. And to ensure reliability, their gear selector mechanism carried a more durable MGB spacer. Nonetheless they passed scrutineering.

Acid-dipping of bodies for lightness was commonplace. Ford even admitted to it and claimed it was within the spirit of the rules. The ARDC and CAMS brought in specialists to match the team's ingenuity: carburettor experts to measure jets, suspension experts to test spring rates. Years later, after Harry Firth retired from racing, they employed him as chief scrutineer—setting a thief to catch many.

There was a gentlemen's agreement between the lead teams, the turning of a mutual blind eye. But in 1974 Firth, then with Holden, broke the code and entered a fifteen-point protest on Allan Moffat's Ford. Moffat, incensed, agreed to take his car to Gurdon's mid-practice for a complete scrutineering check. The interruption, and the stress, cost him the race.

Some of the cheats were blatant. A mechanic disappeared under his team's Ford Escort to drop the gearbox out of the car for official checking. He pulled a standard gearbox out of his toolkit and pushed that from under the car for the checkers. The box that had been in the car left Gurdon's garage locked in his toolkit. There were always rumours of a six-speed Mazda that had reverse activated by a separate lever hidden beneath the shift hood. Its existence was never proved. Kevin Bartlett's Chevy Camaro, which inverted into the Reid Park fence in 1982, was fitted with an ingenious water injection system on its brakes, activated by an Audi headlight washer motor hidden in the boot. Peter Brock was caught directing water from the nozzles of his onboard fire extinguisher onto the intercooler of his turbocharger. It wasn't technically against the rules but he was fined $5000 for infringing the 'spirit' of the regulations.

The small car classes were alive with innovation. Both the Toyota and Datsun (Nissan) teams suffered Monday-morning disqualifications. Blueprinting—the art of building an engine to the absolute maximum tolerance allowed by the workshop manual and going to the spare parts shelves to find the most suitable parts—was okay. But it could be a fine line. Some people were even cheating the manuals that they'd present to scrutineers. Homologating components for racing but not necessarily for the road was a black hole intended to mystify race officials.

Technical checkers needed a fine eye for dimensions. The race-winning Ford Sierras of Swiss engineer Ruedi Eggenberger were ultimately excluded, after international appeal, for having wheel arches that were marginally too large. They'd been spotted by a scrutineer in the Mount Panorama paddock. It cost the Eggenberger team not only the Bathurst win but the World Touring Car Championship. Holden proved it was possible to expand an air intake by 10 per cent and still have it look like it came off the showroom floor. The valve springs in Ford's first race-winning V8 GT, according to the engineer who built them, distorted so a sturdier version was constructed and powder-coated to look like the original. After Gurdon's scrutineering, Ford's 1967 race win still stood.

Years later, a senior police official insisted he saw Firth walk into the local Holden dealership with 'a bag load of axles which he had placed in official parts boxes so that if scrutineers brought any to check against the ones in the race cars they would be identical'.

Firth masterminded four of the first five 500 wins for Ford. In 1965 he devised the Cortina GT500, a blatant Bathurst special even named for the event, which qualified for the race only because Ford contracted Firth to build all 117 of them off-line at his workshop in Queens Road, Melbourne. 'They'd arrive by truck from the factory but had to be driven back because they wouldn't get up the ramp,' Ian Tate recalled. Firth didn't get to race his creation. 'Ford was concerned that if they let him, there'd be 116 built one way and a 117th for Harry.' Instead Firth won the small-cost class in a Cortina 220.

But Firth's Falcon GT changed the race, and a new sponsor transformed the race image.

Start-up tobacco company Gallaher had become race sponsors in 1966. They'd bought a Ferrari 275 GTB as their halo promotional vehicle and insisted their showroom stock race become more of a spectacle. In 1967, Firth and his new recruit Fred Gibson delivered a race win—but only just. The Geoghegan brothers, Leo and Pete, took the flag in their GT only to be relegated to second after a lap-scoring protest by Firth. Incredibly, he actually protested a car of the same make, from the same team.

Both Falcons were only marginally ahead of two Alfa Romeos on the same lap, and one of them was in the same minute. But it would be the last time a small car got that close.

Lap scoring was an issue. Timekeepers would sit in the control tower and manually call the cars as they went past. Over 130 laps the chance of error was immense. The Geoghegans had caused confusion in the 1967 race by entering the pits via a back gate, unseen by the timers. Ray Morris, racer and father of later winner Bob, devised a system that required teams to do their own lap scoring under official supervision. A massive lap scoring structure was erected on the infield at Murray's Corner; designated team members turned over paddle boards every time their car went past. It didn't improve matters.

In 1969 IBM arrived with a massive computer it had built four years before to serve the Bank of America. They dragged it up to the first floor of the control tower and installed it alongside the timekeepers. Teams were able to see a flickering progressive result—Channel Seven pointed a camera at the IBM screen—and within half a decade the computer company had embraced the concept to such a degree that it had relays around the track to provide progressive scoring.

In 1969, Mount Panorama created three new heroes—Colin Bond, Peter Brock and Allan Moffat. Two of them would endure into perpetuity. The third, arguably the most naturally talented of the trio, would suffer a marginalisation born of the others' ambition. Bond won in 1969, but would not win the Bathurst race again. Over the next eighteen years, Brock and Moffat would claim it thirteen times between them. The pair would become the superheroes of Australian touring-car racing. In an eleven-year period from 1973 they would claim the Australian Touring Car Championship seven times. Over twenty years they would win the Sandown long-distance race, the precursor to Mount Panorama, no fewer than fifteen times. By 1987, Brock's last Bathurst win, they had sequestered 52 per cent of all Bathurst long-distance victories between them.

Moffat came to Ford Australia as a direct result of his immense track-testing ability. The Canadian-born and later Australian-naturalised driver had set his sights on a career in the US, but when that faltered he was employed by the Ford Motor Company to be a high-speed test driver in its Kar Kraft division in Dearborn, Michigan. Over a year his test-lap count in Boss Mustangs was immeasurable. He held the lap record among the test team.

'When I got back to Australia, Al Turner hired me to develop the Falcon GTHO,' Moffat said; Turner was the new boss of Ford

Australia's motorsport, displacing Harry Firth. When it came to racing the GTHO, there was an understanding that Moffat would be the lead driver. It would become Australia's most iconic production car of the period.

Bond's win in '69 was due to his first-lap pace. He was ahead of the pack when Sydney newsagent and part-time racer Bill Brown rolled his Falcon GT over Skyline. Brown made a habit of it. He did the same thing just a bit further back up the track two years later. This first time, twelve cars piled into him. John French in the Alfa Romeo went upside down too. 'I was hanging there, waiting for the banging to stop,' French told me, 'when there was a face at the window. It was Dick Johnson, not yet racing at Bathurst. He'd been spectating at Skyline with our wives and he jumped the fence to help me. He told me when it was safe to get out.'

The ARDC made a curious decision post-race. Under pressure from teams it determined there were not 120 top-flight drivers in Australia capable of driving the Mountain, so it allowed teams to nominate one driver only—someone who would be strapped in for the full 804 kilometres. Fifteen of the 60 entrants took up the offer and Moffat won it solo in 1970 and '71. It came with some unusual implications, Moffat recalled: 'My pit stop would take two minutes. I couldn't leave the car but I figured I could time a necessary comfort break. I was doing that, belts loosened, zip undone and feet up on the pedals so they wouldn't get wet, when a TV reporter arrived at my window. I conducted the interview while urinating.'

Moffat's second win occurred 'despite the best efforts of Ford management to stop me'. A beer carton had jammed across the radiator grille of the car and the team, at Ford CEO level, was indicating for him to come to the pit. 'I stayed out. The car's vital signs were good. I was in charge of my own work space. I did raise one finger to the pits. I later explained it meant I intended to win by one lap, which I did.'

Colin Bond might have won in 1972; instead, he crashed mightily. 'It was raining at the start and Harry Firth only had one set of wet-weather tyres,' Bond said. (Firth had moved to Holden when Turner took over Ford.) 'He offered them to me and I accepted. But when the cars were pushed onto the grid at the start, Brock had the wets and I had a set of intermediates. "There you go, Cock," Firth said. "The weather will clear soon."' Two laps later Bond, master of car control but still skating like an Olympian, was in the trees—his only serious crash at the Mountain. Brock won by a lap from John French.

'Firth was hard on Bond all the time,' Ian Tate mused, a faded Colin Bond poster behind him in his cavernous workshop. 'His reaction was, "Send Bond to the Frank Gardner School to learn how to drive [Australian international Gardner was a noted driver trainer]."' Brock, according to Tate, had the easier ride. 'Maybe it was because Brock was living in Melbourne and required by his contract to come in every day. [Holden boss] John Bagshaw said to me, "Work him hard, he's lazy."'

According to Tate, 'Brock was full of himself.' For the Firth mechanics, it all came to a head as they were preparing for the Sandown prelude to Bathurst in 1972: 'Brock was in the pit whinging that his dad reckoned Bond's car was quicker up the back straight,' Tate said. 'Brock was giving us a hard time, and we'd had enough. One of the mechanics, Peter Byrnes, got up from under the car and hit Brock hard. It left a painful bruise and caused a swelling across his left arm and shoulder. He had to be helped in and out of his race suit and gear changing must have been agony. Harry never knew, but Brock was better after that and his dad was banned from the garage.'

Neither driver stayed too long under Firth's regime—Brock fled at the end of '74, Bond two years later when Moffat offered him 'the price of a house' to jump to his Ford team.

It must have been a substantial amount; Bond gave up winning Bathurst for it. In the 1977 race, Moffat had run out of brakes and Bond, who could have gone past him, fell into line behind. 'Can you imagine how Colin felt?' Moffat asked me. 'When you're a racing driver, you want to win again and again. Both of us craved this win and the race was his for the taking.' But Moffat needed the win for the survival of his race team with Ford. 'Into the last corner Colin ranged up alongside—his moment of truth. It was in that final 100 metres I confirmed what I'd always known—he was a gentleman.' The race timing said it all: Moffat and Jacky Ickx, his highly credentialled co-driver, at 6 hours 59 minutes 0.8 seconds; Bond and Alan Hamilton at 6 hours 59 minutes 0.9 seconds. Bond was philosophical, and remains so even now: 'If I'd passed him to win and someone asked who won Bathurst in 1977, the answer would probably be "Brock—didn't he always win?" That formation finish is something everyone remembers. It's part of history.'

It was Moffat's last win at the Mountain. He ran himself close to bankruptcy with his Falcon team, came close to victory with Mazda, and in 1988 saw a 'certain' win slip by in his Ford Sierra. In 1986, in a masterstroke of promotion, Brock hired him as co-driver in his Commodore. Moffat turned left at 200 kilometres an hour and mounted the fence at McPhillamy ('I thought I was about to become Australia's first astronaut'), and the pair finished fifth, one lap down. Moffat's last drive at Bathurst was in 1990. He'd moved on to team management but had still entered himself in the Sierra: 'I suited up and took both cars for a sighting lap. I remember it as surreal, an out-of-body experience. At the time it was just another lap, total concentration, feeling out the car, always respecting the track. That night I played the laps back in my head. It was like I was hovering above each car, critiquing my own performance. I knew I'd driven Bathurst for the last time in a race car and I was okay with that.'

Brock played on a while longer. He was never one to give up. Moffat said it best: 'Peter and I discussed retirement. My view was absolute: quit while you're ahead. His view was typically optimistic—the best was yet to come.' Brock had six partners in his nine Bathurst wins. There were three each with Jim Richards and Larry Perkins, one with Brian Sampson, and two controversial shared wins. The first of these, with John Harvey in 1983, came when Brock and Perkins commandeered the team car of Harvey and Brock's brother Phil; the second was in 1987 when Brock took over the car of David Parsons and Peter McLeod. Phil Brock, known as 'Split-pin' because of his height and thin frame, still holds a grudge.

Peter Brock was the only driver to win at Bathurst in the mighty A9X—the last and best of the Toranas—both times with New Zealander Jim Richards. His magnum opus was their 1979 win, six laps (37 kilometres) ahead of the field; Brock set a new lap record on his final lap.

The rules changed seemingly incessantly, and Brock adapted every time. Holden fell in and out of love with him (and vice versa), and their eventual divorce over his use of a box of crystals that he called the Energy Polarizer lost him not only a race seat but his ability to partner with General Motors in their performance road-car program. It cost him, potentially, millions in opportunity. He was, according to Moffat, 'the only person I ever knew to fire General Motors'.

Holden and Brock got back together again, though not at the same level, and he was driving for them in 1997—at age 50 if you subtract, as he did, the two years he spent in National Service—when he decided to retire. He was angling for his tenth win in what he thought would be his last Great Race, and the signs were good. But not for long. He was sitting quietly in the pits, sipping his never-ending mug of tea, when his co-driver Mark Skaife stopped on top of the Mountain at one third distance with engine failure. It was an ignominious way for such a great career to end but Brock was philosophical. He went back, that day, to signing autographs—the queue of fans so great that they had to illuminate the area at the back of the pits with car headlights to carry on after dark.

Brock came back, of course. In 2002 he accepted an offer from a privateer team to rename themselves Team Brock, and he got a glimpse of what life was like on the other side—they qualified twenty-sixth and finished twenty-third. Then he won the Bathurst 24 Hour the year after. Three years later he was dead, driving, as Moffat put it, 'in a damned car rally in Western Australia'.

Colin Bond pulled the pin on his Mount Panorama driving career in 1994. He drove his last 1000 for Fred Gibson Motorsport, sharing a Commodore with the Swede Anders Olofsson, and they finished sixth. Bond had not missed a Great Race since his 1969 win. He'd stood on the podium seven times in 28 starts, to net two seconds, four thirds and his one victory. He'd driven everything from a Toyota Corolla (in his penultimate year) to Kevin Bartlett's massive Camaro (in the year it went upside down). He'd raced his own Alfa Romeo team, with a best-placed eighth shared with Gregg Hansford. Mount Panorama is unrelenting in its cruelty: he'd suffered eleven failures to finish.

It's not possible to define Bond's career by Mount Panorama alone. He became one of the sport's greatest all-rounders—an Australian Touring Car champion and an Australian Rally champion, and the only driver to achieve both. He may not have ascended into the dizzy clouds of fame and infamy that engulfed Brock and Moffat, but he'd stamped his mark on Australian motorsport, race and rally, with an honest dignity.

He became the president of the Australian Racing Drivers' Club at a time when it needed a high-profile spokesperson to guide it through a period of financial uncertainty. And when it was all over, he volunteered as driving standards officer for the newly formed Supercars Group, to help others gain a little knowledge. 'It's just what you have to do,' he cackled, with that laugh that had become his trademark.

The face and the pace of the race changed when it became the 1000. Ford and Holden regarded it as the most important and public of all their showrooms. The escalation of their efforts was rapid. In 1972 both factories embarked on projects to build the fastest car either factory had ever produced—for Ford, a Phase IV Falcon, and for Holden, a Torana. Chrysler, never really a major contender, was developing an eight-cylinder engine for its Charger.

On 25 June 1972, Sydney's *Sun-Herald* newspaper ran a front-page splash: '160 MPH "SUPER CARS" SOON'. The rules of the Bathurst 1000 required 200 of each car to be built for road registration—and that meant these cars would be available for sale. The story sparked outrage. The New South Wales Minister for Transport, Milton Morris, said he was 'appalled at bullets on wheels being sold to ordinary motorists' and called for a national ban on their registration. Within a week Holden had announced it would abandon plans to build and race a V8-powered Torana and the next day Ford dropped the axe on its GTHO. Chrysler, which may have one day become a key participant, pulled out of Bathurst. The teams ran barely changed cars in their 1972 assault on the last 500, and the new rules for the 1000 were developed not because the race had become longer, but because authorities, like the car makers, had wised up to the awesome influence the Mount Panorama race was having on, as Milton Morris called them, 'ordinary motorists.'

It didn't take long for people to lawyer up. As soon as there's money involved it's the natural next step. 'I got a call from Brock's solicitor asking would I like to race with him at Bathurst—$5000 and a share of the prize money,' Jim Richards said. It was the start of a partnership that netted their three successive victories. 'Peter was a fantastic, friendly guy. If I could go as fast as him I was rapt, but I didn't have to try as hard. It was *his* team.

I was the co-driver. They said to me: "In the race we'll hold out a board for you and tell you the time we expect you to do—a little arrow, up or down." That's all I had to do.' Richards, typically, understates it. But he's also his own man. Frank Gardner, the fast-quipping Australian who'd won the British Touring Car Championship three times and starred in European Formula 5000s, had been contracted to run the works BMW team in Australia. In 1982, 'Frank offered me a full-time drive—$30,000 flat and $500 expenses per meeting,' Richards said. 'I never did one test lap between 1982 and 1987. Frank did it all and I never drove a BMW for Frank that wasn't better than the one before.' Richards came tantalisingly close to a podium with the BMW—three fourths, a fifth and a sixth. 'But in 1987 [BMW boss] Ron Meatchem took Frank and I to lunch and told us he was dissolving the team. The Ford Sierras were pulverising us. But that wasn't the real reason. Frank's health was not the best and Ron adored him.' Meatchem arranged for Brock to take the cars.

Larry Perkins had contracted to Brock. It was a rolling one-year deal. 'I was more interested in running the workshop than driving,' Perkins said, although he was the next to claim three Bathurst wins with Brock, in succession. 'The contract stated that [Brock] would not interfere in the workshop or the preparation of the cars. The workshop was a dirty pigsty. I cleaned it up—and a few people as well.' Perkins doesn't muck around.

In mid-1985, things changed. 'I got a phone call from [mechanic] Neil Burns at a race meeting, saying, "He's sticking magnets on the race cars".' Brock had overstepped the line Perkins said he had drawn. It was one thing for him to apply his Polarizer science to his road cars, but another to put them on the race cars. 'On Monday we had it out. "Well, if you want to end the contract, you can do it," Brock said. I was massively overpaid. He spat the dummy when he had to pay me out.' Perkins went on to live his dream—start his own race team and win at Bathurst three times.

Jim Richards moved on to Fred Gibson's Nissan team in the late 1980s—finally a lead driver in his own right—and he won for two successive years until the mighty Nissan GT-R, the car christened Godzilla, was banned. Gibson was one of the most influential people in motor racing and ultimately, sadly, the one in most frequent contact with the legal profession (an argument over team ownership). Gibson had been Firth's winning co-driver in the 1967 Falcon GT. The year before he'd come second in a Mini. Firth had offered him a seat in the new Holden Dealer Team but his family business was contracted to prepare Ford's fleet cars in Sydney and he wasn't going to pass that up.

He raced for Nissan's works team, then bought it. There's a story about Gibson and twenty-year-old Mark Skaife at Bathurst. It was one of the great Mount Panorama myths but it's now been confirmed. 'It was my first Bathurst and I was driving a class car,' Skaife said. 'Both drivers had to qualify above a cut-off time and my co-driver was having difficulty. So the garage doors came down and when they opened again I was in his helmet and I qualified as him. Fred was across it.' It was strictly illegal but harmless.

In 1991 and '92 the mercurial Skaife partnered Richards in both Bathurst race wins for the Nissan GT-R and it was their success that brought the shutters down on open-class racing.

It was so hard for the privateers to compete in an atmosphere of increasingly big money. The last year of the clash between true privateer entrants may have been 1974 when John Goss and Kevin Bartlett in their Falcon XA GT beat Bob Forbes and Wayne Negus and their Torana. 'Gossy was always knocking on the factory door and it frustrated him he never got in,' Moffat and Gibson once told me.

Goss contracted Bartlett at his bedside at Royal North Shore Hospital. 'I'd just returned from New Zealand where I'd broken my legs badly in an F5000 crash,' Bartlett recalled. 'Gossy turned up with a bottle of stout and talked me into going to Bathurst with him.'

Goss backed up again to win in 1985 but this time as a paid driver in Tom Walkinshaw's Jaguar team. Allan Grice and Graeme Bailey came close to privateer status in 1986 when they brought the Les Small–prepared Commodore home first. But the ambitious Grice put his amateur status in peril when, after winning the Tooheys 1000 in 1990, he went to tear open his race suit on the dais to reveal the logo of his private sponsor VB, a rival beer company.

Dick Johnson was an enigma. He looked, spoke and acted for all the world like a privateer but for more than a decade he was Ford's favourite son, a position he has recently reclaimed. Like Brock, Johnson went to Mount Panorama young as a spectator. He drove overnight with a friend to the 1964 Bathurst 500, risking death. 'The car had a throttle cable under the dash and I was able to pull at it whenever my mate was going too fast,' he said. 'We watched the race from Skyline and I thought, "I'll be here one day."'

Sixteen years later, when a great big boulder rolled down the side of the hill just out of the Cutting and Dick ploughed into it, eliminating him from the lead of the 1980 race, his doleful response as he perched on the corner's concrete wall touched the hearts of a watching nation—and especially that of Ford Australia's vice-president Edsel Ford II. The man with his name on the hubcaps pledged dollar-for-dollar support to a hastily organised Channel Seven telethon. Johnson may have had a wrecked car but he also raised $72,000—twice the prize purse. 'When that happened I knew my days at Ford were numbered,' Moffat said. 'They had a new hero.'

Johnson was accident-prone at the Mountain. In 1983 he plunged off Forrest's Elbow and down into the trees in qualifying. The footage of the crash and the overnight rebuild have become part of Johnson's legend. Another famed episode is the denial of his victory on countback in 1992, when Jim Richards' Nissan crashed in rain, the race was stopped, and the crowd bayed for Johnson to be awarded first—even though the rules gave it to the Nissan. Those Nissan wins were the final straw for the key stakeholders in what had become entrenched as The Great Race. The tribes—Holden and Ford—were massing against upstart intruders.

In 1987 the entire event had been put at risk when organisers fell for the lure of making the race part of the inaugural world championship. The cost of upgrading the facilities, including building the Chase—which added 43 metres to the circuit length, so it was remeasured at 6.213 kilometres—had been immense, and it drove the ARDC into virtual bankruptcy. It took a consortium of Channel Seven, the Bathurst City Council and CAMS, which was dragged reluctantly into the melee, to bail the circuit out. There was too much investment in Mount Panorama to let it go under.

The ARDC lost its naming rights sponsor of twenty years over the naked ambition of the world title promoters. James Hardie Industries, through its chairman John B. Reid, was the company every sport covets. When Prime Minister Malcolm Fraser arrived late for the 1977 race and was stranded on the outside of Pit Straight trying to get to the pits, to perform his official duties, he finally pushed his wife Tamie out into the race traffic and strode purposefully across himself. Officials who had been holding him back in the hope of finding a safety-gap in the traffic were horrified. Reid, watching from the balcony of the VIP area, which was Fraser's destination, turned to his promotions manager and said, 'Bruce, build a bridge.' It was there the next year. The ARDC didn't understand the below-the-line support they were receiving. They demanded more money up-front and Hardie walked.

In 1992 some of the stakeholders, now armed with more power than they'd expected, took a proactive role in the future of the race. Channel Seven convened a meeting with sponsors and manufacturers. They issued an ultimatum: all future races would be for Holden versus Ford, V8s only—or nothing. That's what the public wanted and what they'd respond to; the time for division and confusion was over, they said. Seven, the ARDC, key sponsors and manufacturers effectively formed a V8 consortium to guide the future of the race.

CAMS got the message. It moved to separate 5-litre V8 racing from the small-car classes. The decision created opportunity. Massively wealthy Queensland entrepreneur Terry Morris, along with Sydney promotions czar Peter Adderton, started the Australian Super Touring Car Championship for 2-litre cars, not as an adjunct but as a direct alternative to V8. It was based on the hugely successful British Touring Car Championship, which, at its height, had boasted direct involvement from ten manufacturers. Alan Gow, the British series' Australian-born promoter, was instrumental in assisting Morris and Adderton to set up. Terry Morris's son Paul won the inaugural series in 1995.

The Two Litres raced at Bathurst—in 1996 as a support race to the 1000. But then the split between the categories became a schism. Positions were taken and the Two Litre Series became pivotal in the battle for who would control racing at Mount Panorama. The ARDC backed Two Litre (as Julia Roberts said in the hit movie of the same era *Pretty Woman*, 'Big mistake. Big. Huge.'), and the door was left wide open for a new promoter—the kind motor racing in Australia had never experienced before.

After 33 years of running their long-distance race with an iron hand, just as Jack Hinxman had conceived it, the ARDC was already losing its stranglehold. The V8 consortium had appointed, for want of a better term, an administrator. Channel Seven sales executive Greg Eaton put his hand up and got the job. Eaton had his own office in a demountable in the pits and it was his responsibility to protect the investment of his stakeholders. In 1996 I was sitting with him in his office at the Bathurst 1000 when a man arrived at the door, red faced, belligerent and literally spitting out his demands. He wanted to call a conference of the media and the competitors and he demanded it occur now. His name was Tony Cochrane and, on behalf of the competitors, he was in high dudgeon over the hold 'promoters' had on their races, including Mount Panorama. He was going to stand up for the teams' interests.

10

Supercars

'I like thinking big. I always have. To me it's very simple: if you're going to be thinking anyway, you might as well think big.' US President Donald Trump, in his book *The Art of the Deal*.

Visiting Team Triple Eight's headquarters in the decidedly industrial Brisbane suburb of Banyo, it's as if you have been teleported to the Model Room of the New York Yacht Club. The walls are lined with trophies behind glass, all brilliantly lit, immaculately polished and proudly displayed. It's an impressive show of strength and yet there's something very personal about this presentation, evocative of a private club to which entree is desired and exclusive.

Roland Dane is the principal of the most successful motor-racing team of the V8 Supercars era—eight manufacturer series, nine drivers' championships, and seven victories in the hardest race of all to win, the Bathurst 1000. Dane acknowledges he could not have done it without Tony Cochrane, the impresario who built V8 Supercars brick by brick and who elevated domestic motor racing to a commercial viability it was unlikely to otherwise attain. 'Tony was very good for a while,' Dane said, with the understandably guarded tone of a man who lives in an unrelenting political environment. 'There were no subtleties or nuances about him. He was a bull in a china shop. But he really helped.' Cochrane, the immodestly self-proclaimed 'father of Supercars', has gone now, forced out by his own success when he could not get along with the venture capitalist who bought his shares and made him wealthy. 'I don't think he wanted to get out,' Dane mused, 'but he was never going to fit with their methodology. I can't say I do either.'

Supercars Australia—the V8 has been dropped to broaden its catchment area of entrants—is unquestionably the public face of motorsport in Australia. Formula One, MotoGP and the World Rally Championship titillate with their annual visit, but Supercars has created Aussie heroes and Mount Panorama is the rock on which it has been formed.

'The day Mount Panorama is not the grand final of the Supercars series is the day car racing doesn't exist in this country,' proclaimed Mark Skaife, six-time Bathurst winner, four of them in the Supercars era, and now the sport's most lucid and erudite spokesperson. His office, in Melbourne's Como Centre, is not on a Dane-scale but there are trophies and posters and—most importantly—blueprints for future projects that tantalise with opportunity. This is motorsport central. Skaife shares his office with Michael Masi, deputy race director of Supercars and just-appointed Formula One race director, globally, following the death of long-term boss and legend Charlie Whiting.

Skaife grew up with the 'folklore of Mount Panorama'. His dad Russell, also a racer, was a junior member of Bruce McPhee's 1968 winning team. 'Bathurst was like Christmas,' Skaife said. 'It wasn't a place for a kid, so as a five- or six-year-old I'd be in front of the TV all day. When I finally got there it blew me away.' Skaife has been everything in motor racing. He was national champion, in touring cars and open-wheelers. He became a team owner when he bought the Holden Racing Team, after its English owner Tom Walkinshaw Racing took it to the brink of receivership, 'to save 30 to 40 people losing their jobs'. He's a circuit architect—Supercars' Townsville and Newcastle tracks are his design—and a Supercars rule maker, leading the Car of the Future program that sought to radically change technical regulations to achieve the impossible dream of reducing costs and creating performance parity. And he's now lead commentator on Supercars television. But it's the racing that lights him up. 'Bathurst 2005—it was the best drive I ever put on,' he said. 'I broke the lap record lap after lap and then there was the overtaking move on Jason Richards to win.' (He dived under Richards on top of the Mountain.) 'Personally, that was the best.'

'I was wrong.' The astonishing admission from Tony Cochrane, a man not short of self-belief, came while he was travelling, typically, at 100 kilometres per hour. 'I told the bosses of motor racing that there was no such thing as the Holy Grail, but there is—and it's Mount Panorama.' Cochrane was driving from his home north of Surfers Paradise, where he is chairman of the Gold Coast Suns AFL club, to a meeting in Brisbane. 'Formula One has Monaco, the Indy 500 has Indianapolis, NASCAR has Daytona. Mount Panorama will always be the big moment in Australian motorsport.' Cochrane was vice-president of the Australian arm of then-giant American promotions company IMG (International Management Group) when motor racing first crossed his path. IMG was hired by the New South Wales Government to run world championship MotoGP at Sydney's Eastern Creek Raceway after the initial promoter, Bob Barnard, supported by the Auto Cycle Union, ran out of funds. 'We rejuvenated the event,' said Cochrane. Soon after, Queensland premier Wayne Goss contacted Cochrane to run the Gold Coast street race for IndyCars. 'They'd lost $82 million in four years. We signed up and made it a pretty strong financial success.'

Cochrane's attention turned to domestic racing. 'In my spare time I drew up a white paper to create an organisation I called the Australian Vee Eight Supercar Company—AVESCO.' He had some powerful help. Through motorcycling he'd formed a close friendship with twice world champion Barry Sheene, one of the absolute giants of motorsport, who'd emigrated to Australia because the steel plates holding his broken bones together hated the English winter. Sheene was a corporate chameleon, an astute businessman who could be as rough as bags or smooth as silk as the occasion demanded. He knew an opportunity when he saw it.

In Melbourne, six-time Bathurst winner Larry Perkins had long before called a meeting of touring-car owners: 'We observed that Brock and Moffat were paid a lot of money and we got nothing.' They formed the Touring Car Entrants Group (TEGA). 'We had a PR company tell us they could help us for a sign-on fee of $500,000,' Perkins said. They didn't need that and couldn't afford it. Cochrane backed himself. He proposed a share of the action. Team owners, too, became shareholders. IMG took 25 per cent.

To be on the other side of a Cochrane negotiation is one of life's great experiences. 'The track operators were getting their show for nothing,' he proclaimed. So, in 1996, he hit them between the eyes with a startling proposal: 'I told them I'd discovered most air force bases are closed Friday night to Monday morning. We could turn them into racetracks—cut out the existing circuits.'

Cochrane's stock-in-trade is a combination of guile, cunning and bluff. 'I waited for them to blink. When a few did, the others followed.' Except for Mount Panorama. 'They thought the best form of defence was attack.' Cochrane attended a meeting of the Mount Panorama consortium, made up of the Australian Racing Drivers' Club, the Bathurst City Council and Channel Seven. There were, he recalled, eighteen people in the room. ARDC general manager Ivan Stibbard was very vocal, Cochrane said, arguing that 'V8 touring cars were dinosaurs', and that the ARDC would adopt 2-litre cars, the kind raced in Europe. 'They were prepared to run us as a support category,' said Cochrane. He was not pleased, and he does rage better than most: 'I was pissed off and you don't want to get me pissed off.' He invoked the Trade Practices Act and the ramifications of a lock-out from Mount Panorama.

It was then, according to Cochrane, that the Council 'blinked'.

'I got a call from the mayor'—who was Ian Macintosh, formerly a prominent Canberra lobbyist mainly on rural matters—'who said he'd like to meet in Sydney. I said I'd come to Bathurst. I offered him an olive branch. "You're in the business of renting your circuit," I said. "Don't back anybody. Rent it to the ARDC for their 2-litre race and on a different day to us for the V8s. A strictly commercial proposition. If they're right [about crowd numbers] we'll be embarrassed. But you can tell the good citizens of Bathurst that you've not taken sides."

'"You're a helluva salesman," he said.'

In 1997, on its traditional NSW Labour Day weekend, the ARDC ran its AMP 1000 for 2-litre cars, covered by Channel Seven. Two weeks later AVESCO ran its Primus 1000 for V8 cars, covered by Channel Ten.

'They didn't make it easy for us,' Shane Howard, now the chief operating officer of Supercars Australia, said. 'Just getting the keys required a bit of work.' Howard shadowed the ARDC throughout its race meeting, trying to learn as much as possible but mainly 'making sure they bumped out and we were able to bump in'. One of the unexpected challenges was the enthusiasm of motorsport fans: 'They went for the 2-litres and stayed on in our camp ground for the 1000. We had to knock on tent flaps to collect our entrance fees.'

The ARDC's 2-litre cars endured for three years at Mount Panorama—or, as Cochrane put it: 'Their event was a dismal failure. Ours was a success.'

By 2001 the Australian Super Touring Car Championship had been wound down, but it's disingenuous to give Cochrane too much credit. Internationally the series was also losing support. Kelvin O'Reilly, the series' Australian chief executive, saw it diminish in Britain to just two car makers and in Australia to a privateer category. 'Costs had escalated and the return on investment wasn't there. It cost Nissan tens of millions of pounds to win the British championship,' said O'Reilly. He was quick to point out that the Two Litre 1000-kilometre races at Bathurst were not his. 'The ARDC approached us and asked us to provide a field. But it was their financial risk, not ours.' O'Reilly, now head of Karting Australia, remains a dedicated observer of the battle for Bathurst that set the future direction for Australian motor racing.

'Our series gave their series something to hate,' he said. 'And it made the TV companies very competitive.' O'Reilly credits Cochrane's business partner James Erskine and Channel Ten sports director David White with striking the deal that gave V8 Supercars a platform for growth. 'White is as much a father of V8 Supercars as anyone. Channel Ten did not have good programs and he bet it all on V8 Supercars. He invested in it and he made it a success.' It helped that White was a motorsport tragic.

On 12 September 2001, the day after New York's Twin Towers fell, Two Litre Touring Cars extracted themselves from their broadcast agreement with Channel Seven and wound down the series. According to O'Reilly, neither Terry Morris, now an inductee in the Gold Coast Business Hall of Fame, or Peter Adderton, now the California-based global owner of Boost Mobile, suffered financially. Morris's son Paul went on to win the V8 Bathurst 1000 in 2014.

IMG ran the Bathurst V8 race for the first four years but Cochrane was no longer there. With a small group of colleagues, he'd left the most successful event management company in the world to form a start-up, Sports and Entertainment Limited (SEL). 'IMG thought I was wasting my time and my money on the V8 Supercars series. They didn't understand it.' So they sold him their 25 per cent share in AVESCO for $52,000, 'the best deal I've done in my life'. But IMG wanted to retain management rights of Bathurst. 'Their eyes were on the prize of Mount Panorama.' That caveat became part of Cochrane's separation agreement.

Through AVESCO, Cochrane was happy to charge IMG a fee ('they paid a lot of money') for the rights to run the 1000. 'It gave our organisation an opportunity to set up a company called V8 Supercars Events. When IMG's contract expired we moved in and became our own promoter. The CEO of IMG, Martin Jolly, would say he was bullied into it, but I believe I mounted a persuasive argument. My plans didn't include working with another promoter at Bathurst.' He admits: 'We got the lion's share of the upside.'

Cochrane's crowning glory at Mount Panorama is the circuit's world-class pit complex. He conducted a media conference in the old pits—constructed only in 1987 as part of the upgrade for the World Touring Car Championship—'and ruined a good pair of shoes standing in a running puddle of water'. Cochrane told the media: 'This is a disgrace that any government could allow this to take place. It's as if we are a third-world country.' New South Wales treasurer Michael Egan agreed to match any amount of funding Cochrane could raise from the federal government. 'He expected it to be zero.' But Cochrane mounted a three-year campaign, lobbying known motorsport enthusiasts in Canberra—the federal president of the Liberal Party,

Shane Stone; the government leader in the Senate, Robert Hill; and the Minister for Foreign Affairs, Alexander Downer. 'They stumped up $10 million. The state government matched it and the Council put in $4 million. Mayor Macintosh told me our handshake those few years before was the best he'd ever had.'

Craig Lowndes was in tears on the Mount Panorama podium, barely holding it together.

Lowndes, still today called 'The Kid', rates his 2006 win at Mount Panorama as the one he most cherishes. That was the first Bathurst 1000 since Peter Brock's death and Lowndes, who freely identifies Brock as his hero and mentor, drove a near-perfect race to ensure his name would be the first engraved on the Peter Brock Trophy. There are psychologists who would not have let him race that day, but they weren't consulted. He was in a fragile state of mind. Just an hour before race start, Lowndes had led a parade of Brock's race cars on a lap of Mount Panorama. At the wheel of the 1972 Torana XU-1 that Brock raced to his first Mountain victory, he was in tears. He and Bev Brock embraced on the grid, the emotion raw. He was wearing a black 05 armband—Brock's racing number. On his helmet visor were the words 'Brock Always With Us'. Team owner Roland Dane considered getting Lowndes' co-driver, young Jamie Whincup, to start but Lowndes would have none of it.

Lowndes had won The Great Race only once—ten years before, in the pre-Supercars era—with Brock as a teammate, not a co-driver. Lowndes and Greg Murphy had won. Brock and Tomas Mezera had come fifth. There'd been a changing of the guard.

As Lowndes brought his Team Triple Eight Ford Falcon across the finish line, he slowed and drove past the pit wall in salute, 'on the day he farewelled his friend', commentator Leigh Diffey said. On the podium, announcer Greg Rust referenced Brock, and Lowndes struggled: 'I've got to personally thank [Ford Australia managing director] Tom Gorman for allowing me to drive the Torana around this morning. It was very emotional.' Even at a time of high anxiety, the politics of Ford versus Holden tribalism had to be observed. Ford had been asked for special permission to allow Lowndes to drive Brock's Holden.

Lowndes broke down as he lifted the Brock trophy aloft. 'It was all about the man,' he told Rust at the microphone.

Lowndes is the most successful driver at Mount Panorama in the post-1997 Supercars era. Every one of his six Supercars wins has been with Team Triple Eight. With seven wins in total, he's second on the all-time winners list, tied with Jim Richards; unlike Richards, he is still an active competitor at the Mountain. His win tally could increase. Twenty-four drivers had won the 22 races held in the Supercars era, up to but not including the fiftieth anniversary year of Brock's first appearance at the Mountain. Nine were multiple winners; fifteen had stood on the top step of the podium just once. Only eight spanned the two eras. Sixteen had driven only under the new regime.

Few had Lowndes' credentials or his good fortune: 'The first time I saw the Mountain I was driven around by Tim Schenken,' Lowndes said. Schenken is the powerful Supercars race director, a former top driver with 36 Formula One career participations and a member of Ferrari's winning team in the 1971 World Sports Car Championship. On Mount Panorama that first time, Lowndes said, 'I was thinking, "How do they remember where to go?" But in one lap I was hooked on the place.' The Lowndes family are not motorsport royalty; they weren't born to leadership. For years—to keep the regal analogy going—they were courtiers. Craig's dad Frank was a mechanic, later a scrutineer and always an enthusiastic volunteer. The Kid was a pit pest. 'I'd dive into Dick Johnson's pit to borrow some car polish or hang around the Holden team getting in the way. I was a pain.' At Mount Panorama, Frank and Craig slept in the pits— no motels for them. It's a habit Craig still maintains. He prefers to take a caravan to the Mountain rather than join his team in town.

'Our big break came in 1994 when we got a call from [Holden team manager] Jeff Grech asking us to co-drive with Brad Jones.' Rickard Rydell, the team's import, had a licensing issue. 'I think Brad wondered who was this guy and why should he be lumbered with a rookie. And he was right. I was way out of my depth and I was struggling.' Peter Brock had been reunited with the Holden team that year; Lowndes said he 'sat me down and talked me around the circuit'. It helped settle the twenty-year-old, although not totally. In the Sunday-morning warm-up he hit the wall at Griffin's Bend. Repairs were required.

And then, just six laps into his first race stint, he had a massive spin across the top of the Mountain, flat-spotting all four tyres, which triggered an unscheduled pit stop. Yet with just thirteen laps remaining Lowndes was nose to tail with John Bowe (Falcon), fighting for the lead. To everyone's amazement, at the top of Mountain Straight he pulled out and passed Bowe around the outside of Griffin's Bend. Bowe said later he'd been 'blinded by Lowndes' bravery'. In reality, the youngster had missed his braking marker, gone in far too hot and scrambled to miss Bowe and stay on the track. Two laps later, Bowe redressed the position in lapped traffic. But in his debut drive Lowndes, with Jones, was second, less than 6 seconds adrift. Two years later he won.

Lowndes controversially crossed the great tribalism divide not once but twice in his career. His first defection, from Holden to Ford, sparked massive public controversy, even a program on *60 Minutes*. He received death threats and at least one arrest was made. His Mount Panorama tally is four wins for Holden, three in the Supercars era, and three wins for Ford in succession from 2006. In 2009, as a Triple Eight protest against Ford's withdrawal of support, his Falcon ran unbranded. That year he came fifth.

Craig's return to Holden, through Triple Eight, netted three victories in 2010, 2015 and 2018. Just as tennis great Roger Federer did, when his grand-slam career seemed over, Lowndes gathered new momentum.

'Driving Mount Panorama has changed a lot with the Supercars rules,' he said. 'Tyres and aerodynamics are the difference. We're not as fast down Conrod but we can be 10 kilometres per hour faster through McPhillamy Park. It used to be that we had a steer tyre for the front, and a drive tyre for the rear with different construction and characteristics. Now we have one control tyre. There's not the grip level we had back then.'

Steven Richards, two years older than Lowndes, has achieved all five of his Mount Panorama victories under the Supercars regime, the last two of them partnering Lowndes. Richards and his father Jim claim an outstanding family record—between them, over a period of 40 years, they have won The Great Race twelve times, a family win rate of better than 28 per cent. The figure is a little controversial because one of Jim's wins was in the 2-litre race: 'But it was still 1000 kilometres at Bathurst and I'm claiming it,' Jim said. Father and son have driven together only three times, with their best placed second in the initial V8 Supercars 1000 in 1997. But their most memorable race was 2002 when they finished first and second, just two seconds between them, with Jim in front. They share a high degree of trust, more than most drivers: 'I gave Steve a tap, not to put him off, but I got a good run on the inside and I tore his mirror off on the way through.'

There's not a lot that's complicated about the Richards family. While some drivers and teams immerse themselves in the politics of the sport, the Richards live simply to race. 'Bathurst was our annual holiday,' Steven said. He first went when he was four years old—two years before Jim's first win. 'We'd stay at the Gold Panner Motor Inn outside town, and I used to tear around with the other kids—John Harvey's son Gavin and Ron Harrop's son Tim. You'd find us up around the King George Tavern'—a pop-up pub in the pits—'and it was full of pinball machines. We knew how to get in through the canvas and how to get a free game.' Steven's son Clay is an up-and-coming kart driver. 'It's history repeating itself,' Jim said.

'People think because you're a racing driver that you have plenty of money. It's not true. I sold up everything in New Zealand to come to race in Australia and arrived with just $12,000. Steve hasn't had funds from me.' (Not quite true: 'I saved up everything to buy my first go-kart, and Mum and Dad went halves with me,' Steven recalled.) But it was no easy ride. 'Motor racing is very selfish. Fay brought up the kids while I was away,' Jim said; Fay is Jim's wife of more than 40 years. Steven agreed: 'Very rarely did Dad come to see me race.' And yet the Richards name, and importantly its reputation for integrity, stood for something. It opened doors that would be difficult if a driver was cold-canvassing. Steven's first drive at Mount Panorama was in a Formula Ford—with not a lot of help from Jim, who hadn't driven one before. Steven felt his way across the top of the Mountain: 'It took a while to get the speed up; down the mountain vision is so limited, and you need confidence to go faster.' Three years on, in 1994, Steven won the Australian Formula Ford Championship and the right to race in the prestigious Formula Ford Festival in the UK, a showcase for future stars. Steven and Jim went, but as spectators. The cost of competing was too great.

The Richards have never owned a race team—not like Larry Perkins, Brad Jones, Glenn Seton, Mark Skaife, Wayne Gardner or the guys from the pre-V8 Supercars era. The overheads are high and the sponsorship too precarious to make the prospect attractive to them. Steven provides a service that looks after the race cars of gentlemen drivers, but he operates with contractors. Team ownership has become a very specific business proposition, made possible by the support provided under the Supercars management banner. 'I prefer to be a professional driver,' Steven said.

Until very recently Jamie Whincup, four-time Mount Panorama winner (all in the Supercars era) and the sport's most capped V8 champion—seven national titles to his credit, all with

Team Triple Eight—was archetypically a racing professional. Then, aged 36, he looked at his future and decided he needed more. He negotiated with Roland Dane to buy a small share of the Triple Eight team. 'It wasn't so small,' Dane confessed. 'Fifteen per cent and he paid a seven-figure sum.' Dane already had strategic shareholders: Tim Miles, a top-end investment adviser who had played an integral part in V8 Supercars' evolution; and Paul Dumbrell, a Bathurst 1000 winner with Whincup and chief executive of a leading industrial tool franchise. And there's another shareholder in waiting; Dane's daughter Jessica, already deeply embedded in the family business, is part of his succession plan. 'Tim and Paul will sell [at some stage]. Jessica and Jamie are the future,' Dane told me.

'I want to be in motor racing until I'm 60, but I can see myself being good for only another two or three years driving,' Whincup said from his Gold Coast island home. Spending time with 'majors' like Miles and Dumbrell would be good for him to prepare for a future after he hangs up his helmet.

Like most at the top of the new crop of drivers, Whincup credits Mount Panorama as his inspiration. 'The first race I watched was the 1992 Jim Richards and Mark Skaife Nissan victory in the wet.' Jamie was nine, and a family gathering of young go-karters saw it unfold on TV in the garage of his friend's home. Eight years later he was at Mount Panorama with his Formula Ford, 'out the back of the pit area with a little truck and a tent off it'. It was wet again. 'We had to pull the car through the mud with ropes to get to the dummy grid.' And the circuit? 'You never forget the first day you drive onto Mount Panorama, eyes wide open, trying to hit the apexes.' Whincup walks the Mountain every year—'it's always changing'—but apart from that he simply enjoys the experience. 'It's the quality of the circuit, the surface, the walls. I have more respect for Mount Panorama than any other circuit.'

Whincup's mentors are wisely easing him into the team's business operations. He is taking his time—unlike Mark Skaife who, two decades before, found himself operating simultaneously as owner of the Holden Racing Team and its lead driver. 'It was too much,' Skaife admitted. 'I was doing everything and it created fragility within the race team. If I had my time again, I would definitely have put in a CEO.' Skaife relinquished team ownership, not because he wasn't competent but because it was the only viable means of breaking an impasse among the teams—allegations that Holden was bending the rules over how many teams it could support—that was destabilising the sport. Politics have never been far from the surface in Supercars racing. Skaife's action, said to have cost him dearly, further elevated his status in a sport that was fast becoming a business.

In 2011, Tim Miles acted as corporate adviser when Sydney-based private equity company Archer Capital purchased a 65 per cent share in V8 Supercars, taking Tony Cochrane's SEL off the board—although Cochrane would stay on as chairman. The money provided funding for the development of a Skaife-led Car of the Future program, the next phase of the sport's development.

'It was an amazing offer,' Cochrane told me. 'They paid 10.8 times earnings, and that focuses your attention.' Archer's offer valued Supercars at more than $300 million. SEL's $52,000 purchase of 25 per cent, sixteen and a half years before, looked a pretty smart move. But why sell? 'You could ask twenty people and get twenty different answers,' Cochrane said. I asked him if it was burn-out. 'That's not the right answer,' he said. 'Within SEL the four partners had decided to go different ways. I wanted a change of scenery.'

Roland Dane believes the move to sell was precipitated by SEL. 'They'd been 95 per cent good for us and because of the relationship we had to do something to help them sell down their stake, if that's what they wanted to do,' he said. The upside for the teams was an ability to cash out if they wanted, or to invest further in their businesses. 'Each Racing Entitlement Contract, the right to field one car in the championship, earned about $4.5 million from the sale,' Cochrane recalled; some teams owned two or more. Some sold; most stayed. 'What you had in the past was a board that was making operational decisions, rather than a board that was giving governance and setting strategy,' Tim Miles told the influential motorsport publication Speedcafe.com at the time of the sale.

Sean Seamer is the very model of a modern chief executive. He is the fourth CEO at V8 Supercars in the seven years since the Archer purchase and the sixth in ten years. To an observer it seems a tough gig: balancing the sometimes divisive requirements of team owners ('There's not many shy people in the sport,' Roland Dane said) with the need to maintain and grow a fan base, all in an ever-changing economic and political environment, the tectonic plates of new media—the foundation on which all sports promotion is based—shifting constantly beneath his feet. 'It's refreshing,' Seamer said.

Our conversation was conducted on the telephone in the thoroughly contemporary way, with a 'minder' on the call, too, as a witness to what was said. There's nothing unusual in that. Wise corporate operators do it all the time. But it's likely to be a first for Australian motor racing. The lines were also drawn. Seamer was loath to talk about home or family, but he was happy to talk up a personal interest in motorsport. His background is in drag racing and motorcycles; he has competed in Targa events and club-raced a Porsche.

Seamer came to Supercars from a large and once-troubled media company, its goal 'to help brands unlock growth through media'. He had a fair bit of reputational rebuilding to do on behalf of that company but not so, he said, at Supercars: 'It doesn't need to change.' Seamer's experience in media was no doubt central to his appointment. A contract renewal for terrestrial and digital rights was upcoming and Supercar needed a master strategist and negotiator.

Seamer had landed at a time of really good news at the top end of his newfound sport. US billionaire Roger Penske, a powerhouse of the international automotive and motorsport business, had taken a substantial stake in Dick Johnson Racing and DJR Team Penske had won the 2018 Supercars Championship—with Bathurst still an unfulfilled goal. 'Roger is a global, shining example of how you use motor racing to build a brand name and a business around it,' said Neil Crompton; the former racer, now category manager and commentator, had quickly become a fan of the Penske operation. Penske was building an entire business structure in Australia and using motor racing as its promotional fulcrum.

'Probably only Brad Jones and ourselves are pure racing teams,' Roland Dane said. 'The others have something hanging off them'—to spread costs—and Penske had taken that to the extreme. Dane had been quick to seize on Penske as his logical competitor, raising both their profiles. When Penske said he'd be happy to continue with redundant Ford Falcons until his new Ford Mustang became available, Holden man Dane retorted that 'we don't want to look like a second-hand car yard'. Black hat versus white hat always works with the fans.

Seamer had been methodical in learning the business. 'It's unique. It takes a full twelve months to see everything just once.' He'd been to Mount Panorama, of course, once before his appointment purely as an enthusiast, and he'd been to the top of the Mountain and met the fans. 'Our primary objective is to reach out to as many people as we can and to make their experience better.' He rated Supercars' relationship with Bathurst Regional Council as 'a true partnership . . . perfect.' He'd been impressed with the Bathurst 12 Hour: 'It's becoming a special event, something like the 1000.' But would it ever supplant it? Seamer thinks not. 'We'll not see that happen in our lifetime,' he said.

So what does the future hold? Archer Capital has retained its shareholding long past the use-by date that private equity companies normally impose on their investments. They buy, build and sell on. It's a proposition Seamer acknowledges. 'There are multiple different scenarios—it's too early to tell,' he said. But: 'Archer will exit, ultimately.'

Tony Cochrane was restless and perhaps a little frustrated. 'All the great motor-racing series in the world have benefited from having a character leading them. They need a strong personal touch. They need to stand for something socially.' He's right, of course. Bernie Ecclestone built Formula One, Tony Hulman saved Indianapolis from extinction, Bill France Sr raised NASCAR up out of a Daytona sandpit. Jean Todt engineered himself as the global face of motor racing and road safety. But with the exception of the Napoleonic Todt, the others had all seen their influence diminished by the very contemporary requirements of governance. There was not much room left for knee-jerk reaction or even for individual judgement calls.

'We would hold a war meeting every week after a race to see how we could energise the next one,' Cochrane said. 'We were very single-focused.' Would he ever consider a return? There is a long pause: 'My old mate Dick Johnson told me the only thing you get from looking back is a sore neck—but I'd never say never.'

Cochrane had just returned from attending his first motor race in four years—the Australian Grand Prix—when we spoke. 'I was there to support my wife,' he said. Thea Jeanes-Cochrane had just been appointed to the board of CAMS, the governing body of motor racing in Australia. 'They wanted her for her expertise in marketing, communications and media.'

11

Jump Over Your Shadow

In Australia, the rarefied atmosphere of sales of sports and GT cars costing above $200,000 is inhabited by only 2000 new-car buyers each year. Their volume makes up just 0.2 per cent of the entire motor industry. All sports cars—from the smallest Mazda MX5 upwards—comprise less than 3 per cent of the total market. And yet the health of the sports car segment is a litmus test for the Australian economy. When high-net-worth individuals are buying sports cars it's a sign they're not troubled by other issues. It's the same across the world. An entire industry has grown up around keeping them happy. The Bathurst 12 Hour is an integral part of the push.

With just 9 minutes remaining in the 2019 Mount Panorama 12 Hour race, over the greatest distance ever held, Matt Campbell, a 23-year-old from rural Warwick in Queensland who'd learned to drive on the racetrack his grandfather 'owned', saw a gap and went for it. His works Porsche 911 GT3 R, racing for the first time under the Silver Fern colours of New Zealander Earl Bamber (Le Mans 24 Hour winner and fledgling team owner), had already outdistanced a field of the world's fastest GT3 cars built by Mercedes-Benz, BMW, Audi, Nissan and Ferrari. Millimetres ahead of him and blocking—because victory depended on it—Jake Dennis's Aston Martin was performing better than anyone had expected. The Aston, not rated coming into the race, had been the surprise of the 1938-kilometre race. By the time they got the chequered flag, the lead teams would have covered 312 laps of the mountain circuit, fifteen laps more than the previous record.

Suddenly there was an opening. Hard braking into Forrest's Elbow, Dennis took a marginally wider entry and Campbell thrust the nose of the Porsche alongside the left rear of the Aston, daring Dennis to cover further. On that downhill left-hander—100 kilometres per hour right on the apex—a hard hit on the rear axle of the Aston would have spun it out, and Campbell would likely have gone too. All their hard work, sprinting ahead of the brilliant yellow works Mercedes of world GT champion Raffaele Marciello, would have been for nothing. Dennis, disciplined, yielded. The cars still touched but it was a kiss, not a clout, and Campbell was through. Down Conrod at 260 kilometres per hour, the Aston used the slipstream to try to come back in the Chase, but a lapped car fouled his overtaking opportunity. And it was over. Campbell, driving without a cool suit, helmet fan or a drink bottle—all of which had failed early in the race—was too pumped to notice any discomfort and he raced unrelentingly to the chequered flag. His co-driver, 38-year-old Porsche professional Dirk Werner, exhaled a long-held breath and said: 'He's jumped over his own shadow.'

It's a German expression and it means that you've gone faster, stronger, harder than ever before; you've overcome your own fears and exceeded your own limits. Campbell, jockey-sized and with the cheeky grin of an apprentice who's beaten the bookies, just said, 'It's good to win on your home track.' It wasn't. Mount Panorama had been the pinnacle of his local ambition but his home track had been Morgan Park, a patch of rural land that started out as a 730-metre dirt circuit and grew to be a 3-kilometre club track, with its latest extension in 2010. Matt held the lap record.

Matt was extremely close to his grandad Bill, the president and driving force of the local race club, and he worked as an apprentice builder in Bill's business, spending every spare minute flogging around what was to all intents and purposes the family racetrack. Bill, and Matt's aunt Teresa 'TC' Campbell, had hot Torana XU-1s. Matt got the Datsun 1200.

Matt arrived at Porsche via a path already proved successful by New Zealand's multiple Indy 500 winner Scott Dixon—he turned himself into a company and opened his prospectus for investors. There were 50 of them, none expecting great riches, but all to be paid back with interest as his career progressed. The money he raised bought Campbell a drive in the Australian Porsche Carrera Cup, and when he won that it earned him the right to try out for Porsche's global young driver development program, the best in the world. He had no aspirations to pursue

Formula One. 'Formula One is all about politics,' he said from a two-week training camp in Germany. Porsche's program offered a clear path—as long as he remained successful. Campbell entered a shoot-out with eight other young hopefuls from global Porsche series around the world, and he won. 'There was a race simulation—two short practices, a qualifier and a race, plus debriefings, media interviews, photo shoots—everything you go through in a normal race weekend,' and he was judged on it all. Two weeks later he was part of an intensive program to turn him into a professional race driver. By the time he returned to Mount Panorama he'd won the amateur class at the Le Mans 24 Hour race, his driving services provided by Porsche as an asset to one of its customer teams. He was still not on the top step of the ladder. He was a Porsche Young Professional, one level beneath being a Porsche factory driver. There are 24 of those, none keen to retire, and the competition to get to that level is intense.

Campbell's 2019 victory confirmed Mount Panorama's status as one of the world's greatest motor-racing tracks. Several years earlier, Stéphane Ratel—the genius promoter of GT racing worldwide—tapped what he called the 'classic' circuits on which to run his Intercontinental GT Challenge. 'The circuits are those which attract iconic interest,' Ratel told me from his home in Rome, where he'd recently moved with wife Marie and their first child, baby Victoria. For the unceasingly restless Ratel, still youthful in his fifties, not being on the road is a frustration. When we spoke, it was the first time since his organisation SRO (Stéphane Ratel Organisation) had engineered control of the Bathurst 12 Hour in 2015 that he hadn't attended. His baby daughter came first.

'Mount Panorama is one of the greats we've chosen,' he said. 'The others are Suzuka, Spa and Kyalami. All have existing long-distance races. The only new event which needs to be established is Laguna Seca.' It's a massive line-up and it puts Mount Panorama in perspective: there's the 5.8-kilometre Suzuka circuit in Japan, with its near-to-unique figure-eight configuration and its seemingly never-ending sweeper 130R (named for its 130-degree radius); the awesome 7-kilometre Spa-Francorchamps in Belgium, with its uphill Eau Rouge corner named for the creek over which it passes; Kyalami in South Africa, in and out of bankruptcy and now owned by the country's Porsche distributor; and Laguna Seca, nestled behind Monterey in California, within touching distance of the Pebble Beach Concours d'Elegance and renowned for its left–right downhill-plunging Corkscrew bend. They're all on the bucket list of every race enthusiast, and for the high-net-worth team owners and race drivers who populate Ratel's GT championships, it is an invitation to nirvana.

Ratel started his company in the mid-1990s; gained support from both the FIA—the governing international motorsport body—and from Formula One's dictator Bernie Ecclestone; and, with patience and the odd financially threatening stumble that is inherent in motorsport promotion, he built a formula that provided the world's great high-performance brands with cost-effective access to their most enthusiastic customers.

Some people buy a Porsche or a Ferrari to park prominently at their golf or yacht club, but, increasingly, enthusiastic owners want to explore the potential of their cars. Ratel built a pyramid of performance opportunity, starting with instructor-attended track days and peaking with the Intercontinental GT Challenge.

By the time Matt Campbell won Mount Panorama, Ratel had brought eight big brands on board by convincing them that his complex protocols of achieving parity between vehicle performance, driver ability and economy of operation were the key to brand enhancements in major markets across the world. It was no coincidence that the five circuits he'd chosen for his Challenge were all on different continents.

Four years before Matt Campbell was born, Vince Tesoriero set the wheels in motion to build the twelve-hour-race concept into an event that would become the inaugural round of Ratel's grand vision. It started as a race strictly for production cars and lasted four years at Mount Panorama before its orphan status robbed it of any chance of economic success. Tesoriero and his partners from the advertising agency that had helped fund motorcycle racing at the Mountain took a substantial financial dive. They ran it once more at Sydney's Eastern Creek Raceway, but it was never going to succeed there. A big idea needs a big circuit. And Mount Panorama was its natural home.

When setting up the race, Tesoriero had argued with the sport's controlling body. CAMS was keen to run the 12 Hour according to its own modified production car rules. Tesoriero, guided by the success of his Castrol 6 Hour motorcycle experience, insisted on the cars being absolutely showroom stock.

'The tipping point in getting it over the line was Peter Brock,' Tesoriero recalled. 'He was fantastic to me.' Brock, as he so often did, ignored the negative vibes and ploughed ahead to join his young touring-car teammate Neil Crompton in a bog-standard

Holden Commodore VN. It was Crompton's idea and he sold it to Brock on the basis that it was an opportunity to relive the good old days of motor racing, when you'd drive the race car to the circuit and camp in the pits. Brock, Bev and the kids got on board so much that they drove their Ford Maverick from Melbourne, towing their caravan, and spent the weekend in the Mount Panorama paddock.

Brock was hard on the car, and Crompton—along with motoring writer and occasional race driver Peter McKay—did the hard yards to ease the anything-but-robust car home fourth outright and first in class. 'I'm as easy to flatter as the next guy,' the lanky, laconic McKay said. 'In that car, because of what it was, we were able to match Brock. But I'm also a realist—put me in a supercar against him and it would be a straight-sets victory.' The next year Brock returned to the 12 Hour in a two-car Peugeot team Crompton had put together, this time with enough money to make the deal financially attractive. 'In practice, Brock was passed up Mountain Straight by the second team car,' McKay recalled. There was no skill in it—it was simply the faster car. 'He came back to the pits and said, "That's my car," requiring a massive shuffling of teams to put him in the quicker unit.' Twenty-five laps into the race he'd cooked the brakes.

Economy of scale is what makes Mount Panorama work. It's like the Sydney Harbour Bridge, imposing and iconic, but incredibly expensive to maintain. To function, racing at Mount Panorama needs input from a synergy of sources—entry fees from competitors, commercial support, television and now live-streaming arrangements, and of course revenue from the gate. The fixed costs remain effectively the same and the skill is in amortising those as much as possible. Tesoriero couldn't get the balance right. Even when manufacturers started to grasp the concept and the value of the 12 Hour—particularly Mazda, which won the 12 Hour at Bathurst for three consecutive years with a rotary-powered RX-7 that could have been purpose-built for the Mountain—the event was bleeding its promoters dry. It was particularly galling for Tesoriero when the event moved in 1995 to Eastern Creek, owned by the New South Wales Government and leased by the Australian Racing Drivers' Club. If either body had pulled its weight at Bathurst, Tesoriero could have realised the success he deserved.

It's the oldest of clichés—the only way to make a small fortune out of motor racing is to start with a large one. On the overnight QF22 flight from Narita to Sydney, travelling economy because there's no point in wasting money on business class, Australia's independent steel-producing mogul Ross Palmer was jumping out of his skin with ideas about how he was going to transform motor racing in Australia. Neither of us got much sleep. Palmer—short, stocky and a bundle of energy—had grown up in the next street in Brisbane's southern suburbs to Dick Johnson, who went on to three Bathurst 1000 wins and was Australian Touring Car champion five times. Their mums were good friends. Palmer was super-smart, according to Johnson, topping the classes they shared at school, and he was entrepreneurial just like his dad Les. The Palmers used to build steel steps and patio posts from a workshop at their house, but the problem was that BHP, which got a horrible and deserved public pasting for its arrogant self-promotion, wouldn't provide the roll-formed products with the timely delivery Les Palmer needed. So he bought his own roll former and started sourcing steel from Japan. Pretty soon he was making more steel products than he needed for his own business. 'Ross and his old man came to fisticuffs over it,' Johnson recalled. 'Les wanted to run his business his way; Ross wanted to sell Palmer products to the world.' Ross won, and Palmer Tube Mills was born. Pretty soon he had a strong Australian business and had started another in the US.

Ross Palmer was named in the Australian Rich 200 list with a fortune estimated in the mid-1990s to be close to $180 million. He'd be even wealthier today, according to Johnson, if he hadn't caught the motor-racing bug. Palmer was never going to be a top driver but he was certain he could be a promoter. He sponsored Johnson, cleverly using some of his product names rather than simply the company name to promote to his specific markets. When Johnson's Greens-Tuf Falcon plummeted into the trees at Forrest's Elbow during qualifying for the 1983 Bathurst 1000, he made Palmer's business famous. If only Palmer had stopped there.

With encouragement from others, in 2002 he reconstituted the Tesoriero 12 Hour—except, with great ambition, he decided to double its distance to become the Bathurst 24 Hour. In 2002 and 2003 a massive 7-litre Holden Monaro, the biggest, fastest and most brutish Holden ever built, dominated both 24 Hour races. The first year it covered 532 laps, 3305.3 kilometres, to defeat an American-built Mosler MT900R by 23 laps (just under 143 kilometres). The next year the Monaro was there again, this time with Brock sharing the driving. In appalling weather and with allowance for safety-car intervention it covered five laps

(31 kilometres) less to complete a virtual 1–2 formation finish with the second car in its team.

There'd been one 24 Hour race in Australia before. It had run in 1954 at the old Mount Druitt circuit in Sydney's West. Twenty-two cars started and, by decree, 22 finished—those that had stopped were allowed to be pushed across the line. That may have given Palmer's 24 Hour ambitions some hope. To his credit, the two races they started had comparatively healthy fields—36 in 2002, with 25 finishing, and 45 the next year with 33 across the line. But there were precious few spectators, scant commercial support and little media. The lesson of scaled economies had evaded Palmer and not even his vast wealth, which had diminished somewhat through his motor-racing efforts, could sustain another year's race. It was a great disappointment to the motorsport community, which, while it applauded the concept, hadn't turned up to support it.

Career soldier James O'Brien, who'd moved on to promotion after leaving the military, was ready to desert. After five years with IMG and a variety of forays into motorsport under the giant sports management company's banner—including running the 24 Hour race for Ross Palmer, adding one more layer of cost to the already cash-strapped event—O'Brien had been close enough to the action to see an opportunity at Mount Panorama outside the Bathurst 1000. And he knew how to make it profitable.

'Bathurst Council knew me and knew what I could do,' O'Brien explained. We were in the meeting room of an impressively modern Brisbane apartment block that functions as both his home and his office. Keeping overheads to a minimum is part of his strategy. O'Brien and the Council became partners. 'Mount Panorama is an important part of the fabric of Bathurst and it needs to be utilised,' he said. 'Mount Panorama could not remain viable on one race meeting a year—no matter how successful.' It was a genius move by Bathurst Regional Council to persuade the New South Wales Government to gazette five full closure opportunities a year for Mount Panorama—in which the entire circuit can be used. 'The thing is, the five full closures don't necessarily specify how many days at a time can be used,' O'Brien said. 'As long as you're mindful of the residents, you can run a weekend race meeting and plan commercial track days either side.' It was an opportunity too good to miss.

In 2006, as an independent working with the Council, O'Brien turned Easter into the Bathurst International Festival of Motorsport—an all-in celebration of high-performance action based loosely on Britain's world-renowned Goodwood Festival of Speed. It relied on providing enthusiasts with cost-efficient access to Australia's most revered motor-racing track, without the high costs of activation that had been part and parcel of running the place until then—fewer personnel, including flag marshals, and less presentation. It was loud, colourful and well supported by a vast untapped cache of enthusiasts who couldn't believe their luck. Mount Panorama had been laid at their feet.

O'Brien opened an Aladdin's cave of opportunity for the mountain track. More than a decade on, the circuit is used for everything from a sprint race up and down Pit Straight accompanied by a show-and-shine event, through to a 6 Hour production race that started low key but is growing in stature, and a full-circuit sprint challenge late in the year, which gives enthusiasts a chance to test themselves against the Mountain and the clock. O'Brien has partnered with Bathurst Regional Council to run corporate days; companies like Mercedes-Benz, Porsche, Lexus and even truck maker Hino have brought high-net-worth guests and media to the circuit to sample their products in what is effectively a money-can't-buy environment. Except, of course, it does.

But O'Brien's masterstroke was to finally make the 12 Hour viable. 'It happened almost accidentally, as a consequence of the success of the Festival of Motorsport, and we ran it as simply one feature of the festival,' he smiled. It's almost as if he didn't plan it. O'Brien's vision was to run a 12 Hour race for a combination of production cars and GT cars—the vehicles many of his supporters drove. He ran into opposition from the controlling body.

'The president of CAMS at the time owned a production-car race team, renting cars to prospective drivers. It was obvious what he wanted and so the first event was for production cars.' Few spectators turned up. The camping area was sparsely covered. TV coverage was achieved on a shoestring; the start was halted on one occasion when a race car and a kangaroo collided before dawn, captured on camera but never put to air; and the race was stopped on another when a giant tree, weakened by wet weather, crashed to the ground and blocked the track. O'Brien persevered with production cars for four years, providing victory twice to BMW, and twice to Mitsubishi with its turbocharged Evo series, but it was going nowhere. In 2010, it looked like the Bathurst 12 Hour was again bound for failure.

'I'd kept closely in contact with SRO in Europe and I was watching them grow,' O'Brien said. He lobbied CAMS, under a different president, and spoke to the organisers of the growing number of GT races in Australia and New Zealand. Then, in 2011, he took the plunge and incorporated GT cars. 'The production-car guys didn't want it. They wanted to win outright and didn't want to become merely class competitors,' he said. 'Many stayed away.' Compounding his challenges, the international teams he craved could not accommodate his Easter date because it clashed with their own programs. So he flipped the date to February. And with that, the all-powerful Joest team entered.

Securing Joest was like getting Usain Bolt to compete in your local club's athletics carnival. Reinhold Joest's team had won the Le Mans 24 Hour race thirteen times. And their Audi R8 LMS GT3s dominated Mount Panorama. Their number 1 car, driven by international race professionals, beat their locally crewed car by just 0.7 seconds over 1814 kilometres (292 laps). It was a controlled finish, but it wasn't staged. Craig Lowndes, in the local car, set a new Mount Panorama GT lap record in pursuit of the leader. 'Without Joest I would have been sunk,' O'Brien recalled. 'They lifted the entire profile of the event.'

Heroes were created in the next races. One of them was enshrined. Danish driver Allan Simonsen set a qualifying lap so fast in his Ferrari that he was penalised with a 50-kilogram lead weight bolted into his car, supposedly to equalise him with the rest of the field; instead it prevented him challenging for a race win. Five months later Simonsen died at Le Mans when his Aston Martin hit a lethally immovable safety fence. The Bathurst 12 Hour now presents the Allan Simonsen Trophy for pole position.

Four years after O'Brien's first GT event, Supercars Australia took over the 12 Hour. It was a royal command. Stéphane Ratel was about to begin his Intercontinental GT series, with Mount Panorama as the cornerstone of its 'classic circuits' concept, and he needed to partner with the company that could provide him with certainty of support. Supercars' investment in its 1000-kilometre flagship event guaranteed that—more so than O'Brien operating out of a briefcase. It was a wonderful irony. Only twelve months before, Supercars had done its best to sink the 12 Hour by running its mandatory test day at Sydney Motorsport Park (the renamed Eastern Creek circuit) on the same day as the 12 Hour, preventing many of its star drivers from competing in the GT cars. It was an act of extreme aggression and it did not go down well with the fans. It also was a clear message that for the first time Supercars, which had held itself invincible in Australian motorsport for two decades, saw the GT category as a real threat. Stéphane Ratel, a seasoned diplomat, sees room for both.

'Supercars is a national phenomenon,' he said. 'Our two concepts are entirely different.' He would, he said, never want the two to become competitive, but they can complement each other. 'It's a case of being patient. Nothing comes overnight.' Ratel is deliberately cautious with his metrics. While Supercars Australia talks up its 1000-kilometre race meeting with claims that it draws more than 200,000 spectators, and TV viewers across its free-to-air, pay-to-view and regional channels of close to 2 million, Ratel identifies 40,000 paying spectators and local coverage of less than 1 million for the 12 Hour, but importantly points to live streaming of around 1.4 million online views—about equal, he says, to that of the Spa 24 Hour.

There's a lot of bullishness at the Mount Panorama 12 Hour and Chris Reinke, head of Audi Sport Customer Racing, is the most ebullient of the manufacturers. 'As long as Ratel sticks to his plans, our clear intention is to manufacture and sell 1000 customer cars a year within the next five years,' he said. Like its competitors, Audi is investing strongly in a multi-tiered customer support program. It has built a special test facility at Neuburg, outside its Ingolstadt headquarters, available to owners and customers who want to join its motor-sport program at entry level—the Audi Driving Experience. From there, it's onwards and upwards until you hit one of the fourteen GT motor-racing series run by Ratel, the pinnacle being the Intercontinental Challenge.

But it's a long way from Australia to Ingolstadt. Could there be room for a facility locally that could feed into the Bathurst 12 Hour? Bathurst Regional Council mayor Graeme Hanger spent the weekend of the 2019 Bathurst 12 Hour entertaining the competing brands and their guests in his Council's pit-lane suite—not as opulent as the suites of Bentley, Porsche or AMG, but a local council can't be seen to be spending money unwisely. And the topic of a potential new track, just over the hill to the west of Mountain Straight, was never far from his lips.

Part 5

Tragedy, Triumph and Turmoil

Big venues magnify events. A goal scored on the paddock of a regional football ground, no matter how brilliant, will never have the same gravitas as one scored at the MCG. So it is with Mount Panorama. Anyone who enters the Panorama precinct, whether competitor or spectator, expands to fill the space. Somehow the stories of great success there are more compelling, those of tragedy more distressing, and mischief on the Mountain—the perennial bane of promoters—more visible.

12

The Laps of the Gods

Mark Larkham never won the Bathurst 1000, but he did come third in the first year of V8 Supercars competition. Two years later, in 1999, he claimed pole position. That one magic lap—2 minutes 9.51 seconds—gave him all the credibility he needed to forge a career as Australia's foremost technical TV commentator. Being fastest at Mount Panorama on any given day is a badge worn proudly. Larkham once did a piece for TV on how to lap the Mountain. He called it 'visualising' and he did it with his eyes shut, talking his way around the circuit from memory, with feel and determination. At the end, he said, 'If you can do all that, and cross the line first, you will, for that moment, feel like the greatest racing driver in the world.'

Craig Lowndes is the only Australian to have lapped Mount Panorama at an average speed greater than 200 kilometres per hour. The car he drove in 2011 was the Formula One McLaren MP4-23 that had carried Lewis Hamilton to his world championship three years before.

Lowndes lapped the circuit in 1 minute 50.088 seconds (203.17 kilometres per hour) and he was just 0.678 seconds slower than 2009 Formula One world champion Jenson Button. Button's average of 204.43 kilometres per hour is likely to stand forevermore, or until another promoter decides to show off its Formula One prowess. For Lowndes, three laps in the most advanced aerodynamic car of its time was, in part, the fulfilment of his unfulfilled open-wheeler ambition.

The 'double ton' (200 kilometres per hour) is something no one dares speaks of in normal terms in relation to Mount Panorama—not yet, anyway. It's too fanciful for words. And yet every year, records are being challenged. The 2-minute lap barrier—once thought impossible to reach—has been broken twice, or four times if the Lowndes and Button demonstration drives are taken into account. A lap of 1 minute 55 seconds (194.49 kilometres per hour) is now locked into the simulation traces of the first Australian-made supercar—the Brabham BT62.

For the people who watch it, motorsport is all about human endeavour—skill and bravery. For the people who do it, it's all about the numbers. In 1954, when super athletes John Landy and Roger Bannister broke the 4-minute mile, one of the most famous and revered of all sporting goals, Mount Panorama competitors were talking up an 80-mile-per-hour (128-kilometre-per-hour) lap. Reg Hunt and Lex Davison achieved it two years later. So rapid was the development of technology that

Jack Brabham posted an average of 90 miles per hour (144 kilometres per hour) just four years after that. Seven years on Kevin Bartlett, with a massive lunge, recorded the first 100-mile-per-hour (161-kilometre-per-hour) lap. A year after his achievement, at the 1968 Mexico Olympic Games, the 10-second barrier was first broken in the men's 100-metre sprint.

'If you're a competitor, you just want to keep going faster; it doesn't matter what the sport,' said Allan Grice, the first touring-car driver to break the Mount Panorama 100-mile-per-hour barrier.

Heroically, motorcycles matched the cars. A motorcycle has nowhere near the corner speed of a car and it lacks the aerodynamics that make a car stick to the track. It's all about the contact patch—the amount of rubber that is glued to the ground at any one time. In terms of corner speed, four wheels are better than two.

And yet in 1939, when Mount Panorama was first sealed, Senior TT winner Bat Byrnes, on his Norton 500, broke the 70-mile-per-hour (112-kilometre-per-hour) barrier with a lap time of 3 minutes 14.05 seconds (71.10 miles per hour/114.50 kilometres per hour). Jack Saywell, in his supercharged Alfa Romeo 2900, did it in 3 minutes 9 seconds (73.05 miles per hour/117.56 kilometres per hour). Not a great deal of difference.

Then the rubber band began to stretch. In the 1956 Bathurst 100 Lex Davison (Ferrari 500) and Reg Hunt (Maserati 250F) broke the 80-mile-per-hour barrier simultaneously with 2 minutes 51 seconds (80.69 miles per hour/129.93 kilometres per hour). It was not until 1961 that Eric Hinton (Norton) recorded 2 minutes 50.99 seconds, just 0.01 seconds faster, to become the first motorcycle to beat 80 miles per hour on a lap.

In 1960 Jack Brabham returned to Mount Panorama to celebrate his two world championships and beat 90 miles per hour. In his Cooper Climax he left the record at 2 minutes 30.4 seconds (91.74 miles per hour/147.73 kilometres per hour). It was another twelve years before Bill Horsman used a Yamaha 350 and Ginger Molloy a Kawasaki 500 to spur each other on in the combined Senior and Unlimited TT of 1972 to record an equal time of 2 minutes 32.77 seconds (90.31 miles per hour/145.44 kilometres per hour). Horsman won.

But the big one was the ton. In all of motorsport, in all of enthusiastic motoring, doing the imperial ton has been a badge of honour. 'I was ton-up over the mountains' was a frequent boast at campsites and motels throughout Bathurst. For most enthusiasts, right up to the present day, 100 miles an hour (160.934 kilometres per hour, to be precise) has been—depending on time, location and the potential of being caught by police—a quest as compelling as breaking the sound barrier. But to do it as an *average* speed around Mount Panorama? That's something else again. Kevin Bartlett and Spencer Martin did it in their epic open-wheeler battle of 1967, although Bartlett did it first— 2 minutes 17.7 seconds (100.20 miles per hour/161.35 kilometres per hour). And then in 1976 Warren Willing broke the ton on a motorcycle—2 minutes 17.1 seconds (100.64 miles per hour/162.06 kilometres per hour), and he did it again and again.

Forty-three drivers hold lap records at Mount Panorama. Because of changed track conditions and altered regulations, some of the records go back almost half a century. Allan Moffat's two records have the greatest longevity for touring cars, both set in 1972—his Boss Mustang did 2 minutes 22.4 seconds (96.89 miles per hour/156.03 kilometres per hour) in his epic race with Pete Geoghegan in the Super Falcon. In the Bathurst 500 the same year Moffat recorded a never-to-be-beaten lap of 2 minutes 36.5 seconds (88.16 miles per hour/141.97 kilometres per hour) in his Ford Falcon XY GTHO—a useful comparison between the modified cars contesting the Australian Touring Car Championship and the standard cars in the 500.

Twenty-two records are above the magic ton. Sydney property developer Neil Allen, a gentleman driver who could have become one of the country's best professional racing drivers, holds the outright record on the original 6.172-kilometre Mount Panorama track. In 1970, he stormed his McLaren M10B Formula 5000 car—the new breed of open-wheelers fitted with stock block 5-litre V8 engines—around in 2 minutes 9.7 seconds (106.38 miles per hour/171.31 kilometres per hour) and, like Moffat's, his time will stand forevermore. In 2014, young Simon Hodge from Adelaide, driving a 2-litre Formula Three car, became officially the fastest open-wheeler driver around Mount Panorama. On the 6.213-kilometre track, incorporating the Chase on Conrod, he put down a time of 2 minutes 2.67 seconds (182.33 kilometres per hour). Hodge won the Formula Three championship and proudly became the last person to be awarded the coveted CAMS Gold Star as Australia's best driver. CAMS retired the award, awaiting a series that it believed better reflected the status and intent of the honour.

Kevin Bartlett, twice Australian Gold Star champion, winner of the Macau Grand Prix, winner of the Bathurst 1000, Indy 500 aspirant and horribly injured in a massive Formula-5000 crash, first beat the magic ton at Mount Panorama in 1959. 'It was downhill and I was racing my mum's soft-top Morris Minor,' he smiled, stretching back at his home in the Sunshine Coast hinterland. The previous year, on debut, he'd done 87 miles per hour (140 kilometres per hour) through the flying one-eighth of a mile on Conrod, with the ragtop flapping in the breeze, but with the help of Frank Kleinig, to whom he was apprenticed, he managed to extract enough horsepower from the 803-cc Morris that he cracked the ton the following year. 'It was 102 miles per hour'—164 kilometres per hour—'and I set a lap time of 4 minutes 5.5 seconds' (averaging 56.20 miles per hour/90.50 kilometres per hour). It was a lifetime away from the ton-up lap average, but it was good enough to trounce another young aspirant—Brian Muir in an Austin A30. Within the next half-decade, the talented youngsters would be driving for wealthy patrons, contesting the Bathurst 500 and, in Bartlett's case, given control of one of the fastest open-wheeler racing cars in the country.

'I was racing for anyone for no money,' said Bartlett. 'Lotus Super Sevens, TVR sports cars and small open-wheelers—a Lynx Formula Junior and then an Elfin Imp—and I was doing pretty well and I knew open-wheelers were where I wanted to be. Then Glen Abbey, mechanic to Alec Mildren, came up to me and said, "Mr Mildren wants to see you."' Alec Mildren had won the Australian Grand Prix and the Australian Gold Star Championship in 1960 and started his own race team in 1963. 'Next thing I knew I was his local driver. I'd always be number two to [Australian international] Frank Gardner and he'd bring a new car each year for the International series, which I'd inherit after he'd gone back to the UK. I learned a lot from Frank.' Bartlett would win the Australian Gold Star for Mildren in 1968 and 1969.

Spencer Martin was Gold Star champion in the two years before that. He'd raced for David McKay's Scuderia Veloce in the early 1960s but it was when he defected to Bob Jane's team, taking McKay's Brabham BT11A with him ('David sold it to Bob'), that he found the confidence and support he needed to take the titles.

Bartlett and Martin were both paid drivers, not team owners—a huge distinction. They became the major protagonists of the era.

'Spencer never liked me. I was too aggressive in the car,' Bartlett said. 'He'd move over on you, push you into the dirt,' Martin said of Bartlett. They get along today but the needling is still there.

It was 1967 when they fought out the 100-mile-per-hour lap at Mount Panorama. They were competing in the NSW Road Racing Championship—not a big deal. Except Ron Hodgson—former touring-car competitor, wealthy car dealer and soon-to-be-owner of a Bathurst 1000–winning team—put up a case of champagne for the fastest in qualifying and another case if the 100 miles per hour could be broken in a race.

'I didn't know what champagne was,' Martin joked. Bartlett did, and so did Mildren.

The contest was on from the first session of practice: Bartlett in the yellow Repco Brabham Climax, Martin in the red one; Bartlett on Goodyear tyres, Martin on Dunlops. In qualifying it was so close—Bartlett was the fastest ever around Mount Panorama but half a second away from the 100 miles per hour mark. Martin, conserving his car for the race, was a second behind. 'It was a well-used engine, due for refurbishment,' he said.

The first race was a six-lap warm up, with sports cars mixed in. Martin won the dash to Hell Corner; Bartlett was on him. Down Conrod they pulled an absolutely equal speed—157.89 miles per hour (254.09 kilometres per hour). They couldn't be separated. 'Alec Mildren had told me: "When the wheels come off the ground, get off the throttle, otherwise you'll break a half shaft [axle],"' Bartlett said. 'I stayed on it for the first two humps then backed out on the third.' A third hump? In these cars, bouncing around at warp speed, there was a third hump—a small dip just after what most people regarded as the second hump. Martin dove down the inside of Bartlett into Murray's, then Bartlett did the same to him at Hell to lead up the Mountain.

And then, on lap three, Bartlett got the ton.

'I did it too,' Martin recalled. 'But he got it first,' the pain of the moment still apparent.

In the main event, they went at it again. It was wild stuff. Bartlett flicked the Brabham from corner to corner through the Esses, the result perhaps of better-suited tyres. 'At 160 miles per hour Kevin moved to break the slipstream down Conrod,' Martin said. 'He put two wheels on the grass. I just lifted off.' For Martin, the danger of that intensity of wheel-to-wheel racing was too great. Two laps later his car expired to the pits and Bartlett claimed the race. He spent six of the thirteen laps above the 100-mile-per-hour average. 'I did it without aero or adjustments—just a 272-horsepower [202 kW] engine with 420 kilograms of car. There was no mass to speak of, and also no fences to hit.'

Alec Mildren arranged for some of the champagne to be delivered to Bob Jane's pit.

In 1976, three years into the era of super Formula 750 motorcycles, the Japanese factories Yamaha and Kawasaki sent works riders to Mount Panorama to challenge the locals. Warren Willing and Gregg Hansford had every right to be peeved, especially Willing. For two years he'd won the Australian Unlimited Grand Prix and beaten the best riders the organisers could throw at him; he'd masterminded the successful last-corner lunge at Hansford in the '74 race—the one that is enshrined as the greatest of all time. And now the Japanese factory had sent one of their works riders, Ikujiro Takai, on a works Yamaha to take him on. Why? The locals had enough of a challenge among themselves without having to race the factories.

But Willing rose to it. He'd been in the US at Daytona and he'd had his bike prepared by Kel Carruthers. He knew it was good. And he had a plan—for the Unlimited GP over 30 laps (185 kilometres) he'd practised a killer fuel stop that would let him attack Takai, and Masahiro Wada on the Kawasaki—and Hansford too, if necessary.

In the first warm-up race—the Bathurst Unlimited International—it all came unstuck on the opening lap. While Takai and Hansford took off, Willing's clutch began to slip. He had no choice—he pulled to the pits to fix it. Better to use this race as a shakedown for the next day's GP, he thought. He restarted a lap behind, and something inside him snapped. His lap record stood at 2 minutes 23.35 seconds (154.99 kilometres per hour). He'd set it two years before in his epic duel with Hansford. The year before, 1975, he'd nudged it again but was 0.37 seconds slower. Now, with the race in front of him, he settled down to see what his Yamaha would do.

The 750 motorcycle at Mount Panorama was like no other two-wheel weapon ever built. Murray Sayle, Willing's brother-in-law and a member of the Kawasaki works team with Gregg Hansford, knew the dynamics. 'It would pop a giant wheelie up Mountain Straight. With anything but a very special tyre it would turn the kink out of Forrest's Elbow into a wheel-spinning corner,' Sayle said. 'Over the first hump, both wheels would come off the ground. Then over the second hump, at 280 kilometres per hour—faster than the cars—the front wheel would paw at the air. The rear tyre would wheelspin in a straight line and if it got traction into a braking area it would jump forward before the rider put the brakes on.'

Willing kept a close eye on the windsock on Conrod. The circuit had been resurfaced for 1976, sparking speculation of sub-record lap times, but it was still bumpy on the straight. 'The smoothest line was down the left-hand side,' Sayle told me. 'Anyone who stayed on the crown of the road would suffer from the accentuation in dips and hollows in the road contour. And the right-hand side was simply not as smooth as the left.' No one expected what happened next.

The clocks stopped at 2 minutes 17.1 seconds (100.64 miles per hour/162.06 kilometres an hour). Without working down to it, Willing had bravely and miraculously carved 6.25 seconds off his own lap record and set the first ton-up lap of Mount Panorama on a bike. He was the first to do it, but he wasn't alone. Takai, supposedly Willing's brand-teammate but

Twelve-year-old Bill Buckle watched the 1938 Australian Grand Prix at Mount Panorama with his parents, then came back thirteen years later to race this Citroën Light Fifteen in only the second year sedan cars competed at the Mountain. (Bill Buckle collection)

A Holden first won at Bathurst in 1955. Three years later Holdens were under threat from imported Jaguars. John French leads Leo Geoghegan in their Holden FJs up to the Cutting, with David McKay's Jaguar 3.4 stalking. McKay won the first Australian Touring Car Championship in 1960. (National Motor Racing Museum)

The immaculate Reg Hunt celebrating his ninety-sixth birthday, 63 years after retiring from motor racing at his peak. (David Zeunert)

Five-time world champion Mick Doohan won his first major trophy at Mount Panorama in the 1988 1000-cc Grand Prix. (The Project Group)

Mike Raymond (left) coined the term 'The Great Race', and hired Allan Moffat (right) to provide expert commentary, an innovation as important as Channel Seven's RaceCam. (Chevron Library)

When Larry Perkins (right) and Gregg Hansford won the 1993 Bathurst 1000, they had no money for matching race suits so they borrowed Castrol rain jackets to appear in uniform. (The Project Group)

Margaret Halliday, the first woman to win an Australian Grand Prix, teamed with Doug Chivas Jr in the 1984 Sidecar GP. (The Project Group)

Rodger Freeth won the Arai 500 twice at Mount Panorama in the 1980s on the mighty McIntosh Suzuki, one of the best handling and fastest bikes ever to cross the top of the Mountain. (The Project Group)

The author interviews 1985 Arai 500 winner Rodger Freeth for Channel Ten. Freeth was also a land speed record-holder and international rally co-driver. He was killed during a World Rally Championship round in WA in 1993. (The Project Group)

He was King of the Mountain. Peter Brock won The Great Race nine times, never more convincingly than he did in 1979 in his Torana A9X, shared with Jim Richards. They finished six laps ahead of second-placed Peter Janson and Larry Perkins. (Ray Berghouse/Chevron Library)

Allan Moffat claimed the first of his four Bathurst 1000 victories in 1970, driving solo for 500 miles in the works Ford Falcon GTHO. In that same race Peter Brock placed thirty-seventh, his lowest ever finish. (Chevron Library)

Peter Brock's debut at Mount Panorama in 1969, driving this Holden Dealer Team Monaro GTS350 to third place with lead driver Des West. If not for an 'off' by Brock, they might have won. (Bill Forsyth/Chevron Library)

Peter Brock is immortalised on 'his' mountain. His statue stands proudly in front of the National Motor Racing Museum at the entrance to Mount Panorama. (John Smailes)

Allan Moffat's most memorable Bathurst 1000 victory was in 1977—the (in)famous 1–2 form finish in which he and Jacky Ickx led home teammates Colin Bond and Alan Hamilton by 0.1 seconds after Moffat's brakes failed. (Ray Berghouse/Chevron Library)

After Peter Brock was killed in a rally crash in 2006, his protégé Craig Lowndes drove Brock's 1972-winning Torana XU-1 on a tribute lap, then strapped into his Falcon and won The Great Race. (Chevron Library)

Gregg Hansford (no. 02), the only person to win at Mount Panorama on two wheels and four, in 1974 came second to Warren Willing (no. 85); Ron Toombs (no. 63) was third. With them is Tony Hatton. (The Project Group)

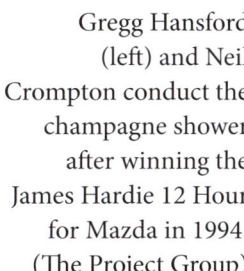

Gregg Hansford (left) and Neil Crompton conduct the champagne shower after winning the James Hardie 12 Hour for Mazda in 1994. (The Project Group)

When Bill Brown rolled his Falcon GT in 1969, mayhem followed in his wake. John French, later to win with Dick Johnson, is upside down in his Alfa Romeo (no. 72E) as the field concertinas. (Chevron Library)

In the 1980 Bathurst 1000, Dick Johnson, co-driving with John French, hit a rock and then the fence (note the flag marshal diving for cover), sparking a spontaneous public appeal that raised more than the first place prize money. (Chevron Library)

Two-time Bathurst 1000 winner Allan Grice was the first person to break the 100-mile-per-hour lap average in a sedan car. And he did it twice: in the Group C and Group A eras, in different-specification Holdens. (Ray Berghouse/Chevron Library)

How the Mountain has changed: in 1985, Tom Walkinshaw (Jaguar) leads Dick Johnson (Ford Mustang) and Robbie Francevic (Volvo 240T). The Hardie bridge is there, but the new pits are not. Both the bridge and the pits have been replaced twice since then. (Ray Berghouse/Chevron Library)

In 2003 Greg Murphy was credited with 'The Lap of the Gods' in the Top Ten Shootout, but later admitted he'd lost 0.2 seconds with a missed gear change. (Ray Berghouse/Chevron Library)

Twenty-two-year-old Matt Campbell, a full-time Porsche Young Professional based in Germany, snatched victory in the 2019 Bathurst 12 Hour. (Porsche AG Motorsport)

Mark Skaife registers disbelief as Jim Richards delivers his critique of the crowd ('You're a pack of arseholes') after winning the 1992 Bathurst 1000 on lap countback. Commentator Garry Wilkinson keeps his race face intact. (Ray Berghouse/Chevron Library)

Three generations of the Davison family have won at Mount Panorama. Lex (not shown) won the 1958 AGP; his grandson Will (right) has won the 1000 twice, and grandson Alex (left) won the Carrera Cup. Lex's son Richard (centre) won in Formula Ford at age 65. (Davison family)

James Brock won the 'forgotten' V8 race—the Bathurst 300—at Mount Panorama in 1999 only six months after his first motor race, while dad Peter watched on nervously. (Chevron Library)

Nine-time Formula One Grand Prix winner Mark Webber (no. 14) in a massive 1995 Formula Ford battle with Gavin Monaghan (no. 2) and eventual title winner Jason Bright (chasing). (Ray Berghouse/Chevron Library)

More than a car, it's the spirit of motor racing: the Brabham BT62. The sight and sound of the car across the top of Mount Panorama brought the crowd to the fences. (Ray Berghouse/Chevron Library)

On the fastest hill climb track in Australia—from Mountain Straight up to Reid Park—Formula One race designer Malcolm Oastler is four-time national champion in his self-designed car. (Oastler collection)

Five-time Bathurst 1000 winner Steven Richards hangs off the pit wall to cheer lead driver, seven-time winner Craig Lowndes, to victory in the 2018 race. (Team Triple Eight)

Craig Lowndes (left) and Steven Richards each have their names engraved on the Peter Brock Trophy, the most prestigious prize in domestic motor racing since the Australian Grand Prix went international. (Team Triple Eight)

Supercars' most successful team owner is considering his succession. Team Triple Eight boss Roland Dane and his heirs apparent, daughter Jessica and star driver Jamie Whincup. (Team Triple Eight)

Tony Cochrane, the impresario who created V8 Supercars, applauding at the pre-race tribute to Peter Brock in 2006. (Supercars Australia)

In the National Motor Racing Museum, Bathurst mayor Graeme Hanger sits in the 1951 AGP-winning George Reed Ford. (Bathurst Regional Council)

Reverend Garry Coleman has been chaplain of motorsport for almost 40 years. On the grid at Mount Panorama, his words of encouragement have become part of the rich pageant of the race. (Supercars Australia)

Mount Panorama is like no other show on Earth. The 2019-winning Bathurst 12 Hour Porsche drives into the fiery dawn with 11 hours 30 minutes remaining. (Porsche AG Motorsport)

The Bathurst 12 Hour is now a round of the Intercontinental GT Challenge, showcasing Mount Panorama on a global stage. The race begins half an hour before dawn; the 2019 start is shown here. (Porsche AG Motorsport)

Supercars boss Sean Seamer (white shirt) on the grid in 2018 with Prime Minister Scott Morrison, flanked by four-time Bathurst 1000 winner Jamie Whincup (left) and Australian Supercars champion Scott McLaughlin (right). (Supercars Australia)

Brock's legend lives on. Each year Sydney enthusiast Glenn Quinlan circles the 05 wagons at the top of Reid Park to celebrate all that makes Australian motor racing great. Naturally he has christened his son Brock. (John Smailes)

World champion Jenson Button and Craig Lowndes are the only two drivers to have achieved a Mount Panorama lap of more than 200 kilometres per hour. Both drove the Formula One McLaren MP4-23, with Button faster than Lowndes by just 0.67 seconds. (Scott Wensley)

Along with the Hollywood sign in Los Angeles, there is probably no branding more anticipated than the giant white 'Mount Panorama' etched into the side of the Bathurst circuit. It's the first thing enthusiasts see as they crest the hill on the Great Western Highway at Kelso, 15 kilometres from the track. (Ray Berghouse/Chevron Library)

also his nemesis, in an epic duel with Hansford was over the ton too.

In the Unlimited GP, Hansford and Wada were overwhelmed by the Yamahas—Takai in the lead, Willing shadowing. 'Slipstreaming made a big difference down Conrod,' Murray Sayle said. 'You didn't have to be right up the bike in front. You could slipstream from 50 metres back and as your speed increased [in the vortex] you'd be able to pull out and go past them at such a speed they couldn't catch you.'

Willing was certain Takai would succumb to exhaustion over the second stint after their fuel stop and perhaps he'd use up his rear tyre too much. The stop came exactly midway and Willing's rehearsed refuelling was several seconds faster. He still tailed Takai and it was now time to attack. His ride was one of the most pin-sharp pieces of two-wheeled mastery the Mountain had seen. By lap 28, when the rain came, he'd lowered the lap record to 2 minutes 15.68 seconds (101.69 miles per hour/163.76 kilometres per hour). As the rain fell and Mount Panorama turned into a skating rink, officials prematurely held out the chequered flag. Willing was not able to complete his mission. He finished second to Takai, with Wada third.

Willing's record would never be surpassed on the 'short' Mount Panorama circuit. In 2000, in the last motorcycle meeting ever held at Mount Panorama—an ambitious but star-crossed affair that left the promoter broke—Kevin Curtain, on the state-of-the-art Yamaha R1 superbike, bravely threaded his way through the concrete fences on the longer track to win six races on the card and post a lap time of 2 minutes 15.45 seconds (165.12 kilometres per hour).

The first time I met Allan Grice he was hanging upside down in his racing harness, spitting teeth. He'd just rolled his white MG TC special across the right–left flip-flop at the old Oran Park track and as a flag marshal I was first to him. He was inverted, and he was in mortal danger. 'Just get it back on its wheels,' he shouted from underneath. 'I can still catch them.' Grice has never been anything other than self-assured. Twice Bathurst 1000 winner, twice Australian Sports Sedan champion, he became the first touring-car driver to lap Mount Panorama at 100 miles per hour—twice.

His ton-up laps bridged two changes of regulations so legitimately he can claim the record successively. On both occasions he was co-driving Holdens with wealthy team owners and patrons, a classic pro-am relationship. And he did them proud. He took the lion's share of driving in both races and brought them home second and first in each race.

Grice was just recovering from a double knee operation when we spoke at his Queensland home. 'I put it down to the old Hardie-Ferodo 1103 brake compound,' he quipped. 'Those pads were so hard that you just pushed on the pedal with such force that sometimes your race seat would break. Not good for the knees.'

Grice set his first 100-mile-per-hour lap in 1982 in a Group C Commodore owned by trucking company owner Alan Browne. Group C had been introduced as a new touring-car regulation ten years prior to enable manufacturers to circumvent road-registration rules. It would soon be replaced by Group A—an international requirement that opened Australian sport to global competition.

'Browney had been driving only a couple of years. He was a bloke in his forties and loved the sport. He commissioned a new car from builder Les Small on the condition I did a few fast laps in it to prove that the car was capable. They only told me that later.' Grice did a near-record lap at Amaroo Park; Browne took delivery of the car and hired Grice to co-drive it in the Bathurst 1000. Grice had just split with Frank Gardner—was in court with him—and happily took the drive. It was a lifeline.

'We were in a drivers' meeting when race organiser Ivan Stibbard made the comment that the 100-miles-per-hour record could be broken in this qualifying session. Browney was a sportsman. He put up his hand and said, "I'll give $5000 to the first one to do it."' It was incentive enough for Grice. He laid down 2 minutes 17.8 seconds (100.13 miles per hour/161.24 kilometres per hour)—'much to the chagrin of Peter Brock', who managed 2 minutes 18.1 seconds (99.91 miles per hour/160.89 kilometres per hour). For all intents and purposes they'd both done the ton, even if the converted calculation of Brock's time was just under, but Grice was the quicker and to this day he swears he was the first. He lowered his time by a further 0.25 seconds in the Top Ten Shootout.

In the 1000, Browne spent just 1 hour 15 minutes behind the wheel. Grice drove to the maximum allowed and they came second, a lap behind Brock and Larry Perkins and just half a second ahead of Brock's teammates John Harvey and Gary Scott.

Three years later Grice was back, this time with poultry farmer Graeme Bailey in the Group A 'Chickadee' Holden Commodore, once more prepared by Les Small. By reputation, the car was the strongest ever built for Bathurst. Grice bristles at the implication: 'Anyone who cheats going to Bathurst is a retard. We didn't have hand-grenade engines. We had a fresh engine, that's all.'

Grice puts that new ton-up lap down to tyres, not horsepower. 'I was doing development work for Yokohama and I was good at it,' he said. 'Brock was hired for development too and they'd send two teams of engineers from Japan to work with us, one for each of us. They'd give us a questionnaire to fill out, rating turn-in, side-stability and power-down—the three critical components of a tyre.

'After they got Brock's assessment, they'd just roll it up in a ball and throw it away. Anyone who says Brock wasn't quick is an idiot. He'd simply drive around any problem. If the car wasn't performing for whatever reason he'd just modify his driving style to suit. My testing added up. Engineers could see where it was going. His didn't.'

Grice went to Mount Panorama on Yokohama's renowned Compound E—the tyre he'd helped develop.

'The trick to being quick at Mount Panorama is turn one [Hell Corner]. If you can be 2 kilometres per hour faster out of it, you'll build to being 25 kilometres per hour faster by the time you reach the top of Mountain Straight. That's all down to tyre control.'

Grice's theory of exponential speed held true. He laid down a lap of 2 minutes 16.6 seconds (162.65 kilometres per hour). It would be another two years before a Group-A car went faster. Graeme Bailey completed one 30-lap stint in the race and Grice did the rest to win, one and a half minutes ahead of John Harvey and Neal Lowe (Commodore).

'I never begrudged my co-drivers,' Grice said. 'They drove as hard as they could and if they made a mistake they didn't mean to do it. Without them I wouldn't have been there at all.'

THE LAPS OF THE GODS

People have subsequently been faster, but in 2003 no one had done a more complete or competent job than New Zealander Greg Murphy, a three-time Bathurst 1000 winner. His flying lap of 2 minutes 6.8594 seconds (176.31 kilometres per hour) in the Top Ten Shootout was hailed as 'The Lap of the Gods'. It remains today as the quintessential single-lap achievement. Murphy—now a respected commentator—remembers it with millimetre precision and understandable pride.

'It had been an amazing qualifying session,' he recalled. 'For the first time ever we'd broken into the 2-minute-7-second bracket. No one had done that before and there were three of us on it—John Bowe [Falcon], Mark Skaife [Commodore] and myself.' Just 0.04 seconds separated the three. Murphy was quickest on 2 minutes 7.9503 seconds. At their most optimistic, no one could contemplate dipping lower than 2 minutes 7 seconds.

'The track was good, the cars were fast and the conditions were great. I've always relished a shootout and Mount Panorama is a special spot—iconic.

'I was sitting in my car at the end of pit lane ready to go. I didn't want to know what the others had done. There's no point. You have to drive as fast as you can. I could tell from the crowd reaction that John Bowe had done well [2 minutes 7.956 seconds] and Skaife was still on track when I headed out. My confidence level was huge.' (Skaife would be seventh-fastest.)

Murphy was driving a hybrid of a Commodore. It had started life as a VT Commodore for the Holden Dealer Team in 2000 and had been converted to VY specification when it transferred to Holden's second team—K-Mart Racing. It had changed front suspension to suit new regulations and it still had extraneous assemblies under the bonnet. 'But they had done a beaut job building it,' Murphy said.

'I never intended to do a six. My interest was in beating the fastest time. That's all. I got a good clean run through turn two (Griffin's Bend)—corner speed is so critical—and as I was heading up the hill the shift lights were coming up earlier than usual. It felt good.'

Mount Panorama is divided into three sectors so people can judge progressive progress. The first is at the entrance to McPhillamy. At this point, incredibly, Murphy was 0.4055 seconds faster than Bowe.

'Through McPhillamy the car was feeling light and when I was coming up to Skyline I was on the rev limiter [7500 rpm] and doing so well I thought I might try for fifth. But I'd never done it before and I knew it could be a disaster and I could crash, so I held it in fourth.

'Over Skyline and into the Esses I was hearing little chirps from the front tyres—telling me I was right on the limit of turn-in.

'I was in second through the Dipper, stood on the gas and went to flat-change and shift across the gate'—in those days cars still used a standard H-pattern gear shift. 'I took a small dip of the clutch and went straight back to first. The engine over-revved to 9500 rpm.' NO. 'I grabbed second again, then third. I thought I've ruined the lap. I had to quickly settle myself.'

Murphy had been so fast across the top that in the second sector he'd actually gained more time, a further 0.289 seconds, so was now 0.6944 seconds faster than Bowe.

'I tried too hard through Forrest's Elbow, got on the gas as quick as I could. Our gear ratios were too short for Conrod. I was on the rev limiter a long time into the Chase; I decided to brake later than I'd ever done before. It was beautifully balanced. I took fifth gear into the run down into Murray's, pulled up later again and then powered up to the flag.'

Murphy knew he'd done everything right—even with the missed gear, which his team later calculated cost him 0.2 seconds. 'I looked down at my dash read-out and it came up as a 2.06.85. It took a few moments for it to sink in. I'd been hoping for a high seven.'

After the shoot-out, cars re-enter the pits from just after Hell Corner and drive in the opposite direction down the lane. As Murphy turned in, the entire pit rushed out to cheer and wave him. No one has ever had that reception before. 'That's what made it. Without their reaction, it wouldn't have been as special, or remembered.'

That night Murphy's team changed the valve springs in the car as a precaution after his over-rev. The next day he and Rick Kelly won the race.

His Lap of the Gods time remained the fastest ever for another seven years.

James O'Brien, the father of the current-day Bathurst 12 Hour, had an idea. Near the end of each year—November or December—he'd hold a Challenge Bathurst day to give owners of performance cars a unique track-day experience at the Mountain. It would also, O'Brien reasoned, provide teams in the following year's 12 Hour with invaluable set-up opportunity. The Challenge Bathurst event was sanctioned by CAMS, so a lap record would be official.

Audi rose to the challenge. It removed the technical restrictors from its GT3 car and went for the outright record—the first lap under 2 minutes.

The restrictions are called the Balance of Performance (BoP) and they ensure all GT cars, regardless of make, are, with the right driver input, able to lap a circuit within 0.3 seconds of each other. Weight penalties, and restraints to the air intake into the engine and engine mapping, make up a complex formula of artificial impairment. Take the restrictions off and a car should fly.

When the first Challenge Bathurst was held in 2018, the lap record for GT3 cars around Mount Panorama, with BoP applied, was held by New Zealand's Shane van Gisbergen (McLaren 650S). He'd set it in 2016—a time of 2 minutes 1.567 seconds (183.98 kilometres per hour).

German Chris Mies is an Audi professional driver, available to be loaned or hired to Audi GT teams throughout the world. He had won the Bathurst 12 Hour in its first two years as a GT category. He'd backed up to win the Australian GT championship in 2015 and a year later he'd won the Nürburgring 24 Hour event.

Audi gave him the keys to the car.

'The first time I came to Mount Panorama I was surprised by the concrete walls,' Mies told me, leaning back on the pit wall in his shining white driving suit—lean, compact, light on his feet. 'I didn't want to be the first one to make a mistake. I didn't take the Chase flat until the race. Once I'd done it once it was easy.'

Now he's a Mount Panorama veteran, at ease with the track. But a non-BoP lap was new: 'I was surprised how much more engine horsepower I had when they took the restrictor off. I was up to 610 horsepower from 530 (454 kW from 395 kW). But it was the torque that really mattered. I was able to exit the slow corners—Murray's, Hell, the Cutting and Forrest's Elbow—so much better.'

Mies took three laps to do the job. His driving partner on the day, three-time Bathurst 1000 winner and Australian Touring Car champion Garth Tander, stood down to give him the chance. He overdrove the first two laps, 'wide at turn one', both times. Then on lap three he nailed it: 217 kilometres per hour up to Hell Corner, sixth gear and 267 kilometres per hour into Griffin's Bend, second gear and 96 kilometres per hour at the apex of the Cutting, fourth gear and 224 kilometres per hour at McPhillamy, 205 kilometres per hour over Skyline, 94 kilometres per hour on the apex of Forrest's Elbow, on the rev limiter for some time down Conrod, and 291 kilometres per hour flat through the Chase, fifth down to Murray's at 220 kilometres per hour, picking up slower traffic.

He crossed the line in 1 minute 59.291 seconds (187.49 kilometres per hour).

'It felt quite good.' There's not a lot of emotion from the German racing driver. But he set up a new challenge, likely to become an annual feature of O'Brien's Challenge event.

Le Mans 24 Hour winner David Brabham, the youngest of Jack's three sons, had decided to do something special to honour his father.

He'd become part of a consortium that had put the Brabham name to an aerodynamic customer sports-racing car—the Brabham BT62. They intend to build 62 cars—equal to the number of years Jack had been in the racing game when the project started—and each car would be painted differently in one of Jack's many liveries. There was a veil of secrecy over the car. The engine, for example, was a 5.4-litre, naturally aspirated V8 but Brabham is coy about its source.

Customer relations at this level—and price—remain confidential, but the posted price was $1.8 million, higher if you wanted the car modified for the road. At Mount Panorama in January 2019, David Brabham was celebrating acquiring his first customer—a European delivery.

The Brabham team had been testing the car at the new circuit at Tailem Bend in South Australia, a relatively flat track with wide progressive corners. It's a circuit that suits the Brabham. The BT62 is an aero car, using its body and underbody to generate 1200 kilograms of downforce to glue the vehicle to the track, in the same manner as a Formula One machine. Supercars and GT3 cars rely mainly on mechanical grip, the connection with the road made by chassis and suspension tuning. Aero for them is limited by regulations. Supercars allow just 330 kilograms over the total of front and rear axles.

The Brabham had both—good mechanical grip, and aero that added another dimension.

Luke Youlden, racing driver and engineer, winner of the Bathurst 1000 in 2017, had been doing the development driving. He and Brabham brought the BT62 to Mount Panorama at the 12 Hour meeting in 2019 to show it off.

'I came here with a sub–2-minute clearly in mind,' Youlden said. 'At Tailem Bend it had been about 7 seconds faster than an Australian GT car.' That record was held by Youlden's Bathurst 1000–winning partner David Reynolds in an AMG GT3.

THE LAPS OF THE GODS

The aero effect across the Mountain staggered Youlden. 'We eased into it—going up in throttle availability in increments from 60 per cent to 100 per cent. [When we opened it up] it was about 20 kilometres per hour faster than a GT car everywhere.' Youlden estimated he was pulling close to 3 g— three times the car's weight—in longitudinal deceleration and anything up to 2.5 g in lateral cornering force. 'It will take a fair bit of gym work for a driver to train to handle that.' But perhaps that was not the point. 'For a gentleman driver, there's a lot of leeway to be able to go really fast without pushing the car to its limit.' Down Conrod, Youlden said the car 'shook and rattled' over the bumps. There was so much downforce that the team had installed special packers in the suspension to hold it firmly in place.

Into the Chase, Youlden's telemetry was showing 300 kilometres per hour on the front right wheel and 299 on the rear left. 'We'd been having some difficulty with the electronic traction control being too intrusive, so on the last run we switched it off.' That's when Youlden put in a 'conservative' lap of 1 minute 58.68 seconds (188.46 kilometres per hour), the fastest any car other than a Formula One has been around Mount Panorama. 'I think there's a 1 minute 55 second [lap] in it,' Youlden said. 'Maybe next time.'

Mount Panorama taught Australian Formula One star Mark Webber about racecraft. He raced there just once, in a Formula Ford previously owned by Craig Lowndes.

Lowndes had wanted to race the Formula Ford but his father Frank thought the track was too dangerous: 'The kerbs were made for the road, not the track, and they could launch a formula car,' Frank said. 'I told the Bathurst council about it and they changed the kerbs but by then Craig had moved on.' Craig's car was sold to another father-and-son team—Alan and Mark Webber—and Mark drove it in the 1995 Australian Formula Ford Championship series in which he came fourth.

'That weekend taught me a lot,' Webber, winner of nine world championship grands prix and twice winner of Monaco, told me. The Formula Ford is a non-aero car—no wings, no artificial aids. It's all about mechanical grip. 'The car moved around a bit but you could take McPhillamy flat and you could leave it super late on brakes over Skyline.' The man who had driven the fastest cars in the world was getting animated with the recollection.

'It was over-geared, so first gear was very long and it was only a four-speed box. It took a long time to get down Conrod. But across the Mountain it was quick. It popped a wheel up through the Dipper and the walls were so high it was difficult to get a reference point.'

And then there was slipstreaming. The golden rule in Formula Ford is never to lead at the beginning of the last lap. Just like in a bicycle race breakaway group, it's best to let someone else lead and then pull out of their draft at the last moment. 'It was the last lap and I came over Skyline where there were double yellow flags out [a warning that caution is required, and no passing]. I decided to ignore them and went for it. By the time I exited Forrest's Elbow there was no one in my mirrors and I definitely knew I could win. But then I saw the peloton coming.' Their collective mass was propelling them far faster than a single car could go.

'They swamped me into the Chase and I salvaged a third.'

In 2011 Craig Lowndes was about to make good on driving an open-wheeler at the Mountain, except it wasn't a Formula Ford—it was the archetypical aero car, the McLaren MP4-23, the car so equipped with aerodynamic aids that it triggered a new set of simplified regulations in 2009 a year after Lewis Hamilton used it to win his first world championship. The car was now a demonstration unit, run by McLaren's test team manager Indy Lall, and it had been brought to Mount Panorama as a promotion by telco Vodafone, which sponsored both McLaren and Lowndes' Supercar team.

Jenson Button would drive Craig's Supercar and the Formula One. In return Craig would get two laps in the Formula One.

'Jenson was so excited about being at Mount Panorama,' Lowndes said. 'And a bit nervous. I spent an hour driving him around in a road car, explaining some of it to him.' Button agreed: 'Normally I can learn a track in one or two laps. This one has taken me half a day.' He had a smile on his face.

When Button went out for his installation lap, Craig went to a place at the bottom of the circuit where he could watch Button's braking points. 'He did that all the time,' Frank Lowndes said. 'He never sat still—always watching others and learning.'

Button put in three laps in the McLaren—his best at 1 minute 49.41 seconds (204.43 kilometres per hour). His top speed down Conrod was just on 300 kilometres per hour, a little slower up the Mountain. In two laps Lowndes achieved a time that was 0.678 seconds slower. It was a trade-off between them—this was Button's first time at the Mountain and Lowndes' first time in a Formula One car.

'Look at the traces,' Lowndes bubbled, with his trademark enthusiasm. (Traces are a moment-by-moment description of speed and dynamics, generated by computer, that are a team's guide to performance.) 'I'm used to mechanical traction so I was quicker than him in all the slow corners, 6 to 8 kilometres per hour better mid-corner. He was much quicker in anything that was high speed.' But not by much, and Lowndes knew the track's limits: 'I wasn't taking any risks—I took a wide line into the Dipper and the left-hand front wheel was still a foot in the air.'

A sizeable crowd had gathered that day for what was nothing more than a promotion. But what they saw and heard, as McLaren's turbocharged V8 screamed out to 19,000 rpm, was something very special. 'It was amazing,' Lowndes grinned.

13

Sky Pilots

'Motorsport activities are inherently dangerous recreational activities and there is significant risk of injury, disability or death.' The disclaimer is on the back of every entry ticket and credential at every race meeting.

'Today we are more than Ford and Holden fans. We are a family, shrouded in the loss of a father, a grandfather, a brother, a friend, a hero, a colleague, a competitor, a fellow traveller.'

These were the opening words of the tribute to nine-time Mount Panorama winner Peter Brock by the sport's chaplain, Reverend Garry Coleman, on the grid, just before the start of the 2006 Bathurst 1000.

'For us, when we follow a champion, we often feel that their victories are our own,' Coleman said. 'We see ourselves lifted above our own lives, gliding across the top of the Mountain, down through the twisting Esses, and telling the world we ran the Chase and we won.'

Twenty people had died as a result of race incidents at Mount Panorama when Coleman delivered his eulogy to the hushed and hurting crowd. Sadly, the twenty-first would pass away later that afternoon as a result of injuries he'd received two days before.

Brock hadn't died at Mount Panorama; he'd *lived* there. He'd perished in an impact with a tree in a tarmac rally in Western Australia a month before. A millimetre each way and he may have survived. A sterling silver memorial award was behind Coleman as he spoke: the Peter Brock Trophy, inscribed 'King of the Mountain', the product of 200 hours of work and a cost of $75,000 yet designed and completed in three weeks. It would be offered in perpetuity to the winners of The Great Race.

It had been a bad week for heroes. Four days before Brock died another national icon, eco-adventurer Steve Irwin, had taken a stingray barb through his heart, diving on Batt Reef in northern Queensland. Although Coleman was referencing Brock, he wanted to embrace Irwin as well. 'I intended my speech as a means of healing a vast audience,' said Coleman, a senior member of Sports Chaplaincy Australia. 'Share your talents and help others climb higher. Give of yourselves and make life for living, rather than enduring . . .'

People don't go racing to have a bad time. But twenty-one people have died in 80 years of racing at the Mountain. That's one every four years; one every three years, if you measure first fatality to last; but there have been none since the day Garry Coleman made his speech.

'Motor racing is one of the safest sports I know,' Coleman said, en route to the first round of the 2019 Supercars Championship where he would head a team of three ministers—'peer support coordinators' in corporate-speak. 'Lap for lap, race for race, it's safer than most sports you could name.' Reliable figures on motorsport trauma through the ages are not available. Motorcyclists say the tally at the Isle of Man is up to 270 deaths since the race was first held in 1910. Formula One counts 51 driver deaths since the championship began in 1950. NASCAR—accurately, because it counts everything—claims 28. The statistics drive a common resolve from all branches of the sport to achieve meaningful improvement in safety standards, and in the last decade especially they've achieved that. The FIA, world governing body of four-wheel sport, has an Institute for Motor Sport Safety and Sustainability, and it is constantly introducing innovations and upgrades. Motorcycling, a little more limited in its scope for improvement, has done likewise. The dark days of the 1960s and '70s are behind them.

But more people have died in pursuit of their sport—or by simply watching it—on Mount Panorama than on any other circuit in Australia. The toll is split about 50:50 between cars and motorcycles. Ten motorcycle riders and one spectator have died over a period of 58 years. Eight car drivers and two spectators have died in 57 years. Incredibly, eleven of the eighteen incidents occurred not on top of the Mountain but on some part of Conrod Straight. And for every fatality there have been miraculous escapes; because they had a happy ending they've been replayed almost on rotation. People like a 'good' crash.

The Mountain, under threat of closure after its first post-war fatality, has been fortunate to escape sanction.

When motorcycle racer Ray Fletcher, by all accounts a totally innocent party, slammed fatally into jaywalking Bathurst citizen Bernard O'Halloran at the base of Conrod Straight in the first post-war meeting, he triggered a reaction in the police department and New South Wales Parliament that could have closed Mount Panorama right then. To the credit of the motorcycle and car clubs, and the Bathurst City Council, the improvements promised and delivered after that first incident—a double fatality—were of sufficient magnitude to enable a permit to race to be issued.

Jack Johnson's crash in 1949, when his MG TC spun and rolled under brakes into Murray's Corner, caused scrutineers to tighten up safety regulations. It appeared Johnson had chromed his brake drums both inside and out, and the peeling chrome had caused the front brake to lock.

The introduction of clubman racing to Mount Panorama swelled the motorcycle fields, kept the books balanced and paid the prize money. In 1953 a rider lost control between Reid Park and McPhillamy Park; after he was spat off, the bike continued on—off the side of the mountain and through two cattle fences before it exploded in flames. Perhaps that unsettled Billy Baldry, who also came off and hit the bank on the outside of McPhillamy with fatal consequences. The winner of the clubman race was Barry 'Doc' Halliday, one of the most popular members of the motorcycle club and an unceasing and uncomplaining worker as well as rider. Five years later, in Friday practice, Doc became the next motorcycle fatality.

In a period of just six months three incidents, seemingly unconnected, occurred that could have shut Mount Panorama for good.

It was Easter 1955 and seven-year-old Gavan Larnock of Bathurst, full of excitement, was a spectator at the bottom of Conrod Straight. It was the Bathurst 100 and the best open-wheeler cars in Australia were wheel to wheel. Reg Hunt, in the works red Maserati, was slicing through the field. The 1954 Australian Grand Prix winner Lex Davison in the HWM Jaguar, and Ern Seeliger in the fearsome Maybach, had been nose to tail, passing and repassing. The crowd was six deep on the fence in the braking area.

Newcastle racing enthusiast Gordon Greig was driving his ex-Scuderia Ferrari Alfa Romeo that day. It was the same car that had been driven by Jack Saywell to sixth in the 1939 Australian Grand Prix, then fitted with a new 4.3-litre Alvis engine and driven by Bill Murray to third in the 1952 GP at Mount Panorama. The Alfa was handicapped eleventh in the field, four minutes in front of Hunt's Maserati. It was a difficult car to drive, touchy under brakes. Greig started and on lap sixteen handed the car to Tony Burke. Down Conrod into the braking area, the Alfa started to fishtail—more violently with every correction. It got up on two wheels, then snap-spun and went backwards into the crowd.

Young Gavan died instantly. Eighteen spectators were injured and one was later to die. The race continued even as four ambulance wagons ran in shuttle to the hospital with a police escort, their sirens blaring. Burke, uninjured, was treated for shock.

Viewed in isolation, the Alfa crash and its consequences were horrific.

But just three months previously, Gnoo Blas had suffered a similar tragedy. An open-wheeled racing car had clipped a barrier and somersaulted through a barbed-wire fence into a small group of spectators, who were standing in what organisers had deemed a prohibited area. One died instantly, six were injured, and the driver, Ian Mountain, succumbed to his injuries in hospital.

Then just months after the Mount Panorama fatalities, in the Le Mans 24 Hour race of June 1955, a works Mercedes driven by Pierre Levegh was catapulted into the crowd lining Pit Straight. More than 80 people died and another 180 were injured. It was the worse motor-racing catastrophe ever. The race continued—in order to keep crowds stationary and leave roads clear for emergency crews—but motor racing in Europe was temporarily halted. In the US, major car makers voluntarily withdrew their teams from NASCAR, fearing they were only one wrong turn of the wheel away from a similar fate. Surely that disaster, covered around the world, must have impacted on Mount Panorama and all motorsport.

But no one, it seemed, had made a connection between all three. To do so, potentially, could have brought motor racing to a halt.

The ARDC and Bathurst City Council were already at work on their specific reaction. Spectators were banned from Conrod Straight except for its last 300 metres, and they were kept well back, now behind a steel fence. The countermeasure satisfied authorities. In 1957 the New South Wales Government gazetted the *Speedway Racing (Public Safety) Act*. It applied to cars and bikes. The Act eliminated doubt and interference by well-meaning figures of authority, and it imposed ironclad responsibility on promoters under threat of government penalty. The fines were more a wrist slap—£100 for a first offence by an organiser, £10 for a competitor. The more important imputation was that government and its designated authority—the police—required a close working relationship and agreement with organisers if motor racing was to continue.

In 1960, Victorian car dealer Reg Smith was competing in the inaugural Australian GT Championship. It was an odd field, made up of proper GT cars like Smith's Porsche and Leo Geoghegan's Lotus Elite. But it was also the repository for the touring and sports cars that were looking for a home in the changing CAMS classifications. While Leo fronted with his Lotus, brother Pete was in their black Holden, no longer a touring car. Bill Buckle was there in his own Ford Zephyr–powered Buckle.

It was a wild race. Leo Geoghegan led across the line for the first of thirteen laps, but Tasmanian Gavin Youl in a Porsche took over, with Leo second and Pete dropping back. The weather conditions were blustery when Smith, in the middle of the field, crested the last hump on Conrod. He'd just been timed at 123 miles per hour (197 kilometres per hour) when, apparently, he was shifted sideways by the wind. His Porsche, its brakes fully applied, left the track, scythed down a tree and came back, upside down, onto the track. Officials pulled him from the car as it caught fire, black smoke forming a pyre above it, but he was dead. The race continued under a yellow warning flag on the hump, restricting passing at that point, and Leo Geoghegan went on to win his first national title from

Youl and brother Pete. It's unlikely they felt much like racing each other anyway.

In 1969, the 22-year-old Victorian Bevan Gibson—son of the race driver they called Hoot, after the Hollywood cowboy-film star—was hired to drive Bob Jane's massively powerful Elfin 400 Repco. He was up against Neil Allen's Elfin Chevrolet and Frank Matich in his self-named Matich SR4 Repco. Gibson was a real talent. When Spencer Martin first moved to Melbourne to drive for Bob Jane, he and Gibson had shared a flat together and Martin was all too aware of the youngster's exceptional ability and ambition. 'We'd go out to Calder [which Jane owned] and speed around in a Valiant—not a soul there. We were both faster than Bob and we didn't think it was a good idea to tell him.'

Gibson was worried about Mount Panorama. This was the year aerodynamic wings first appeared on cars; their purpose was to apply some sort of downforce to compress the cars on the track. It was an inexact science and Bob Jane's Elfin didn't have wings. Matich's car did—but it was really a moot point. The technology was so rudimentary that no one really knew whether it worked.

'The night before the race Bevan asked how to drive Conrod,' Spencer Martin recalled. 'He was asking everyone, really concerned. I said [world champion] Graham Hill had told me when I was looking after him with McKay's Brabham at Longford in Tasmania that it was always a good idea to lift before you crested a hill. It settled the car and got the wind out from underneath.'

The race was called the Mount Panorama Trophy for Sports Cars and it was only six laps—just a support to a round of the Australian Touring Car Championship and the open-wheelers' Gold Star race. But the so-called 'Big Banger' sports cars brought the crowd to the fence. Matich struggled for traction from the start and Allen led away, followed by Gibson. Going up the Mountain for the first time, Matich simply put his foot into it. He passed Gibson on the run-up to Griffin's Bend then bided his time until they got to Forrest's Elbow and moved past Allen. Pushed hard by Gibson, Allen spun at the Cutting and Gibson was up to second. On the next lap Gibson set a new record and ranged alongside Matich into Murray's Corner but couldn't get through. Matich, who later said he had fuel pick-up problems, moved ahead up the Mountain. At Forrest's Elbow they were separated by 80 metres and Matich, not on full song, was vulnerable. Perhaps Gibson, caught up in the pursuit, neglected to lift the throttle. Eyewitnesses said Matich was moving over to let him through when, on the last hump, the Elfin simply took off.

Years later audiences saw something similarly graphic on TV when Mark Webber 'flew' the works Mercedes-Benz not once but twice at the 1999 Le Mans 24 Hour. Spencer Martin, a great supporter of Webber, was there too. In both instances Webber went high in the air, flipping and landing (mercifully) on a roof structure so strong that it saved his life. When air gets under the underbody of a big sports car, the vehicle becomes an aircraft—not because of aerodynamic lift, but simply from the sheer gale force passing beneath its bodywork. In Webber's case, he'd been promised efficient aerodynamics—by then they were available—and after another of its cars took flight Mercedes, embarrassed all the way up to board level, withdrew their team because of their failure.

Gibson had no such guarantees. His car scraped down Conrod, upside down, initially at something well over 200 kilometres per hour. 'I will never forget Bob Jane running to the scene,' Martin recalled. 'We were standing in the pits and we saw it all. Then Bob was off. He was fit back then, a former competitive cyclist, and he outdistanced everyone across the paddock. But when he got to the car he just turned away, his head hanging. I've often thought: if I hadn't retired from Bob's team, would it have been me in the car?' Matich, Allen and others pulled out of the race. Officials didn't stop it. Once more, in a sort of macabre ritual that went on for years, cars went by at reduced speed, and it was Glyn Scott in a Lotus 23B who ultimately took the chequered flag.

Tom Sulman, son of noted architect Sir John Sulman in whose name the Art Gallery of New South Wales's coveted Sulman Prize is awarded, died at Mount Panorama. It was a year after Gibson's crash and Tom Sulman was 70 years old, the senior statesman of the sport; he had been a member of the 1955 Kangaroo Stable to Europe tour, and had raced everything from a tiny NSU Prinz to a works-prepared Aston Martin.

The crash occurred at almost the same place as Gibson's but in a different manner. It was unlikely Sulman's Lotus Eleven was hit with the same underbody tornado, but speculation was that he had been affected by a side wind that caused him to back off and be glanced from behind by another car.

He hit a bank, cartwheeled upside down into the fence post of a farmer's locked gate, then skidded down the track. A later examination of the wreck found cracks around the front disc brake so perhaps a mechanical fault contributed. Tom had been motor racing since 1923 when he had built the Sulman Simplex cycle car and driven it at Sydney's Victoria Park. He had entered Mount Panorama consistently since 1947 and had come sixth in the Australian Grand Prix at the Mountain in 1952. When he didn't have a car he'd be flag marshalling. He had the coveted number one flag spot at Sydney's Warwick Farm. The ARDC named a section of Mount Panorama after him—Sulman Park, between Reid and McPhillamy Parks—and the Bathurst Light Car Club erected a Sulman monument on one of the stone entrance gates to their clubhouse beneath Forrest's Elbow.

Ron Toombs should never have returned from retirement. He was four years out of competitive motorcycling and 46 years old; motorcycles had moved on, but to a degree he hadn't. Tyre technology had advanced and where bikes used to slide they now gripped. But Toombs wasn't disconnected. I used to ghost-write a column for him in Sydney's *Daily Telegraph* and it was a privilege to get his perspective on the young guns of the sport, half his age and younger, who were risking it all—and yet, in his view, not risking enough. 'They were too processional,' he said, 'too willing to tuck in behind one another and wait for a mechanical advantage to open up.' His preference was for a bit of knees and elbows body contact.

Ron was in a relatively new relationship then. He was no longer with his childhood sweetheart Mavis and had started a relationship with the former wife of a team manager. We'd sit at his home in Epping, Sydney, on the slopes overlooking a valley and he was quite open about the turmoil he was experiencing. He was torn. Perhaps it was his personal life, at least in part, that made the prospect of getting back on a racing motorcycle so appealing. He was the master of motorcycle racing. Behind the fairing there are no distractions. In 1979 he was offered the use of a TZ350 Yamaha by the manager of one of Sydney's biggest motorcycle distributors. It was only three months before the Mount Panorama Easter meeting.

On Easter Sunday morning Toombs pulled on his old familiar and somewhat scarred green leathers for the Australian Senior Grand Prix. He was up against 500-cc machines in the hands of guns like the Kiwi duo of John Woodley and Stu Avant. But Ron was never anything but optimistic. He got away mid-pack and began a relentless progression through the field. Photographers say that on the lap before his crash they saw him brush the fence with his shoulder on the way out of the Dipper, not as pin-sharp as he'd been a decade before. Next lap through, now lying eighth, he was off-line again and went straight ahead on the right-hander below the Dipper, highsiding into a tree. As is the norm in motor-racing crashes he was pronounced dead on arrival at hospital.

The grief in the pits and around the circuit was palpable. People, even those who didn't know him personally, were crying and couldn't function. In those days, before Garry Coleman and the sports chaplaincy, race organiser Arthur Blizzard was left to bear the burden of the grief, including his own, and to run a race meeting. It was a huge responsibility.

Arthur and Jan Blizzard endured the emotional distress of five motorcycle deaths at Mount Panorama in the space of eight years. In 1972 sidecar rider Ian Hogg, a South Australian veteran of solos and sidecars, speedway and circuit, hit the fence in the Esses and died instantly. It was the last race of the meeting, late in the day when people were winding down, and it was all the more poignant because of it.

Four years later Ross Barelli, a high-profile member of a motorcycling family that included his brother-in-law Bob Rosenthal—who was entered at the same meeting on the ex-Giacomo Agostini Yamaha TZ750—went straight on at the bottom of Conrod. He was going too fast to make the escape road and way too fast to make the corner. His speed when he hit the fence appeared to be undiminished. It was claimed later that he had drilled holes in his brake discs for lightness. The Friday time trials in which he was participating were brought to a halt, engines were shut down and the rescue workers, doing all they could, were all too apparent as they clustered around the fallen rider at Murray's Corner before the ambulance arrived.

The year after Ron Toombs died, two fatalities occurred at the same race meeting. Ian Dick, a superbike rider, lost control of his Kawasaki on Conrod and died during practice. Rob Moorehouse—known as Moose to his mates—was renowned for his eccentric taste in tow cars. He'd driven to Mount Panorama in an old Rolls-Royce Silver Shadow (they weren't that expensive) with a Union Jack painted on the roof. On the third lap of the main feature, the Australian Unlimited GP, his Yamaha TZ750 arrived at Skyline with its front brakes inoperative. Later investigation showed that the hydraulic brake line had been chafed through by contact with the front tyre. By then Mount Panorama was increasingly becoming a circuit built for cars. Safety fences were erected to deflect the big sedans, not to catch motorcycles. Moose's Yamaha launched over the steel fence. He went beneath the barrier.

It was time for motorcycle racing to take a deep breath.

Reverend Garry Coleman got his job in motorsport when he responded to a story he'd seen on a new concept called sports chaplaincy. In 1982 Baptist minister Mark Tronson, who went on to become chaplain for the Australian cricket team, formed a voluntary organisation called the Sports and Leisure Ministry to bring pastoral assistance to a whole range of sports. Coleman had been a mechanic, worked at the old speedway at the Sydney showgrounds, and through family connections in evangelism had studied at the Moody Bible Institute in the US. Back home he'd been the pastor at three churches and he thought he could help.

At his first outing, Coleman attended a fatality at Sydney's Amaroo Park. A racing car had been launched into the crowd; it went over the heads of spectators at the fences and struck a woman who was sitting, knitting, in a deckchair. He was able, professionally, to assist in counselling, beyond prayer, with practical issues. 'In these circumstances people are sometimes beyond rational thought—where are the car keys, who to call, what to do,' he said. 'But we also help people who need to cry.'

In the early days Coleman believed he needed to go to the scene of the trauma: 'I'd jump on the back of the rescue truck and go out there.' He doesn't do that anymore. The standard of professionalism in first intervention has improved markedly. Supercars racing has a full-time doctor who is the best person to be at the scene. He reports back to the appropriate people who will take the steps for which they are qualified. Coleman is part of the Supercars management program, but he may still be the immediate responder at other events, like speedways, club rallies and motorcycle races—anywhere one of the 50 motorsport chaplains, among the 700 sports chaplains in Australia, are needed.

In 1986 Garry Coleman was present when the first fatality occurred in the Bathurst 1000. Mike Burgmann, accountant to the ARDC—and, more than that, a close confidant of race secretary Ivan Stibbard and one of the moving forces in securing the new World Touring Car Championship for Mount Panorama—was jockeying for position at the end of Conrod Straight when his Holden Commodore became slightly airborne over the second hump. It landed a little crookedly; Burgmann stood full on the brakes and the car turned right. A bridge had been built across the track and Burgmann's car hit the stanchion head-on. It was an unsurvivable deceleration. 'I went straight to race control to support them. They needed it. Then, aware that there was family that needed help, I went to them too.' Coleman is aware of the protocol: 'It is the responsibility of the secretary of the meeting to handle all matters of trauma, but [Supercars race director] Tim Schenken relaxes when I show up. After the Burgmann fatality the secretary of CAMS, John Keeffe, issued an edict that if anyone offers to be chaplain at a motor race meeting, accept them willingly.'

In a time of increasing governance and responsibility, the chaplain can act as an intermediary, able to say things to people in distress that governance will not enable an organiser to do because of concern of later liability. It is a grey area to some but not to Coleman. He sees his responsibility as being very human: 'Years after Mike Burgmann's death I came across the mechanic who had built his engine. He was carrying his guilt for the incident, as if he'd been responsible. It's a natural reaction—grief leads to guilt. I was able to help him understand why he was feeling as he did.'

There is a misconception that Mike Burgmann's death led to the construction of the high-speed Chase at Mount Panorama, which eliminated the second hump and turned it into a spectacular chicane. That's not so. Conrod Straight was too long to be accepted by the FIA, the world governing body, for the World Touring Car race the following year—the one Burgmann helped secure—and it needed to be shortened. After 48 years the second hump, scene of so much trauma, was ploughed under. It's ironic that the man who negotiated its removal was also its last victim.

Call it the curse of Conrod.

In 1992, world Formula One champion Denny Hulme died at the top of the straight. The 1967 champion when driving for

Jack Brabham's team, and New Zealand's only Formula One world-title holder, had a heart attack in his BMW M3. His last act was to apply the brakes and steer for the side of the track where he would be out of the way of passing cars. That his yellow BMW then drifted for a while down the track was evidence that Denny—'The Bear', as the 56-year-old was known—was no longer in control. Racing drivers are now required to have annual ECGs when they reapply for their racing licences. The conditions that day had been appalling. The Bear's countryman and good friend Jim Richards was awarded the Bathurst 1000 win on countback after crashing at the top of the mountain. Folklore has it that he was told of Hulme's death just before he mounted the victory dais to give his infamous 'You're a pack of arseholes' response to the baying crowd beneath, who were incensed that he'd won in a Nissan, but that's not how it happened. Richards told me he was informed quietly almost as soon as Hulme's incident occurred. 'I knew about his death at the next driver change. They said, "We think he's passed away." I said, "Shit." I didn't shed a tear. I was just grateful for the time he'd spent with us.' Sitting in his Melbourne workshop, surrounded by trophies and cars, Richards looked wistful even as he said the words.

Two years later Melbourne trucking company owner Don Watson—his big semis are still on the road today—fell prey to the unthinkable. The very safety device that had been installed to save lives was where he lost his. It's thought his brakes exploded. Instead of turning right off Conrod and into the Chase he went straight ahead, never looking like turning. The speed of his car was so great that it managed to surf across the top of the sand trap that had been installed to impede velocity. On the other side was a concrete retaining wall—gone now—surrounded by tyres intended to absorb energy on impact. Nothing worked for him and Watson died. Watson was the ultimate enthusiast, and it could be argued one of the last of the breed. He paid his own bills; he made his own way in the sport. The Mountain had become his obsession. He'd had three attempts in the previous three years and his eighth place on his second try, against the best touring-car drivers in Australia, had given him incentive to come back again.

Six months before Watson's death a double fatality at the top of Mount Panorama broke the heart of the race organiser who had tried so hard to resurrect the spirit of motorcycle racing on the Mountain. Vince Tesoriero had done his best with the 12 Hour production car race. He had found sponsorship, cajoled manufacturers, secured television coverage. He'd done everything possible but the immense cost of mounting the event had worn him down. The 1994 race at Mount Panorama was likely to be his last, he felt, and he would retreat to the more economic Eastern Creek (Sydney Motorsport Park) for one last try the following year. But Tesoriero was first and foremost a motorcycle fan. That's where his heart lay. While other people saw the bike races he ran in conjunction with the 12 Hour as the support categories, he saw them as the equal main event. He'd done everything possible to bring the bikes back to Bathurst. A new Australian invention—an inflatable safety fence that would protect the bikes from the harsh steel and concrete walls built for cars—was installed at key places around the mountain.

It was a mammoth effort because the fences had to be removed again for the car racers.

There were few of the huge names of the past—although the ageless Bill Horsman did turn up to win in the Classic historic races—but in 1992 and 1993 the small number of races Tesoriero held for bikes were a success. He had also secured the Australian Sidecar TT. The sidecars best suited what was essentially a car race meeting. In 1994, in the final sidecar event of the meeting, Ballarat team Jim Colligan and Ian Thornton ran wide at McPhillamy Park and skimmed across the top of the sand trap. Their speed was so great that when they hit the fence they ricocheted back onto the track, where they were struck by following riders. Neither survived. The race was stopped; the meeting was in danger of being abandoned. The silence was immense.

Ultimately they ran the last two races but there was no joy in it. Tesoriero never ran a motorcycle race again.

October 2006 was the Peter Brock tribute meeting at Bathurst. The top of the Mountain was festooned with floral tributes. Homemade banners were raised and the concrete wall along Skyline was a patchwork of fans' signatures, each a personal recollection. New Zealand racer Mark Porter had been born in 1974, two years after Brock's first Bathurst 1000 win, and he grew up during the years of Brock's dominance. He raced for the first time in the 1000 in 2002 and his best result had been three years later when he finished eleventh in a Commodore, knocking on the door of the top ten.

In 2006 Porter was to drive the second car in the main event for Brad Jones Racing, but he was also committed to the V8 Supercar development series in which, after fourteen races, he was lying third, with four events remaining. In the dip on the way into McPhillamy Park Porter's car went sideways, was clipped by a following competitor, and a third vehicle impacted with his driver's door. The driver of that car did all he could, getting it sideways so the point of contact was not a full T-bone. Porter was airlifted to Sydney's Royal Prince Alfred Hospital, where he lay critically injured as Garry Coleman delivered his Brock eulogy. He died later that afternoon. His Bathurst 1000 race car, driven by Michael Caruso who was hurriedly drafted, and with his name still on its side, retired from the race on lap 59.

14

A Day at the Races

Big venues cry out for expressions of unofficial public participation. Some people travel to Milan just so they can sing on the steps of La Scala. Others, while in Athens, make a beeline for the 1896 Olympic stadium, the first of the modern era, to run a lap of the track.

It had to happen. It's not possible to have a racetrack on your doorstep and not make use of it. Brian Nightingale and his mates from Bathurst Technical College couldn't let the chance go by. Mount Panorama was too enticing: 'Occasionally, just occasionally we'd go out there on our lunch break,' the highly regarded committee member of the Bathurst Light Car Club admitted. 'We'd line up on Pit Straight and have a Le Mans start'—where the drivers, on one side of the track, sprint to their cars on the other. 'It would only ever be one lap, and we wouldn't stop at the pits. We'd keep going straight past Hell Corner and up the escape road to Barry Gurdon Drive and then onto the Blayney Road, where we'd disperse.' According to Nightingale, up to twenty cars were involved each time, but that could be an exaggeration of memory. 'Anyway, it all came to an end when one of the blokes—now an equally well-respected business owner in Bathurst—rolled his FJ Holden in the Dipper.'

The drive-in movie theatre on Conrod Straight put paid to night racing. 'Until they built the drive-in, we were pretty right for a night-time lap,' Nightingale said. 'But the police used to enjoy the movies so they'd sit out there watching the screen while waiting for us to come along.' Colour TV killed the drive-in, but by the early 1980s, when the Conrod theatre (essentially just a single screen in a paddock) shut its gates, Nightingale and his mates had grown up and discovered responsibility.

In 2017—a lifetime later—two young drivers had their licences suspended for six months and each was fined $2350 for doing 126 kilometres per hour down Conrod. It's a 60 zone. One was in a Toyota Prado and the other in a Nissan Navara, neither of them hoon-mobiles. The incident rated major coverage in Bathurst's *Western Advocate*, and police provided the paper with a screen grab of their radar readout.

'I always used to get into the races for free,' confessed Michael O'Shea, who grew up to become the police inspector in charge of the region's highway patrol, and a key participant in the policing of the Mountain. 'We kids would ride our pushbikes through the uni [then Bathurst TAFE], cross the creek and sneak in under the fence. We could even make money out of it. Empty soft-drink bottles had a redeemable value and we'd collect them.' There was a lot to be said for growing up in a country town in the 1950s. There was much more freedom. Unsupervised responsibility was not something discussed between parent and child; it was an unsaid expectation. Kids were left to their own devices to test the boundaries. 'About halfway along Pit Straight there was a willow tree, and you could climb it and edge out along the branches so the motorcycles actually went by underneath you.'

O'Shea and his mates—most of them students at 'Stannies' (St Stanislaus' College) just down the road from the Mountain—got to know race secretary Jack Hinxman and his wife Tottie, and later Ivan and Leonie Stibbard, pretty well. Hinxman always tried to get along with the townsfolk, and Stibbard would walk the streets armed with tickets to hand to the locals. When they were young, Hinxman would turn Michael and his friends into program sellers. Mount Panorama gave them early life experiences. 'I was there when the Alfa went into the crowd at the bottom of Conrod,' O'Shea said, recalling the 1955 tragedy. And he was there again, as a teenager, to witness Bevan Gibson's fatality.

Neither dampened his desire to drive fast cars and ride powerful motorbikes. Motor racing, costly beyond imagination, wasn't an option. Joining the police was. 'I had an open door to Mini Cooper S, Torana XU-1 and Falcon GT.' There was also a Triumph Thunderbird 750 twin.

'Some of my earliest memories are in town,' O'Shea said. 'I was standing on the town hall steps when those idiots tried to blow up the Carillon and then went on to stone the police station. I was a kid and I actually saw them putting dynamite under the Carillon.'

Bad behaviour is a questionable by-product of many entertainment events, but for many years it threatened to define racing at Mount Panorama.

In the beginning it was benign, a spot of good fun. Peter Whitehead's 1938 bonfire was about as rowdy as it got. In the 1950s the car crowd did nothing more outrageous than shoving newfangled wet-weather tyres in the shower to see if they worked, or carrying tiny racing Mini Minors into the reception areas of hotels to observe with hilarity their owners' attempts to get them back out. The serious saloon and sports-car racers, and especially some of the early long-distance race competitors, tended to stay at the Canobolas Hotel in Orange, well out of harm's way, so they could properly warm up their cars on the early-morning 60-kilometre drive to the circuit. The motorcyclists camped around town, mostly down on the sportsground and along the river. The Mountain was a place to race but the facilities at the top of the track were rudimentary—not conducive to camping. It wasn't just about accommodation. After the racing, there was nothing to do up there. If you were looking for a bit of action, the city was the place to be.

'In the early 1960s, both sides of William Street would be packed with bikes, and the centre of the road would have another line of them as well,' Michael O'Shea recalled. For a young enthusiast like O'Shea it was exciting—some of the most desirable motorcycles in the world came to Bathurst not only to race but to show off, and their owners were bike-proud and happy to chat.

But then, somehow, it changed, and no one really knows why. The attempt to blow up the carillon war memorial in 1960 understandably captured significant media attention; the running of a Japanese flag up the town's flagpole in 1965, at a time when memories of World War II were still comparatively fresh, was another flashpoint. On the upside, the crowds were spending a lot of money in the town. But the atmosphere was becoming uncomfortable. Unruly crowd behaviour and confrontations with police, far from being unusual, became expected.

Discussions between Bathurst City Council, race promoters and the police determined it would be better for all concerned to move the mayhem to the Mountain. That began a comedy of crowd containment as authorities and so-called experts, some of them working with grants from universities and utility companies to produce grand white papers, applied solutions. In truth, every one of them was nothing more than an experiment. For every point, a counterpoint was made: 'What if we held rock concerts at the top?' 'No, that would only excite them—better to let them get quietly wasted and pass out.' For some time every committee meeting of the Auto Cycle Union was distracted from the job of organising racing and Arthur Blizzard would have to bring the agenda back on track. There were no experts on crowd control on this committee. 'I wish,' an exasperated Blizzard told me, 'that we could run the meeting for the competitors. I'd rather have a few thousand people only watching at the top of the Mountain, and just break even, than go through this drama.' Strangely his words were echoed almost 40 years later by

Roland Dane: 'The Americans have the right attitude: shut the gate and run the race only for family and friends.'

It was necessary only to look at the US, and to a lesser degree the Le Mans 24 Hour race, to put the crowd issue at Mount Panorama into international perspective. The Snake Pit behind Turn One at the Indy 500 had been a problem for organisers for years. The Bog at the Watkins Glen Formula One circuit was a cesspool. At Le Mans anybody sensible, especially if they're driving a good car, knows to stay clear of the Houx roundabout and away from the village of Arnage. Indy solved its problem by building grandstands in the place where the kids used to rampage. Watkins Glen closed down. Le Mans endures, but unless there's an escalation, the hijinks remain pretty tame. Mount Panorama was not unique, but it felt that way.

Throughout the mid-1970s and into the '80s 'bikie riots' at Bathurst became as predictable a newspaper headline as the first great white shark sighting of summer.

The problem wasn't restricted to the bikes. Long after the bikes were gone from the Mountain, promoters of the Bathurst 500 and 1000 were beset by the same challenges. In certain ways it was worse—an escalation—and it wasn't until Supercars Australia took over the organisation of their own race that radical policing measures were put in place to make the Mountain family-friendly.

In 1979 police built a brick station house at the top of the Mountain, right on the perimeter of the racetrack between Reid and McPhillamy Parks. It wasn't received well. Within moments, a simple place to hang your hat and receive visitors had become, in media speak, a 'compound', with all the connotations of confrontation. 'Why go into a rats' nest with a piece of cheese?'

was the reaction of Vince Tesoriero. 'I was horrified when they built the Compound—even more so when they brought in the police Tactical Response Group [with riot shields and batons]. It was a gross overreaction. Yes, there was unruly behaviour, but there were no guns. No one was knifing each other.'

Tesoriero had a partial solution. He began running the Bathurst Rally, a shout-out to legitimate touring motorcyclists to participate in one of the several long-distance events that carry with them a badge of participation—an actual medallion to be pinned to a rider's Barbour oilskin clothing. The rallies exist to this day—the annual Alpine, down to Australia's Snowy Mountains, and the Barry Sheene Tribute Ride, to the Australian Motorcycle Grand Prix at Phillip Island. The Bathurst Rally went to O'Connell, 25 kilometres out of town, and participants could ride or bus in every day.

Tesoriero had firsthand experience of those who contrived to live on the wild side. He'd assisted Australian cinematographer Sandy Harbutt in his production of the 1970s cult bikie movie *Stone* (in which an undercover cop works inside a bikie gang to discover who is murdering its members). The motorcycle industry was convinced Marlon Brando's *Wild One* had spawned the cult of outlaw bike gangs. *Stone* just reinforced it.

Michael O'Shea wasn't so certain: 'There was a group of hardened criminals from south-west Victoria who'd turn up each year to stir the crowd.' O'Shea had returned to Bathurst in 1983 after postings throughout New South Wales. He was a sergeant in the highway patrol and was soon promoted to inspector. 'I was in charge of the day shift at Mount Panorama. Some said that was the easy job—but it wasn't (because they were waking up mean).' O'Shea is a proud citizen of Bathurst and a rusted-on motorsport man, so on a number of levels it hurt him to witness the disrespect of some members of the crowd towards the Mountain. 'We had to meet fire with fire,' he said. 'It was the only alternative.'

The year after the Compound was built, it was surrounded by a new high wire fence—walls had been built around the castle—and to top it off it was illuminated by floodlights. There had never been a more obvious target. 'We had one cheeky young bloke come in to ask, "What time does the riot start?"' O'Shea recalled. 'I said, "For you, it's over—come in here."'

It's important to get the geography in perspective. In those days, there were perhaps 10,000 people camped on top of Mount Panorama. Five hundred metres from the Compound, campers were sleeping. But there was a ring of 'rioters' around the enclosure. Some were serious—carrying rocks, bottles, petrol-soaked rags that they could light and throw. But for every committed participant there were ten more who were playing a game of tip-the-dragon. They'd run in for their adrenaline rush and then scamper away again. How many were there? A few hundred, maybe a thousand. By no means was the top of the Mountain consumed by riot, as the media implied. The police were, in the main, volunteers. 'They were understaffed, so there had to be a show of force. They had to be proactive,' O'Shea said. 'Some police may have overstepped the mark.' After one night of baton charging, more than three-quarters of the 80 or so tactical response police reported they'd suffered injuries.

The low point of the 'riots' was the overturning and immolation of a Channel Seven news van. It remains controversial. Even some from the side of the authorities believe it was a set-up—the van brought to the Mountain to be sacrificial, its road cases nothing more than black painted cardboard boxes. 'I saw it go down,' Tesoriero recalled. 'They removed the cameras and tripods and egged the crowd on.'

Getting to the top of the Mountain was a trial. First there were the official entry gates up Barry Gurdon Drive, the spectator road to the top, where police stopped and searched entrants. 'Official' observation conducted for university white papers alleged motorcyclists were monstered while car drivers were allowed relatively free passage. Charges were laid and court appearances occurred; the Bathurst Courthouse was desecrated.

In the archives of the Bathurst Regional Council is a long-forgotten letter. In 1976, the town clerk received a cheque for $100 from the St George Motorcycle Club in Sydney: 'Our members feel very close to the City of Bathurst, they consider it the mecca of motorcycling in Australia. We were appalled at the disgusting act which took place at the Courthouse during the Easter weekend. They feel they would like to contribute in this small way towards the restoration work.' The letter lies in a dusty file. Perhaps it should have been framed and promoted, because the carnage continued.

On Bathurst 1000 days, it was impossible to drive to the top of the Mountain without being confronted by a gang just before the Reid Park entrance gate, who'd pour water or oil on the road and demand that that the driver 'smoke the bags'. Refusal to comply could lead to their car being stoned; it's incredible that it happened only a few hundred metres from the police inspection point.

It was not a good look. Something had to give.

Damien Codognotto, the politically savvy spokesperson for the Victorian-formed Motorcycle Riders Association, had been vocal in his criticism of the conditions: 'They treat us like animals,' he said. As much as his voice rankled those in charge, he was right. Council responded and, as toilets and shower blocks went up, the Compound began to dismantle. 'I took great pride when I came back to Bathurst to promote the Bathurst 12 Hour, and with [Council engineer] Peter Gannon we used a pair of wire-cutters to pull the fence down,' Tesoriero said.

Policing methods changed.

Police went on foot patrol and spectators were welcomed into what had been tightly held police areas. But the campers had to have their fun. Even as alcohol restrictions were put in place, committed campers made a preliminary trip to the Mountain to bury their cache of alcohol under trees, to be retrieved on race weekend. 'We walked past one tent and I called out loudly, "Love the smell of the coffee." The place reeked of rum,' O'Shea said.

A new police area was built at the back of Reid Park, just behind the TV transmission towers, with a big open front yard 'where police and spectators could talk equally rather than across a desktop'. The area still has a large storage shed for response vehicles, including a mobile water cannon. The Compound finally became an ambulance room.

And yet—the troubles continued.

When IMG took over the running of the Bathurst 1000 from the ARDC in 1997, Shane Howard introduced an immediate edict—no female member of his organising staff was to go to the top of the Mountain. 'Some of it was scary,' he said. 'We'd sit in race control at night and watch the dust and the lights from the bullring, the centre of mayhem, and hear the explosions when they were trying to blow up the toilet blocks.

'After that first 1000 we went to clean up and found 21 burnt-out cars in the bullring where they'd done their donuts.' Their owners had brought the cars to Mount Panorama as paddock bashers with the express intention of torching them.

It had gotten so bad that even the regular campers were staying away. Over the years huge encampments had grown up, each with their own name and character—Smarty's Circus, Pygmy's Palace, Stumpy's Castle, The No Shit Hotel, and the more recent Camp Drinkalot. For all their evocative names, they were legitimate havens of genuine enthusiasts, mainly but not exclusively male, who'd made a tradition of meeting on the Mountain.

'I came to my first V8 race in 1971,' said Glenn Quinlan, whose Holden is decaled as a homage to Brock's 05 and each year sits in a circle-your-wagons compound of similar vehicles. Quinlan still comes to Bathurst, now with his son Brock (there are many young Brocks on the Mountain), and he has seen the best and worst of the madness. 'I first came here when I was seventeen and I still remember Moffat's 351 Cleveland up through the Cutting. It was a mighty engine and a mighty car.' One of his great memories is of the two 24 Hour races—'the headlights coming at us in the middle of the night in the drizzling rain—every aspect of it was mind blowing'. And the friends, too. He pointed out Pat Brennan's caravan in the corner of their circle. It was early morning and it was still locked, with Brennan asleep inside. 'Pat's been coming here every year since 1968. He's only missed one race—when he got married.' Quinlan's look says it all—why hadn't he chosen another date? Quinlan had seen 'the idiots who'd charge through the campground doing donuts'. It was like 'a war zone', he said. Then there was the designated area called the bullring where cars and bikes would race and do donuts. 'The cops would come around and we'd point it out to them, but their reaction would be: "Go over there? Are you *nuts*?"' There's a certain sense of nostalgia as he speaks. In all the time he'd been going up the Mountain 'there's been no theft, no damage'. But, on balance, it was good it had been cleaned up.

'It was the Peter Brock memorial meeting in 2006 that gave us the resolve to finally fix the top of the Mountain,' Shane Howard said. 'There was a massive attendance that year to pay tribute to Peter. It brought a lot of people back to the Mountain from different eras. People were devastated and they all came to pay respect. They saw a Mount Panorama they'd not known before. We'd opened the new pit building and so the venue had changed. It felt different.

'It was at that moment we realised that our motorsport community is truly a family. It gave us the confidence to do what we knew had to be done.' From a strictly financial standpoint, organisers had equivocated. They'd seen what had happened two decades before when the bikes had cracked down on their crowd—it had been the death of the race meeting. So they sought consensus with their crowd.

'We made them part of the solution. We got a lot of feedback from the campers. It turned out they didn't want a rogue presence putting their event in jeopardy.'

And then Supercars struck, with 'a massively increased police presence, more than 200; sniffer dogs, riot squad, 130 private security people. We thought it was overkill, but in hindsight it was the best for the event'. There were 160 arrests in 2007, equal to the most ever at a Mount Panorama motorcycle weekend (back in 1985). An attempt by the rogue element to damage the TV transmission towers was thwarted. An alcohol policy of one carton per person per day was introduced; anything more than that was confiscated from cars on the way in, returnable on exit. Organisers paid $350,000 towards the cost of the action. It was money well spent.

And they kept the pressure up. Each year the police operation got a code name. In 2009 it was Operation Brock. That year 56 people were charged with 87 offences and ten cannabis cautions were issued. Significantly, 43 people were banned from the event. Ten years on, arrests had diminished to just three people—none from the top of the Mountain. One was a charge of offensive behaviour against a racegoer who called Australia's prime minister, Scott Morrison, a 'f—ing muppet'.

In December 1996, Bathurst's first FM station began transmission. It calls itself B-Rock FM. 'Brock did a lot of good for our community, not just for the Mountain,' veteran broadcaster Kerry Peck, one of Bathurst's 200 Living Legends, said. 'Ron Camplin, owner of both the AM and FM station in the city, came up with the idea [for the name] and Brock agreed.' Peck led the team that conducted Camplin's first-ever live broadcast of The Great Race. He clocked up 50 years with the station in the same year Brock's debut drive was celebrated.

Peter Brock was the first of only three racing drivers to be anointed as an Honorary Citizen of Bathurst. He received his key to the city just three months before Allan Moffat. Both were 37 years ahead of Craig Lowndes. It's significant that of the only eighteen Honorary Citizenships ever bestowed, nine were directly related to The Great Race. Arthur Blizzard and Harry Bartrop got it for motorcycles, and Jack Hinxman for cars; the other three, spread over fourteen years, were all related to one sponsor, James Hardie Industries—its chairman John Reid, and operatives George Hibbert and Jim Kelso.

The contribution of motor racing to the city of Bathurst is substantial. The Bathurst Region Economic Development Strategy 2018–2022 talks the circuit up: 'In 2009,' the strategy reported, 'the four events that were held in that year contributed $29.3 million in value added to the Bathurst economy when flow-on effects are taken into account.' That year, Mount Panorama activities made up 1.9 per cent of the gross regional product and, significantly, 19 per cent of the total contribution from tourism to the Bathurst economy.

Bathurst Regional Council Mayor Graeme Hanger is concerned the race is becoming too remote from the city, and it's affecting the economy. 'Supercars have moved everything from the town to the Mountain,' he said. It's a valid point. With the exception of accommodation, the Mountain is so well catered with food, beverage and merchandise that there's little incentive for racegoers to visit the city. Few local caterers get a look-in at the catering rights. The days of the local car club providing the beer truck and having the concession for sales have long gone. 'The last time the V8s came to town was in the days of Brock and Moffat,' Hanger asserted. 'We want them back so we can draw crowds back into town.' He held no immediate fears for the safety of the carillon.

In 2019 Hanger arranged for the major participants in the Bathurst 12 Hour to drive from the circuit for a civic reception in front of the city's Heroes' Walk, the expanse of footpath outside the Council chambers in which the name of each Great Race winner is cast in bronze. It was well attended, and marked the beginning of what Hanger is determined will become a matter of noblesse oblige for the Supercar fraternity.

Hanger is using the Mountain to good advantage. His Council bid for and won the rights to host the World Cross Country Championships in 2021. 'The key reason for Bathurst being awarded the event was the infrastructure already in place for the regular motor racing at Mount Panorama,' said the International Association of Athletics Federations. Hanger was cock-a-hoop that Elton John had chosen Bathurst as the regional base for his farewell concert in 2020.

Mount Panorama is far more than a venue for the Bathurst 1000.

Mike Pilbeam, the most prolific constructor of hill climb cars in the world, with seventeen British Championship victories to his credit, was in awe of the circuit. On the drive into Bathurst, in 1996, he insisted on stopping on the Great Western Highway so he could take in the majesty of the Mountain. Pilbeam had accepted an invitation to enter his car in the Australian Hill Climb Championship. He brought with him former British champion Alister Douglas-Osborn, but it was local driver Peter Finlay who stormed the car to second place just 0.03 seconds behind Peter Gumley, who claimed the first of his record ten national title victories. A slightly missed gear change on Finlay's part was all it took.

Run by the Bathurst Light Car Club, which is allowed to conduct limited activities on the track as long as they do not use the full circuit, Mount Panorama features two of the best hill climb courses in Australia: one that climbs 750 metres up the Esses from the top of Conrod to above Skyline, and the other that starts on the crest of Mountain Straight and ends 1700 metres later at Sulman Park. The Mountain Straight climb is the fastest in Australia.

Malcolm Oastler, one of Australia's Formula One design and engineering success stories who retired back home when he was chief engineer of Jaguar F1, holds the record on the Mountain Straight circuit. He drives a self-made OMS 28, an English carbon-fibre tub that he has fitted up with all the suspension and aerodynamic aids his considerable skill has conceived. 'The car weighs 305 kilograms and develops 350 horsepower [260 kW] from a turbocharged Suzuki Hayabusa engine,' Oastler told me from his farm at Bega on the NSW South Coast. 'It has a rear wing bigger than a bucket from a D9 Caterpillar, and a front wing and diffuser to match. It's probably got more downforce than a Formula One car.'

So what's it like to drive on the Mountain? 'It's like riding a cannonball. It's 300 metres from the start to Griffin's Bend, and by the time it gets there it's maxing in fifth gear at 260 kilometres per hour. Take fourth and then back to fifth for the run up to the Cutting. Because of the torque you take the Cutting in fourth at 7500 rpm, then back to fifth for another 260 before you ease off slightly to finish at 220 kilometres per hour. It's always accelerating—so you rush into corners. It's just a case of hanging on.'

His *average* speed from a standing start on that course is just under 170 kilometres per hour. Oastler would be 60 when he tried for his fifth Australian Hill Climb Championship at Mount Panorama just after the Bathurst 1000 in 2019. Then, he thought, he might consider retirement.

The Bathurst Light Car Club, inaugurated in 1953, had been the home of sprints and hill climbs, including four national titles, each made incredibly special because of its venue. Its fully owned clubhouse perched on the inside of Forrest's Elbow, with its entrance gates dedicated to legends Lex Davison and Tom Sulman, was once the home of motorsport over the Blue Mountains. It's where you'd find engineers and drivers who performed well above expectation. George Reed, son of a local funeral director, dedicated his life to building and racing homemade specials. When his dad, Cam, died, Reed had some investment properties built and retired to his shed to indulge his passion. His best-known car, a flathead Ford, won the 1951 Australian Grand Prix at Narrogin in Western Australia, driven by Bathurst local Warwick Pratley. Fitted with two seats and lights, it was also used by Reed's wife Norma as her shopping car. Reed and a panelbeater from nearby Orange, Brian Keegan, built one of Australia's first slingshot dragsters, a supercharged V8 they called 'The Monster', and for five years it was the Australian champion. Reed drove in the very first Mount Panorama meeting and was honoured as Grand Marshal of the Bathurst International Motor Festival at Easter 2006, three years before his death.

Bathurst's citizens contributed a lot. Barry Gurdon threw his workshop open to enthusiasts and Bill Chadwick, the Light Car Club's first president, built his Vauxhall 30/98 special there (in touring version, its value today exceeds $300,000). Rex Ellis, Gurdon's business associate and brother-in-law, was one of those instrumental in securing the ARDC to take over Mount Panorama. The pioneers and their cars form an important part of the National Motor Racing Museum at the bottom of Conrod Straight.

'In the early days of racing, the Club was deeply involved in the running of the Easter and October meetings,' Brian Nightingale recalled. 'We'd provide many of the officials, take care of catering on top of the Mountain, even sweep the circuit at night to get it ready for the next day's racing.'

But those days have passed.

'We're poor second-grade citizens,' the Bathurst Club's current president Mick Tuckey said, only slightly tongue-in-cheek. 'The big race meetings have nothing to do with us, and contribute nothing to us.' The Club, which was once the engine room of racing on the Mountain, had become at best an auxiliary. Like most clubs in the internet age, it had a tough time maintaining momentum. Although it boasts 403 members, it's 'as if we've missed a generation', and Tuckey had to work hard at times to raise a quorum at club meetings. Tuckey's committee was concentrating on road safety in part to attract a new generation of membership. A motorkhana course on the back face of Mount Panorama was available to local youngsters to learn driving skills. The Club even had several cars that it hired out at $5 a try, 'just enough to pay for the petrol', but it required parents and guardians to come along to supervise and that was proving a struggle.

Tuckey was very aware of the Club's heritage and hopeful that a proposed new circuit on the Mountain would provide an opportunity for more proactive involvement.

'Peter Brock was one of our members,' he told me, almost as an afterthought.

15

Virtual Reality and Real Legends

Half a century ago, at the dawn of the computer age, respected American magazine *Road & Track* published a speculative story about an Indy 500 race run without drivers and controlled by algorithms that could artificially devise real-life challenges. It was sci-fi. *Road & Track* observed that the missing link in its scenario was the heroes.

Twenty-two-year-old Matthew Bink is the Mount Panorama champion few people have heard of. He has lapped the 6.213-kilometre circuit in a time equal to Greg Murphy's Lap of the Gods, he has kissed the concrete walls with the panels of his VF Commodore, and he has withstood immense pressure to win by less than 0.2 seconds.

Bink is Supercars Australia's e-racing challenge winner, and he has laid down a benchmark for future competition that, in terms of active driver participation, has already grown to numbers that are 200 times greater than the real Bathurst 1000.

'Supercars was once an events-based company that had a media arm,' CEO Sean Seamer told me. 'Now we are a media company that does events.' It is an astounding change of primary focus that may shock traditionalists to their bump stops, but it might point to the future of motor racing—not only at Mount Panorama but globally.

'It's part of the pillar of our future strategy,' said Supercars head of television and content Nathan Prendergast, a man who grow up with a Formula Vee in his backyard to drive when he got home from school. (His Dad, Kevin, was general manager of Eastern Creek Raceway and the racetrack was young Nathan's playground.) 'Most sporting audiences are getting older. E-racing gives us access to a younger audience.'

E-racing, sometimes called sim racing (for 'simulator'), is do-it-yourself living-room racing. All you need is a computer, an off-the-shelf game package, a hand controller—or, if you have the money, a full-on seat, steering wheel and pedal box rig—and you're a racer, with all the thrills and none of the expense or the risk. It's not new; it's been around for at least fifteen years. But the increases in available bandwidth and internet speeds have made what was once a clunky arcade game so accurate that real racers are using it to learn circuits and sharpen their skills. Mount Panorama is one of the top ten circuits in the e-racing world.

Supercars put a 'toe in the e-water' in 2017 when they invited eight virtual racers to the Mount Panorama pits to compete online against V8 drivers. They put the challenge to air on their internet channel and it drew more viewers than the Bathurst 1000 qualifier. In 2018 they took it to the next level, established a dedicated set and had one of their best young on-air Supercars talents, Chad Neylon, host it. Racers entered online and qualified in a knock-out competition; their races were called live, just like the real thing. Incredibly, 5000 virtual racers entered the Mount Panorama qualification rounds.

The following year Supercars got really serious. They scoured the world and found the very best platform to host their challenge. 'There's the opportunity for more cameras, better perspective, much better graphics,' Prendergast enthused.

Sean Seamer is quick to offer perspective. 'E-racing is what we can give our fan base when we don't have real racing happening,' he said. It's incremental, not substitutional.

One of the smartest things Supercars did within three years of taking direct control of Mount Panorama's 1000-kilometre race was to launch its own broadcast production. Supercars Media produces over 1800 hours of live and post-produced content annually in 97 countries with a reach, it said, of 232 million households. The figures aren't rubbery, just hard to accept in their enormity. Since the dawn of the Mountain, media have been served up crowd figures that have been decidedly optimistic.

But, according to Prendergast, the Supercheap Auto Bathurst 1000 in 2018 was watched by an average Sunday Australian audience of 1.722 million, which peaked at 2.4 million as Craig Lowndes crossed the line for his seventh victory.

They do it well, despite the bleating of their online critics—paradoxically, using platforms that Supercars have created. By 2018 The Great Race had won a near-record seven Logie Awards for Outstanding Sports Coverage, surpassed only by the AFL. The real metrics lie in the new media of page views, Facebook and Twitter impressions, and apps opened. For its one race at Mount Panorama, Supercars Media registered 4.7 million page views on its own sites, 31 million Facebook impressions and 5.2 million video views. 'When we last negotiated our media partnerships, digital rights were a minor part of the deal,' Prendergast told me. 'You could mount an argument now that they are worth more than the terrestrial rights.'

'When I first came to Mount Panorama as a camera operator, we laid 600 metres of really heavy multicore cable from the Castrol Tower at Skyline back to McPhillamy Park one way and to the Dipper the other,' said Ian 'Fish' O'Brien, who first covered racing at the Mountain in 1973. 'And each morning we'd find the bastards at the top of the hill had cut them up. We ended up with three 100-metre cables, which was as far as we could shoot.' O'Brien is one of the long-term core-coverage team that holds the knowledge of how to present the Mountain at its demanding best. He's called Fish because in 1964 he won gold at the Tokyo Olympics in the 200-metre breaststroke and set a new world record. The Japanese concept of *kaizen*—constant improvement—is not top of his mind but he's impressed when he sees it happen.

'When I walk into the Gearhouse truck [the central outside broadcast unit] I'm amazed at how director Brian Forshaw cuts the race. He's got 32 track cameras, speciality cameras in-ground and on the walls, in-car cameras in twelve cars, choppers. There must be 30 or 40 monitors in front of him.' O'Brien was one of two directors at Mount Panorama in the 1970s. When he covered the top of the Mountain from Griffin's Bend to halfway down Conrod, and another director had the bottom, the cut was sequential. 'My very first job as a cameraman was on top of the Castrol Tower. In the very early days there were no cameras further down the hill so they used to give that camera position an extension lens [a telephoto], which would allow it to follow the cars down Conrod. The camera shake, especially in a wind, was unbelievable.'

New technology continues to amaze him. 'Time was, the best long-distance lens I had was a 13:1. Now we're shooting on 107:1.' The constant quest for higher resolution (in one respect, to keep pace with what's available on e-gaming) is putting more, not less, pressure on operators. Iris openings are narrowing, even in bright sunlight, and a 'camo' has to be on his or her game to keep focus.

'I loved the top of the Mountain,' he said. 'When we drove up the top we'd load the back of the van with beer so when the boys in the crowd pulled us up we'd say, "Have a beer" and they'd let us through. It was like having a day pass. At night we'd sit up there and watch them play "fire footy". One time there was a guy—drunk—who lay on the ground with a plank over his chest and invited the boys on their bikes to ride over him. It was a bit crazy.'

O'Brien had been at the forefront of a health-and-safety upgrade to build proper metal camera platforms, not 'scaffolds made out of timber planks'. 'I remember back in 1982 when [camera operator] John De Ruvo faced down the full force of Kevin Bartlett's upside-down Camaro after he'd blown a tyre. We gave him a round of applause at the after-race party and laughed about it. I think we're a lot better off today.'

British-based Rebecca Jones, one of the smartest communications operators in global motorsport, views e-racing as a threat to motor racing as much as an asset. 'In 2016, 16.5 million people watched sim racing around the world,' she said in the media centre of the Bathurst 12 Hour where she was shepherding the interests of two international brands. She set a frenetic pace. Her team of six was constantly producing content—written, verbal and visual—and punching it out on multiple internet platforms to a worldwide audience.

These days media centres, once a relaxed space where journalists like Mike Kable could visit the pits and write their considered race reports, have become content-central and there is not much time for contemplation. In the manufacturer's mix of promotional opportunities, Jones told me, 'Gaming is becoming increasingly important. It's no secret that manufacturers are all looking for innovative and cost-efficient ways to connect with their customers. Traditional motor racing, in the face of a fresh approach for a comparatively affordable price, is under threat', said Jones.

'The World Endurance Championship is struggling,' she said. Spanish Formula One driver Fernando Alonso had 'just bought a major share in a sim-racing company'.

Roland Dane pointed to the change in the automotive environment. 'The company spending the most money on motor racing in Australia isn't Holden or Ford,' he asserted. 'It's Toyota.' It's a shocking revelation, almost unbelievable, but it came from a team owner who should know. He was, after all, the official Holden Racing Team boss, having won the contract from the beleaguered Walkinshaw organisation two seasons before.

Dane's statement put in doubt the half-century tradition of the two majors—Holden and Ford—fighting out their race for sales supremacy on the contours of Mount Panorama. In truth, sales dominance for the two makes had long gone. When local manufacture of cars ceased in Australia at the end of 2017, Holden and Ford were the biggest losers. At the end of 2018 Ford was number five in the market and Holden was number six. Market leader Toyota was so ascendant that it was delivering 1.6 times the combined total of Ford and Holden's sales.

Clearly all bets were off. 'Toyota has its 86 series and its new rally team in the Australian Rally Championship,' Dane said. Its 86 Racing Series is a one-make category, ostensibly for aspiring youngsters, that runs as a support to Supercars and had created a mayhem of crashes at Mount Panorama. The combination of investment in those two events, Dane estimated, added up to more than Ford or Holden were spending on each of their works Supercars teams.

'Ford and Holden still tap into the passion that exists for them in The Great Race,' Dane said. 'Tribalism still exists. But these days you can drive up to Mount Panorama in your X5 [a BMW] and barrack for a Holden.'

Team owners could no longer rely on the new breed of car distributors. Today, Supercars franchise owners must use their

Holden and Ford alliances as a platform for companies, many of which are outside the motor industry—consumables, telcos and the like, Dane said.

'We need to fish where the fish are,' said Dane. 'We must cut our cloth according to the marketplace to ensure the Supercars racing industry can support itself.' He maintained the natural size of the series should be twelve events a year, not the sixteen it had in 2018 and the fifteen planned for the following year. Mount Panorama was at the top of his retention list. 'It underpins Australian touring-car racing just as Monaco does Formula One'. The challenge was to get that message to the marketplace.

'Supercars has the best social media platform in the world,' Dane said. 'Last year's Mount Panorama race resulted in six million minutes of video online.' (Actually, according to Nathan Prendergast's figures, it was 5,570,141 minutes.) E-racing was part of the Supercars platform. Dane supports the concept, even though he came to motor racing the old-fashioned way. 'I will never forget my first experience at Mount Panorama,' he said. 'I had Derek Warwick with me to co-drive with Peter Brock in the first 2-litre race. Derek was amazed at the number of people queuing for his autograph, and then he realised it was all for Brock.'

So what does the future hold? Dane laughs: 'Only liars know.'

Scott McLaughlin, 2018 Supercars champion and the youngest-ever winner of a Supercars race, is one of a growing band of professional drivers who e-race. 'I've raced F1's Lando Norris,' he said, with more than a bit of glee. Norris, promoted to Formula

One in his nineteenth year as McLaughlin was in Supercars, has several professional simulator rigs in his UK home and regularly goes online to challenge e-racers around the world. McLaughlin e-races to keep sharp. 'The experience is different to the real thing,' he said. 'There's not the same sounds and smells and you don't have the same g-forces. In e-racing a lot of the feel of the car comes through the steering wheel, whereas in real life it's through the seat of your pants.'

McLaughlin's race team, Dick Johnson's DJR Penske, has just installed a fully professional sim at its Gold Coast workshop to address some of those issues. The $100,000 bespoke rig has a hydraulically activated platform that moves on several axes to provide better real-time feel through a purpose-built carbon race seat. McLaughlin, his teammate Fabian Coulthard and their engineers use either a virtual reality headset or a bank of 55-inch surround-monitors, and their program developer has mapped every track on which they compete using data provided by Supercars. Mount Panorama is McLaughlin's favourite.

The key to virtual reality is a phenomenon called latency—the time it takes between the driver's input and the computer's reaction. Low latency is good and the best systems now measure reaction time in milliseconds. 'Ten to fifteen milliseconds of latency allows you to play well,' Sam Barker, Supercars' digital manager, said.

'I've raced an F1 car at Mount Panorama,' Supercars e-racing champion Matt Bink volunteered. 'It was a 2017 R.S.17 Renault and I lapped in just over 1 minute 30 seconds.' That's 19 seconds faster than Jenson Button's fastest lap in the McLaren, admittedly a demonstration car. Sim racing is supposed to replicate real life and, on the sim, Scott McLaughlin usually is tenths of a second within his lap times on the real track. So, implausibly, a lap of 1 minute 30 seconds sets up a lap average of 248 kilometres per hour, just shy of the Formula One lap record at the flat, ultra-fast Monza circuit in Italy—the fastest of all Formula One tracks. Split the difference and call Bink's time 1 minute 39 seconds (225 kilometres per hour) and that would still make Mount Panorama one of the top ten fastest Formula One tracks in the world. 'I crashed many times before I got to that time,' Bink confessed. 'And I'll bet Jenson had more fun.'

On his track walk for his first-ever race at Mount Panorama, Richard Davison, aged 64, climbed the safety fence at the Bathurst Light Car Club on top of Conrod and stood in contemplation before the monument erected to his father, Lex. It was 2018, 59 years since Lex had won the Australian Grand Prix on the Mountain, 53 since he had died at Sandown. The next year Richard made the pilgrimage again and then, full of determination, won his category in the Australian Formula Ford Championship in its fiftieth anniversary season, celebrating a half-century of the spindly-wheeled racing cars in Australia.

'I felt, in my own low-key way, I was completing a circle. I had become the last Davison in my direct line to win at Mount Panorama.' It couldn't have come soon enough. Richard worked out that the combined ages of the three young guns he beat didn't add up to his own.

Richard's two sons—Alex, named for his grandfather, and Will—have both stood on the top step of the podium at Mount Panorama. Will, the younger of the pair, has won two Bathurst

1000s; Alex clinched the 2004 Australian Carrera Cup title on the Mountain circuit. The brothers are close and occasionally race together, but motor racing is seldom amenable to sibling ambition. 'Their careers have taken them in different directions,' Richard said, 'and strangely, when one has been on a high, the other has been on a low.' Alex and Will entered motor racing not because of family tradition, nor because their father was 1980 Australian Formula Two champion. It was because of the father-and-son team of Frank and Craig Lowndes. 'We had just bought a factory outside Melbourne and Frank had a business opposite. He had a trailer parked outside with a sticker that said, "We support junior karting". The boys went across the road, met a very young Craig who was up the back of the workshop assembling a kart, and their careers were set.'

Will won his very first kart race from the back of the grid and then retired. '"I want to finish the cricket season," he told me,' Richard said. 'But he came back after that.' The Davison brothers are the first in their illustrious family to make a full-time living out of motorsport. They have paired three times in the Bathurst 1000; their best result was a fourth for the Erebus Mercedes-Benz team in 2014. On each occasion they'd made the family pilgrimage, stopping by the memorial to their grandfather.

In 2019, Will had arranged to bring Alex back for one more crack. The pair would share a new Ford Mustang in The Great Race. 'I don't want to get ahead of myself, but it feels like our best chance yet,' Will said. 'That would be the ultimate,' Richard concurred, 'to see them on the Mount Panorama podium together.'

VIRTUAL REALITY AND REAL LEGENDS

James Brock single-handedly won the Bathurst V8 race that time forgot. Peter and Bev Brock stood proudly in the background as the shy, ponytailed 23-year-old accepted the trophy for the rain-affected Bathurst V8 300 in October 1999. The race was a last-ditch effort of 2-litre touring-car racing at Mount Panorama to salvage a means of staving off the category's inevitable demise. The decision to run a V8 event as a support race to the Super Tourers had raised howls of protest from Tony Cochrane's fledgling Supercars operation. He needn't have bothered. Weather—arguably the worst Mount Panorama had seen over a full weekend—put paid to any lingering hopes of reprieve. Channel Seven had hired an external promoter, and it had decided to run a 500-kilometre race for Super Tourers and a three-hour race for V8s.

The fields for both events were not good, and the abysmal weather ensured neither went full distance. Paul Morris (BMW) won the 2-litre race—the last at the Mountain—after 310 kilometres, and James Brock covered just 236 kilometres in 2 hours 12 minutes to win the V8 event. James, who became Peter's adopted son while still a baby, had been racing just six months. It was an ambitious project to send him to Mount Panorama so early in his career, but it was James's decision, not his father's. 'He never wanted to be a motor-racing dad,' James recalled. 'There wasn't a lot of direction—but there was a lot of support.'

'I must admit I felt a bit of concern for James because of the difficulties of the conditions, in a brand-new car and the fact that he was still learning the circuit. But what a debut,' Peter told a TV audience that was quite healthy, even if the crowd at the circuit could have fitted into one pit bay. James and Peter would later share a V8 utility at Mount Panorama and they stood on the podium together, but it wasn't the 1000. So, in the pragmatic world of Bathurst 1000-racers, like a tree falling in a forest, did it really count?

Likewise James Moffat's second place in the 2014 Great Race. He missed the win by just four seconds. 'When he stood on the podium of Australia's Great Race—my race—I cried,' father Allan said.

'Throughout his childhood, all he wanted to be was a V8 Supercars driver. It's hard for people to grasp, but in most cases the name Moffat has been more a hindrance than a help. There's a weight of expectation that's unfair.' But to come second by 4 seconds? A generation ago that would have been a trigger for people in the Moffat camp to run for cover. Allan, the most competitive of all racers, would have been inconsolable.

There is no way to quantify a legend. Mere statistics don't do it. The Brabham name, simply, rises above all others in Australian motorsport. Brabham stands for Formula One. Say 'Brabham' and you think of a take-no-prisoners, hardest-of-hardcore racer, with the guts to pull together his own team, build his own car and claim it all for himself. When Jack Brabham raced at Mount Panorama, no one else mattered.

Any one of his three boys—two of them, anyway—could have been stars in their own right, and even Gary, the 'forgotten' brother, can claim some international victories and a brief if unsuccessful Formula One career. Geoff and David have each won the Le Mans 24 Hour race for Peugeot, a decade apart; raced at the top of the categories they chose; and in 1997 stood together on the Mount Panorama podium having whistled their BMW home first in the first 1000-kilometre 2-litre touring-car race. Brabhams—father and sons—had between them raced thirteen times in the Bathurst 1000, but the 1997 win is the only time any have stood on the podium for it. David has had a fourth, Geoff a fifth, Jack a sixth. It's not illustrious. But what do numbers matter?

It was late in the afternoon of final practice for the 2019 Bathurst 12 Hour and all was still. Campfires were beginning to burn across Reid Park and people had moved away from the fences. There was a distant high-pitched wail, growing louder, like some ghostly echo of 80 years of cars and motorcycles on the Mountain. There was no announcement and yet the flag marshals were still in position in anticipation. Listen to it on Mountain Straight—four shifts in succession, minimal hesitation and, with each one, the sound became greater. Like first-onset tinnitus, it invaded the senses.

And then suddenly it arrived in a rush—green and gold, Australia's racing colours, Jack Brabham's colours—and before it truly registered, it was past. The howl was unworldly. Every racing car has its own signature sound. Even the old V10 Formula One cars, spinning up to an ear-shattering 18,000 rpm, had distinguishing features. This was none of that—not a GT car, not a Supercar, not even a re-spool of the greatest sounds of Bathurst. This was unique, and made all the more compelling because the driver did not lift. The car was absolutely flat through Reid Park, across Sulman and into McPhillamy, planted to the ground by engineering that defied the laws of gravity, applied by a driver who was without fear.

And then, there it was on Conrod—flashing through the orchard, gathering speed, faster and faster, until it jinked right into the Chase, never hesitating until it dived deep under brakes into the left–right kink. This was the car David Brabham built in Jack's name—the Brabham BT62—and it stood for everything that was important in motor racing. It was the reason why virtual reality would always be an amusement and why, no matter what commercial constraints the car industry faced, drivers and engineers would always find a way to test their limits.

The last words go to Sean Seamer, like many CEOs, a man some may have suspected to be without a soul. 'This is the purpose of motor racing at Mount Panorama—to provide a unique and exhilarating experience,' he said. 'To fill our senses with sight and smell, to present an element of competition, to combine the best of man and machine. To be visceral.'

Epilogue

The Battle of Bathurst

The rock on which Mount Panorama rests was formed 50 million years ago, a granite outcrop above the rich loam of the Western Plains. It was a stroke of good fortune that its contours lent themselves to becoming, naturally, one of the world's greatest motor-racing circuits. Now its ongoing management needs to be as solid as the rock.

In the view of some local Aboriginal elders, including Dinawan Dyirribang (Bill Allen Jr), Mount Panorama should be known as Wahluu. It should pay the local Aboriginal community a royalty through public admission fees, and refer all future development for the joint agreement of traditional stakeholders.

A group of elders of the Wiradjuri nation—the predominant Aboriginal community in the NSW Central West—has succeeded in having the name Wahluu, meaning 'young man's initiation place', recognised by the NSW Geographic Names Register as an optional alternative for Mount Panorama, but the name does not confer any rights beyond that.

The elders have been pushing for greater consultation, using mechanisms inherent in NSW law to declare Wahluu an Aboriginal place, and requiring an Indigenous land use agreement with the Bathurst Regional Council, which owns much of the real estate on and surrounding the circuit.

'The Wiradjuri claim needs to be addressed.' Bathurst mayor Graeme Hanger's first words were unexpected as he bustled, late, into what the locals call the 'Seat of Knowledge', on the leather chairs against the plate-glass window of the Country Coffee café. The window overlooks Bathurst's war memorial carillon, with a long view down to the Council chambers. Hanger had relatively recently been inducted as mayor after the previous incumbent, Gary Rush, a man with vision, had succumbed to an intensive campaign by radio shock-jock Ray Hadley over matters of personal finance unrelated to Council. A low-range drink-drive charge had been the catalyst for his resignation.

I'd come to discuss motor-racing heritage. Instead Hanger was focused on the future, particularly on the roadblocks that might stand in the way of progress.

Hanger, I'd been told, was a steady-as-she-goes man, but this bundle of energy, repeatedly detaching himself from our conversation to glad-hand locals, had seized the initiatives laid down by his predecessor and was intent on pushing them through. A new circuit had been proposed, additional to the revered mountain track, and it held great promise for the Bathurst region.

'It's cost us several hundred thousand dollars to get heritage and anthropological investigations done of the Mountain. The elders are in a position where they can make any claim they like. Then it's up to us to prove or disprove them.' According to Hanger, no evidence of historic habitation—either Indigenous or settler—has been found on Mount Panorama. 'So now they're going us on spiritual connection'.

It's an issue by no means confined to Bathurst. Nomadic Indigenous Australians left little trace on the land, surely the archetypical environmentalists, but because of the nature of Aboriginal life and of European development, evidence of sacred sites and camps can, by their very nature, be hard to identify.

In 1824, just eleven years after explorers Blaxland, Lawson and Wentworth had cut the first path across the Great Dividing Range, and only three years after the new NSW governor Thomas Brisbane had issued a flood of land grants to settlers on the western side of the Blue Mountains, war broke out between the new settlers and the incumbent Wiradjuri, who had been effectively barred from their traditional hunting grounds and whose source of food supply had been, if not stopped, at least curtailed.

It started as individual skirmishes and escalated. Brisbane issued a proclamation of martial law. It culminated in what became known as the Battle of Bathurst, in which at least sixteen Wiradjuri people and five troopers were killed, and countless more on both sides were wounded before Brisbane called a ceasefire. He commended magistrates in Bathurst for 'the judicious measures' by which 'the aboriginal natives have learned to respect our power'. A statement not even right for its time that seems so wrong now.

The claims of some elders as they relate specifically to Mount Panorama have been questioned from within the local Indigenous community. 'Mount Panorama as a whole is open to everyone,' said Shirley Scott, founding member of the Bathurst Local Aboriginal Land Council, speaking outside the neat nineteenth-century railway cottage that is the Land Council's local headquarters. Scott, too, is a Wiradjuri elder, and says that the elders who would like to claim the land on Mount Panorama 'do not speak for the entire Aboriginal community'.

The Land Council already owns some of Mount Panorama—about 80 hectares on the south-eastern border of the circuit, just behind Brock's Skyline. It had been a Bathurst Regional Council–owned nature reserve, complete with a brick building known as the Snake House, where live reptiles were on permanent display, but when funding ceased the fenced area fell into disrepair. Under NSW law, the Land Council was able to claim freehold ownership. It is, according to Toni-Lee Scott (Shirley's daughter and full-time administrator of the Land Council), the largest of about twenty plots of land between Bathurst and Little Hartley at the base of the Blue Mountains that have been secured under NSW's Aboriginal Land Rights Act.

'We want to turn it into a tranquil place, significant to everyone, with all types of activity on it,' Toni-Lee said.

'Bill [Dinawan Dyirribang] can't touch it. We hold the freehold and he's able only to make a claim on Crown land.'

'What about *our* children? What about their heritage—their needs?' Dinawan Dyirribang's emotions were plain to hear at the end of the phone. There'd been a Council meeting the previous night to discuss the progress of a proposed go-kart track at McPhillamy Park. The members of the Bathurst Kart Club had spoken passionately about the need to nurture young talent. 'It must be said that for the development of the Daniel Ricciardo and Simona de Silvestro of tomorrow'—thus encapsulating both men and women in motor racing—'they need a facility to learn the trade,' Bathurst Kart Club secretary Steve Angelucci said. 'This circuit will be it.'

On the phone, Dyirribang had a multi-tiered response. He spoke of the cultural significance of Wahluu, of the need to preserve it for sacred rites and the passage to manhood that is part of the roots of the Wiradjuri nation. 'The spot where they want to put the kart track is a women's sacred area and [also] a place where boys go to become men.'

But, he said, he was not opposed to motor racing continuing. 'My mum and dad took me to the first Armstrong 500 in 1963. It's a matter of getting the balance right—of the two entities sharing some space.'

The kart club argued at the Council meeting that an international circuit would allow them to run races 'with 400 entrants per event', plus support people, spectators and officials. It would be, Angelucci said, 'a self-sustaining Bathurst sporting facility' like the city's hockey complex, BMX track and football grounds. 'Those facilities become self-sustaining, highly utilised and attract people to Bathurst,' he said. 'The amount of interest in this facility, both in Australia, the US and Europe, cannot be understated.'

The kart track had been stalled both by local protest and by Council seeking more internationally aligned plans. Typically ambitious, they didn't want just a local track. They wanted one where internationals could race.

Dyirribang was unhappy with Bathurst Regional Council and with race promoters. 'They've just got dollar signs in front of their eyes. Council won't talk to us. It's all through correspondence.' And he questions the long-term viability of Wahluu as a motor-racing circuit. 'Where are the figures that show [motor racing] will be around for a long time, for 100 years?' he said. 'Fuel's changing; there's changes in cars. Where will it be in the future?'

Bathurst Regional Council continues to have big plans for Mount Panorama, well beyond a new kart track.

Since its inauguration, the greatest of all Australian public road tracks has been in a state of constant evolution—sometimes cashed-up, sometimes bankrupt. But it's always been too valuable to abandon.

In 2018, its eightieth year of operation, Bathurst Regional Council's ownership of the Mountain was commercially in a good place. Its biggest event of the year, the Bathurst 1000, operated as a lucrative dry-hire to Supercars Australia, and its other events occurred in successful partnership with promoters.

Now it was time, again, to forge forward.

Council extracted a $25 million pledge from the New South Wales and federal governments for future developments of motor racing in the region. It successfully negotiated with a farmer to buy 200 hectares of land to the west of Mount Panorama and it granted rights to UK-based specialist motor-racing architects Apex Circuit Design to come up with plans for a purpose-built track, minimum 4.7 kilometres, which could be used year-round. Apex initially suggested a track that would have no dependence, at all, on the facilities of the existing circuit.

To say the Council had hit new heights of controversy would be an understatement.

Apex's plans would provide for a multitude of interdependent tracks accommodating everything from a World MotoGP (putting Bathurst in competition with Phillip Island as potential promoters of global motorcycling in Australia), through to running sophisticated vehicle evaluation and learner driver courses in an automotive industrial enclave. Mount Panorama, the road circuit and the legend, would be the icing on the cake—used sparingly for the big events, the annual 1000-kilometre Supercars classic and the fast-growing 12 Hour for the world's most exciting GT cars.

Armed with the proposal, Graeme Hanger intended to head for Macquarie Street and Canberra to get the two governments to double their pledges in order to build his council's dream.

If it all went to plan, he thought, the extended Mount Panorama precinct could be up and running by 2025.

Apex Designs had form in Australia. In 2009 it was contracted to redesign Sydney's Eastern Creek Raceway, owned by the New South Wales Government and operated by the Australian Racing Drivers' Club. Its new design transformed the geographic architecture into a spider's web of several tracks, some of which can be used simultaneously. The rebranded Sydney Motorsport Park became a success. The circuit hire schedule, a sure-fire measure of popularity, was jam-packed. Supercars Australia was waiting on a new lighting project, intended to transform the track into a night-time spectacle.

Apex's specialty lies in conceiving multi-functional closed-road facilities that can maximise their owners' return on investment. While Formula One circuit designer Hermann Tilke has spent the last twenty years designing tracks remarkably similar in character so that promoters—usually ambitious governments—can host once-a-year PR extravaganzas featuring the world's fastest open-wheeler cars, Apex and its managing director Clive Bowen have taken a far more pragmatic approach.

Apex's plans are business-like, designed to be applied across a broad range of commercial events up to and including MotoGP and world sports-car racing—everything but Formula One. A city like Bathurst couldn't handle Formula One; the sport's profits exist in the cloud of economic modelling, not in the real world of counting the gate and banking the money from advertising and TV rights.

Mount Panorama is a phenomenon just as it is. It draws bumper crowds to its sedan and GT races, even though it is 150 kilometres west of the closest metropolitan capital, over a goat track of an access road across the Blue Mountains—which truly is a national disgrace.

'What we need is a tunnel straight through the mountains,' Graeme Hanger grinned, 'or a very fast train.' Neither was a likely prospect, so Hanger was bunkering down, preparing to sell with Martin Griffin–like determination the plans that Council had purchased from Apex.

They would be good plans. Taken in isolation, they had the ability to provide a committed business operator with a platform for success. They would work anywhere in the world.

Bathurst's advantage is its contours. The paddocks purchased by the Council are wonderfully, naturally moulded so that a track—or series of tracks—can sweep and sway through an outback setting, providing spectators and TV cameras with a truly magnificent spectacle set against a backdrop of Australian scenery while simultaneously challenging competitors. It would be the best of both worlds. TV would love the new track and tourism boards could sell regional travel off the images.

But the plans would not touch Mount Panorama, and would use none of its facilities. It was an omission so starkly obvious that Hanger's sell-in would be made commensurately more difficult by a groundswell of protest—ranging from a consistent whisper campaign to outright rebellion. Vincent Tesoriero, by then a twenty-year commercial friend of the Council and of Mount Panorama, was dumbfounded by the deliberate separation. Tesoriero had possession of an earlier set of Council plans that displayed the existing comprehensive pit and paddock buildings as the core of a new permanent complex, moving into the orchard behind before heading towards the city, crossing Conrod Straight above the high-speed Chase and then forming its own serpentine loops in the paddocks beyond. The plan in Tesoriero's hands allowed for two circuits: one of almost 5 kilometres, to be a MotoGP track; and a 2.5-kilometre abbreviated version, permanent, on the city side of Conrod, with its own pit buildings and able to operate year-round. The relatively new Panorama Hotel would tower above it, like the hotels at Germany's fabled Nürburgring, providing ready-made viewing and hospitality areas. For Tesoriero, keeping contact with the roots of Mount Panorama had both emotional and—in the case of the existing infrastructure—financial benefits.

Graeme Hanger disagreed. 'We are actively setting up a buffer zone,' he told me from the Seat of Knowledge. 'Any time a property becomes available near Panorama, we try to buy it up.' Hanger knows that Australia's regional cities expand out, not up. Sooner or later expansion has the potential to threaten Bathurst's most valuable asset. Councils before his have been proactive to prevent encroachment on Mount Panorama. His council also recently bought a tract of farming land on the inside of Conrod Straight. And when the grazing property to the west, the Apex site, became available as a deceased estate, the Council bought it—for about $3 million—and saw it as good buying because, comparatively, it is far removed from immediate problems that bedevil all motor-racing promoters: it is neither in sight, nor importantly in sound, of the city. Hanger stepped down from those negotiations because he had distant family connections to the owners.

Hanger acknowledged problems but decided to turn them into opportunities. The new Mount Panorama precinct would compete with Sydney Motorsport Park, not just for weekend race attendance but for the commercial investment they both covet—an automotive-based hi-tech industrial complex of component manufacturers, developers, retailers and educators that would come together to provide each other with synergy. It's the dream of motor-racing developments worldwide. Perhaps only Silverstone, in the UK, has done it successfully. In 2013, it was estimated that the UK's Motorsport Industry Association generates an estimated £9 billion annually, and much of that occurs within a location called Motorsport Valley encircling, but in a 100-kilometre radius, its Formula One track Silverstone. The track itself has industrial buildings on site. One of them, Silverstone Park, boasts more than 50 like-minded tenants.

'Bathurst is a university town,' Hanger said. 'I can see us developing special curriculums that service the motor and motor-racing industries. And besides, our rents are cheaper.' It's a proposition already pioneered by Wodonga TAFE on the Victorian side of the Murray River. A 1.6-kilometre purpose-built track, approved by CAMS, supports TAFE courses in motorsport engineering.

Road safety is another opportunity. The Driver Education Centre at Shepparton has been a pioneer in providing a purpose-built facility for road-safety training—everything from their Careful Cobber program for preschoolers, right up to heavy commercial vehicle certification. But there is always room for more—in fact, every regional city should have one—and nobody has yet put it all together in one place.

Hanger is a fan of decentralisation. At one stage, Bathurst and nearby Orange had been earmarked as major centres to move essential government services out of the Sydney basin. Bathurst got the Central Mapping Service and Orange the Department of Agriculture before the 1980s scheme was, as Hanger put it, 'killed off by crooks'. Perhaps the new Mount Panorama would rekindle such a program.

Bathurst Regional Council had adopted the name 'Velocity' for its new track. The one key word encompassed everything they wanted to say: speed of action and completion, unstoppable motion, and the sheer joy of going fast. But 'Velocity' also happened to be the brand name of the loyalty program run by Supercars Australia's naming-rights sponsor Virgin. On several levels it was unavailable. Instead, the Council settled on an interim working title of Panorama Valley.

'Perhaps we'll do as Martin Griffin did 80 years ago and invite the public to decide,' Mayor Hanger said. There were those who realised, even then, that it might be a good idea to incorporate the word 'Panorama' somewhere in the name.

Acknowledgements

In the Mount Panorama pits, Peter and Bev Brock offered to put me in touch with my father. He had died a little time before. Though their offer was genuine, I declined—their beliefs were not mine—but I appreciated their compassion and their sincerity. Looking back, I wish I'd taken them up on it just to see what would have happened. The Brocks are very special people.

This history of Mount Panorama was not intended to be the Peter Brock story; he wrote himself into it. Brock is such a part of the Mountain's folklore that no matter what turn you take, he's there. The phenomenon of children christened Brock (I met my first Skaife recently) proves his omnipotence.

Bathurst breeds heroes—of bikes and cars. It generates powerfully held recollections; many of them, in the cold light of fact-checking, are unique in their retelling. More than 100 people directly participated in this book. Another 50 books and countless online references contributed. All motorsport is grounded in statistics, the better to tell its story accurately and dispassionately. The Mountain, though, is steeped in mythology. It's not the where, when or what that counts; it's the how and the why. For every fact there's an opinion, so strongly voiced that it bends and twists the original premise like a demon run off the top of Skyline. To acknowledge this is not so much a disclaimer as a recognition that there will be readers who disagree with parts of this story—and, because of their passion, perhaps vehemently so. I've done my best to separate fact and fantasy while ignoring neither. The mystique of Mount Panorama deserves a place in its history.

The overwhelming enthusiasm and support of the custodians of Mount Panorama made this deep dive into the Mountain's development all the more enjoyable. Bathurst Regional Council mayor Graeme Hanger OAM led the team that willingly unlocked archives and provided personal perspective, alphabetically: Alan Cattermole, Brian Dwyer, Brad Owen, Tim Pike, Mark Rayner, Bob Roach and Narelle Stocks. The people of Bathurst, likewise, contributed so much—Dinawan Dyirribang, Peta Gurdon-O'Meara, Brian Nightingale, Michael O'Shea, Kerry Peck (the voice of Bathurst), Shirley Scott, Toni-Lee Scott, John Shanks, Dave Sherley and Mick Tuckey.

There are some wonderful lap-by-lap descriptions of Mount Panorama races through the ages, some of which—like Jim Scaysbrook's *Bikes and Bathurst* and John Medley's *Bathurst: Cradle of Australian Motor Racing*, plus all the works of Chevron (later Next Media) on the Bathurst 1000, mainly

ACKNOWLEDGEMENTS

written by the late Bill Tuckey—I relied on to fact-check, but not to replicate.

I set out to present Mount Panorama through the eyes of people who'd been there—Reg Hunt, for example, now undeniably the senior statesman of the golden era of open-wheeler racing, and Kel Carruthers, who used the Mountain as a springboard to his world title. To both of them, special thanks.

Drivers and riders I spoke to included Kevin Bartlett, Steve Bayliss, Norm Beechey, e-racing champion Matt Bink, Colin Bond OAM, David Brabham, James Brock, Bill Buckle OAM, Matt Campbell, Richard Davison, Will Davison, Peter Finlay, Bob Forbes, John French, Wayne Gardner AM, Fred Gibson, Allan Grice, Kenny Habul, Dick Johnson AM, Craig Lowndes OAM (and wife Lara and dad Frank), Peter Macrow, Jim Manolios, Spencer Martin, Scott McLaughlin, Chris Mies, Allan Moffat OBE, Greg Murphy, Malcolm Oastler, Charlie O'Brien, Larry Perkins, Sue Ransom, Jim Richards, Steven Richards, Murray Sayle, Vern Schuppan AM, Mark Skaife OAM, Scott Taylor, Mark Webber AO, Dirk Werner, Jamie Whincup and Luke Youlden. And to all those with whom the conversation was in passing, my sincere thanks.

Team management and well-connected individuals who set me on paths of knowledge and understanding included Matteo Braga (Pirelli), Benjamin Franassovici (SRO), Sebastian Gulz (Porsche), Brian Gush (Bentley), Mike Jeffery, who enlightened me on the Bathurst/Orange battle, Rebecca Jones, Jens Marquardt (BMW), Ben Nightingale (DJR Penske), Sophie Peyrat (SRO), Chris Renke (Audi), and particularly David Zeunert of the Maserati Club of Victoria who facilitated a wonderful half-day with Reg Hunt and his partner Julia Wood.

Supercars Australia willingly participated. Special thanks to communications director Cole Hitchcock who set up contact with CEO Sean Seamer, long-term operations manager Shane Howard, Bathurst 12 Hour manager Kurt Sakzewski, head of TV Nathan Prendergast, digital manager Sam Barker, and the longest serving camo on the Mountain Ian O'Brien.

Media who contributed directly include Mark Bisett, René de Boer, Ray Berghouse, Philip Christensen, Richard Craill, Neil Crompton (who crosses many streams), Darryl Flack, Bill Forsyth, Will Hagon, John Hindhaugh (Radio Le Mans), Nathan Johnson, Peter McKay, Steve Normoyle, Scott Wensley and Luke West. Thanks to the photographers of the old Project Group team—Jeff Nield, Graham Long, Paul Pearson and Bob Seary. Hugh King of the Australian Motoring Heritage Foundation made his extensive collection available. And to Chris Currie, heartfelt thanks for hours of photo selection and scanning.

Organisers and major influencers deserve special thanks for so many reasons—Jan Blizzard, the Rev. Garry Coleman OAM, Tony Cochrane, Roland Dane, Jessica Dane, Greg Eaton, Allan Horsley, David Johnson, James O'Brien, Kelvin O'Reilly, Stéphane Ratel, Ian Tate and Vincent Tesoriero.

I was particularly delighted to make contact with the owners and curators of the first car to win the Australian Grand Prix at Mount Panorama—Paddins Dowling, its owner/driver, and the ERA team Adam Ferrington and David Morris.

Mount Panorama is a story of families. My thanks to Ryan Hansford and his mum Julie for sharing Gregg's story, Chris Davison for his insight into the Davison family, Sir Jack Brabham for a long discussion we had just before his passing, and to Neil Brock OAM and Bev Brock OAM for their further

ACKNOWLEDGEMENTS

revelations about Peter. Just when we thought there was nothing new to know . . .

On the subject of family I would like to acknowledge with love my own family: Jenny, and our children Andrew and Kate, who for years thought the Easter Bunny only visited the Bathurst Motor Inn; and their partners Karen and Dan. It's only a little while now before grandchildren Cameron and Matilda become Mountaineers.

To Allen & Unwin, immense appreciation to senior editor Samantha Kent, who has managed the manuscript magnificently; the aptly named Emma Driver who negotiated the twists and turns of the story with the precision of a race engineer; designer Luke Causby who has captured the essence of the Mountain; publishing director Tom Gilliatt who continues to be the best writer-coach in the business; and sales and marketing director Jim Demetriou who said in the foyer one day: 'Are you going to Bathurst this weekend?', and so got the book started.

And finally to Glenn Quinlan, the keeper of the flame in the 05 encampment at Reid Park, and to the thousands of campers who join him in homage each year, if only because he christened his firstborn Brock.

Index

60 Minutes 215

1938–1962 racing
  1938 51–69, 135, 162
  1939 70–84
  1940 84–6
  1946 92–6
  1947 96–100
  1948 102–3
  1949 103–4
  1952 142–3
  1954 143–4
  1955 146–7, 165
  1956 147–8, 165–6
  1958 148–50, 159–60
  1960 150–2
  1961 160
  1962 183

Abbey, Glen 246
Aboriginal land rights 319–24
Abrahams, Lou 149
Adderton, Peter 202–3, 210
Adelaide *Advertiser* 52
aerodynamic wings 155, 272–4
Agostini, Giacomo 4, 12–13, 129
Ahearn, Jack 117, 124–7, 130
Allen, Bill Jr *see* Dyirribang, Dinawan
Allen, Neil 155, 245, 272–4
Allison, 'Big Col' 10
Allison, Bruce 10
Alonso, Fernando 309
Amaroo Park 177
Amateur Drivers' Club *see* Light Car
  Club of Bathurst
Anderson, Colin 64
Anderson, Wally 167, 169

INDEX

Angelucci, Steve 323–4
Annand & Thompson 11
Apex Circuit Design 325–7
Appleton, Rob 81
Arai 500 130, 132–3
Archer Capital 219–22
Armstrong 500 *see* Bathurst 1000
Audi Sport Customer Racing 238
Australian Hill Climb
 Championship 299–301
Australian Racing Drivers' Club
 (ARDC) 12, 108–11, 150, 177, 196, 201–3, 208–10, 270–1
Australian Sporting Car Club
 (ASCC) 96–8, 100–5, 107–11, 143
Australian Super Touring Car
 Championship 202, 209–10
Australian Touring Car
 Championship 169
Australian Tourist Trophy 158–60
Australian Vee Eight Supercar Company
 (AVESCO) 207–12
Auto Cycle Union (ACU) 12, 81, 96, 104, 109, 118, 131, 138, 177
Automobile Association of Australia
 (AAA) 101, 104–5, 107–9
Avant, Stu 276

B-Rock FM 297
Bagshaw, John 32, 192
Bailey, Graeme 200, 253–4
Bain, Don xv, xx, 61, 77, 84–5, 92
Baldry, Billy 268
Bamber, Earl 225
Barelli, Ross 277
Barker, Sam 312
Barnard, Bob 131, 207
Barraclough, John 78, 81, 83–4, 95, 100, 102
Barrett, Alf 'The Maestro' 64, 72, 81–2, 83–4, 86, 103
Bartlett, Kevin 30, 34, 153, 187, 196, 200, 243–4, 246–9, 309
Bartrop, Harry 118, 298

Bathurst 12 Hour 18, 21–2, 179, 224–38
 1992 3, 21–2
 1993 22–3
 1994 23
Bathurst 100 108, 147–8, 155, 243, 269
Bathurst 500 *see* Bathurst 1000
Bathurst 1000 3, 18, 27, 45–7, 94, 140, 179, 181–203, 241
 1963 32, 39–40, 185–6
 1965 157
 1966 169–78
 1967 32
 1968 157
 1969 30–6, 40–2, 190–1
 1970 191
 1971 191–2
 1972 192, 245
 1977 18, 193
 1981 166
 1982 252–3
 1983 232
 1984 19–20
 1986 193–4, 279
 1988 20–1, 193
 1992 280–1
 1993 23
 1994 23, 281–2
 1997 209, 317
 1999 241
 2005 206
 2006 212–13, 265–6, 283–4
 2014 314, 316
 2018 306–7
Bathurst City Council xix, 109–11, 201–2, 270–1, 298–9
Bathurst International Festival of
 Motorsport 234–5, 302
Bathurst Kart Club 323–4
Bathurst Light Car Club xii, 74, 182, 275, 300–3
Bathurst Local Aboriginal Land
 Council 322–3
Bathurst Regional Council 234–5, 238, 298–9, 319–30

337

Battle of Bathurst 321–2
Bayliss, Stan 134–8
Bayliss, Steve 135–8
Beechey, Norm 169–74
behaviour 67, 288–97
Behind the Wheel 106
Behra, Jean 69, 158
Bink, Matthew 304–5, 312–13
Bira Princes 56, 58–9
Birkin, Tim 56–7
Bland, Charles 'Dick' 100
Blizzard, Arthur 119, 127–8, 276–7, 277–8, 289, 298
Blizzard, Jan 119, 126, 127–8, 138, 277–8
Blomfield, Warren 159
Bond, Colin 18, 20, 24, 29, 31, 34, 40–1, 176–8, 190–3, 196
Boulden, Moyna 130
Boulden, Ron 117, 130–1
Bourne, Peter 'Possum' 133
Bowe, John 20, 214–15, 255–6
Bowen, Clive 326
Brabham, David 259–60, 316–18
Brabham, Gary 316–17
Brabham, Geoff 316–17
Brabham, Jack 'Black Jack' 30, 72, 84, 103, 140–1, 144, 147, 151–2, 155–6, 242–4, 280–1, 316–18
Brabham, Tom 144
Brabham BT62 259–61, 317–18
Brad Jones Racing 284
Brennan, Pat 295–6
Brisbane, Thomas 321–2
British Touring Car Championship 203
broadcasting 306–13
Brock, Alexander (great-great-grandfather) 38
Brock, Bev 43, 212, 230, 315
Brock, Geoff 36–7
Brock, James 315–16
Brock, Lewis 37
Brock, Neil 36–8
Brock, Peter

1969 Bathurst 500 30–42
1979 victory 28
Bathurst Light Car Club member 303
Bathurst 12 Hour 229–31, 232–3
death 28, 265–6
driving style 254
father/son racing 315–16
Firth's regime 29–33, 192–3
Holden team 29–30, 192–3, 195
Honorary Citizen of Bathurst 297
'King of the Mountain' 42–3, 184, 266
legend 27–8, 190
military service 28–9
monument 26
Mount Panorama victories 184, 190
personality 30
Peter Brock trophy 212–13, 266
'Peter Perfect' 28, 46
pushing the regulations 187
racing partners 194, 197–9
retirement 194–5
ton attempt 253
tribute meeting 212–13, 283–4
upbringing 37–8
Brock, Phillip 37, 194
Brock, Ruth 36
Brown, Bill 157, 191
Browne, Alan 252–3
Brydon, 'Curley' (The Mouse) 101, 108
Buckle, Anne 162
Buckle, Bill 162–4, 271–2
Buckle, Elsie 162
Buckle, William (W.G.) 162–3
Buckle GT 164
Burgmann, Mike 279–80
Burke, Tony 269
Burns, Neil 198
Burrows, Les 65–6
Button, Jenson 242, 263–4
Byrne, Terry 152
Byrnes, Bernard 'Bat' 74–7, 79, 85, 92, 104, 243
Byrnes, Peter 192

INDEX

Campbell, Bill 226
Campbell, Malcolm 131
Campbell, Matt 225–9
Campbell, Teresa 'TC' 226
Camplin, Ron 297–8
CAMS Gold Star 94, 245–9
Capper, Wally 103–4, 109
Carruthers, Jack 119–20, 123
Carruthers, Jan 117, 120
Carruthers, Kel 9, 30, 116–17, 119–20, 123–4, 249
Carruthers, Lil 120
Caruso, Michael 284
Casey, Ron 44–5
Chadwick, Bill 302
Challenge Bathurst 257–9
Channel Nine 44–5, 152
Channel Seven 45, 186, 201–2, 209, 292–3
Channel Ten 209–10
chaplaincy, sport 278–80
Chapman, Colin 174
cheating 181, 186–90
Chesterfield Australian Grand Prix 12
Chevrolet Impala 170–1
Chifley, Ben xvi–xviii, 91
Chiron, Louis 141
Chivas, Doug Jr 138
Cochrane, Tony 203, 205, 207–12, 219–20, 223, 315
Codognotto, Damien 293
Cole, Michael 132, 133
Coleman, Reverend Garry 265–7, 276, 278–80, 284
Coleman, Rod 121–2
Collerson, Barry 155
Colligan, Jim 283
commentary *see* race promotion
commentators 241
Confederation of Australian Motor Sport (CAMS) 109–11, 152, 201–3, 223
Conrod Straight 3–5, 80, 280
construction xii–xxi
Cooper, John 151–2

Coulthard, Fabian 312
Courage, Piers 156
Cowan, Brian 130
Cowley, George 144
Cox, Rod 133
Crago, Alan 64–6
Crick, Diana 94, 99–100, 147
Crompton, Neil 22, 221, 230
Crosby, Graeme 'Croz' 131
Crouch, Cecil 72
Crouch, John 72, 104–5, 144, 162
crowd numbers 14–15
Curtain, Kevin 251

Damman, Peter 162
Dane, Jessica 218
Dane, Roland 205, 212, 218, 220, 222, 289–90, 310–11
Davison, A.A. (Alec) 94
Davison, Alex 313–14
Davison, Alexander 'Lex' 94–5, 99–100, 102–3, 144, 146–50, 152–3, 159, 242, 243, 269, 301, 313
Davison, Chris 94–5
Davison, Richard 313–14
Davison, Will 313–14
Daytona 200 4
Dean, Charlie 141–4, 146
deaths 4–5, 30, 91–3, 103–4, 155–6, 265–84
Dennis, Jake 225
Dentry, Barney 63
Dentry, Bess 63
De Ruvo, John 309
Devil's Elbow *see* Forrest's Elbow
Dick, Ian 277
Diffey, Leigh 213
Dixon, Scott 226
Don, Kaye 56
Donovan, Carolyn 24–5
Doohan, Mick 115–16, 131, 133–4
Douglas-Osborn, Alister 299
Dowling, Paddins 69
Downer, Alexander 211–12

Dowson, Michael 131, 133–4
Doyle, Neville 16, 24
Dumbrell, Paul 218
Dunne, Colin 56
Dyirribang, Dinawan 319, 322–4

e-racing 304–6, 309, 311–13
Easter 1973 meeting 176–8
Eastmure, Joe 10
Eaton, Greg 138–9, 203
Ecclestone, Bernie 223, 228
Economaki, Chris 45
Egan, Michael 211–12
Eggenberger, Ruedi 20–1, 188
EH 179 badge 39
Elbow see Forrest's Elbow
Ellis, Rex 302
Elton John farewell concert 299
England, 'Lofty' 168
English Racing Automobiles (ERAs) 54, 57–8, 64–7, 69
Erskine, James 210
Eyston, George 56

Fagan, Jim 56
Fangio, Juan Manuel 145
Federation Internationale de Motocyclisme (FIM) 7
Ferguson, Barry 186
Ferrari, Enzo 72
Ferrari P4 157
Ferrari 250 LM 156–8
Ferrington, Adam 69
financial contribution 298
Finlay, Peter 300
Firth, Harry 'The Fox' 29–36, 38, 39–41, 176, 183, 186–90, 192–3
Firth, Norm 183
FJ Holden 165–7, 169
Fletcher, Ray Edwin 93, 268
Forbes, Bob 200
Ford II, Edsel 201
Ford versus Holden 172–6, 196–203, 213, 215, 310–11

Forrest, Jack 92, 98, 103, 124–5
Forrest, K.M. xviii–xix
Forrest's Elbow 98
Forshaw, Brian 308
Foyt, A.J. 44
France, Bill Jr 45
France, Bill Sr 223
Fraser, Malcolm 202
Fraser, Tamie 202
Freeth, Rodger 133
French, John 89, 166–9, 174, 191, 192
future plans 324–30

Gall, Stephen 11
Gannon, Peter 294
Gardner, Frank 192, 198, 247, 253
Gardner, Wayne 116, 125, 132, 217
Garlick, Nellie 82
Garlick, Reginald (Phil) 82
Gaze, Tony 103
General Motors US 32
Geoghegan, Ian 'Pete' 5, 155, 157, 169–76, 183, 189, 245, 271–2
Geoghegan, Leo 155, 166–9, 183, 189, 271–2
Geoghegan, Tom 154, 162, 170
German motorcycle racing team 52–3
Gibson, Bevan 5, 30, 155, 272–4
Gibson, Christine 184
Gibson, Fred 189, 199
Gnoo Blas course 107–11, 270
Gorman, Tom 213
Goss, John 200
Goss, Wayne 207
Gow, Alan 203
'Grand Marshals' 45
Grant, Ron 4
Gray, Ted 148–50
Grech, Jeff 214
Greig, Gordon 269
Grice, Allan 'Spicy Gricey' 45, 200, 243, 252–4
Griffin, Mayor Martin xvi–xxi, 60, 67, 85, 91, 330

INDEX

Griffin's Bend xxi
Gumley, Peter 299
Gunter, Anthony 11
Gurdon, Barry 165–6, 181–2, 186–8, 302
Gurdon-O'Meara, Peta 182

Hadley, Ray 320
Hailwood, Mike 'Mike the Bike' 129
Halliday, Barry 'Doc' 268
Halliday, Margaret 138
Hamilton, Alan 18, 193
Hamilton, Lewis 242
Hammond, Frank 76
Hanger, Graeme 238, 298–9, 320–2, 325–30
Hannaford, George 76
Hansford, Edna 10
Hansford, Gregg 3–26, 127, 128–9, 196, 249–51
Hansford, Harrison 24–5
Hansford, Harry 10
Hansford, Julie 10, 17, 24
Hansford, Rhys 24
Hansford, Ryan 24, 25
Harrop, Ron 216
Harrop, Tim 216
Harvey, Gavin 216
Harvey, John 20, 155, 156, 194, 216, 253–4
Hatton, Tony 132
Hawkins, Paul 157
Hayes, Arthur 110
Healy, Geoff 45, 46
Henderson, Tony 125
Henderson Matchless G50 125
Hennen, Pat 4, 7–8, 14
Heroes' Walk 299
Hibbert, George 298
Hill, David 46
Hill, Graham 272
Hill, Robert 212
hill climbs 73–4, 299–301
Hindle, Bryan 12–14
Hinton, Eric 121–2, 124, 243

Hinton, Harry 61–2, 92, 98, 103, 105–6, 121–2, 135
Hinton, Harry Jr 121–2
Hinton, Peter 121
Hinton, Rob 14, 121
Hinton, Tony 121, 131
Hinton, Vienie 106
Hinton family 117
Hinxman, Jack 170, 183, 186, 203, 298
Hodge, Simon 245
Hodgson, Ron 169, 247
Hogg, Ian 277
Holden, Bob 166
Holden Dealer Team 10, 32
Holden versus Austin 165–6
Holden versus Ford 172–6, 196–203, 213, 215, 310–11
Honda, Soichiro 122
Honda motorcycle 122–4
Honorary Citizen of Bathurst 298
Horsley, Allan 21–2, 24–5
Horsman, Bill 117, 125–7, 244, 283
Howard, Shane 209, 294–6
Hulman, Tony 223
Hulme, Denny 'The Bear' 280–1
Hunt, Reg 144–8, 242, 243, 269
Hurst, Charles 93

Ickx, Jacky 18, 193
IMG (International Management Group) 207–8, 210–11
Institute for Motor Sport Safety and Sustainability 267
Irving, Phil 145
Irwin, Mayor John 91
Irwin, Steve 266

Jaguar 168–70
James, Wally 81
James Hardie Industries 202, 298
James Hardie 12 Hour *see* Bathurst 12 Hour
Jane, Bob 13, 154, 160, 171–6, 183, 272–4

341

Jeanes-Cochrane, Thea 223
Jemison, Tom 'The Prof' 101
Jenkins, Peter 93
Joest, Reinhold 235
Johnson, Andrew 117, 130–1, 133
Johnson, David 108–9
Johnson, Dick 'Tricky Dicky' 20, 24, 45, 47–8, 167–8, 191, 200–1, 223, 231–2
Johnson, Jack 103–4, 268
Jolly, Derek 159
Jolly, Martin 211
Jones, Alan 141, 146
Jones, Belf 108
Jones, Brad 214–15, 217, 222
Jones, Rebecca 309
Jones, Stan 141–4, 146–50
Joyce, John 174

Kable, Mike xii, xviii–xxii, 34, 309
Kanaya, Hideo 129
Kane, Clive 164
Katayama, Yoshimi 19
Keeffe, John 280
Keegan, Brian 301
Kelly, Rick 257
Kelso, Jim 298
Kelso camp 86–7, 92
Kessing, Ron 92
Keyes, Graeme 137
'King of the Mountain' 42–3
Kleinig, Frank 57, 64, 74, 79–81, 83–4, 92, 246
Kluge, Ewald 52–3
Kyalami circuit 228

Lago Talbot 140–3
Lang, Jack xvii
lap scoring 189–90
Larkham, Mark 241
Larnock, Gavan 269
Lauren, Ralph 158
Le Mans 24 Hour race 40, 56–7, 59, 68, 156, 227, 236, 270, 273–4, 290
Levegh, Pierre 270

Light Car Club of Bathurst 73–4, 92
Light Car Club of NSW 81
Little, Lindsay 186
Liverpool Speedway 44
Lowe, Neal 254
Lowndes, Craig 'The Kid' 33, 212–15, 235, 242, 261–4, 298, 314
Lowndes, Frank 214, 262, 314
Lowrie, Bill 163
Lucas, Geoff 127
Lyons, Joseph 71

McAlpine, Tony 119
McCrae, Sandy 136–7
McGrath, Sir Charles 'Dave' 141
McGregor, Graeme 137
Macintosh, Ian 209, 212
McIntosh, Ken 133
McKay, Betty 168
McKay, David 'Sir Malcolm' 41, 101–2, 106, 108, 153–4, 156–60, 168–9
McKay, Peter 230
MacKay, William 'Big Bill' 89–92, 96–8, 100
Mackellar, Ron 81
MacLachlan, Bill 96, 162
McLaren, Bruce 155–6
McLaren MP4-23 263–4
McLaughlin, Scott 311–13
McLeod, Peter 194
McPhee, Bruce 33, 40, 42
McPherson, Eric 62, 77, 98, 120, 135
McPhillamy, Walter J. xxi
McPhillamy Park xxi, 13, 32
Macquarie Motorcycle Mafia 10
Macrow, Peter 36
Magee, Kevin 133
Marciello, Raffaele 225
marketing *see* race promotion
Marshall, Rex 96, 99, 101
Martin, George 68
Martin, Gerry 35
Martin, Spencer 34–6, 39–40, 153–4, 156–8, 244, 247–9, 272–4

INDEX

Martin, Vicky 157
Masi, Michael 206
Mason, Nick 69
Matich, Frank 154, 159–60, 272–4
Maxwell, Kenneth 54, 63, 68
Mays, Raymond 58
Meatchem, Ron 198
Meller, Edgar xiii
Meller, James xiii
Menzies, Robert 71, 80–1
Mezera, Tomas 212
Midnight Oil 42–3
Mies, Chris 258–9
Mike Kable 'Young Gun' Award xxii
Mildren, Alec 34, 153, 246
Miles, Tim 218–20
Moffat, Allan 5, 10, 18–21, 24, 40–2, 171, 173–6, 187, 190–4, 244–5, 298, 316
Moffat, James 316
Molloy, Ginger 244
Monza Service 72
Moorehouse, Rob 'Moose' 277–8
Morris, Bob 47, 189
Morris, Milton 197
Morris, Paul 203, 210, 315
Morris, Ray 189
Morris, Terry 202–3, 210
Morse, Alan 91
Moss, Stirling 69, 145, 158–9
motorcycle racing xiiii–xiv, 115–39, 243–4, 249–51
  1940 NSW Senior TT 85
  1946 NSW Victory TT 92–3
  1955 NSW TT 121–2
  1968 Australian Unlimited Motorcycle Grand Prix 126–7
  1974 Australian Unlimited Grand Prix 3–10, 14–16
  1974 Bathurst Unlimited 12–14
  administration 118–20
  deaths 91–3, 267–8, 275–8, 282–3
  safety 115–16, 282–3
  sidecar racing 134–8
  Yamaha TZ750 8–9, 11–13, 249–51

Mount Druitt racetrack 108
Mountain, Ian 270
Muir, Brian 'Yogi' 39–40, 246
Mulholland, Barry 40
Murphy, Greg 212, 255–7
Murray, Bill 96, 99–100, 164, 269
Murray, Jack 'Gelignite Jack' 95–6, 159, 162
Murray's Corner 7, 96, 268
Mussett, Frank 103
Mustang 171
Myers, Jack 165–6

Najar, Alf 95–6
naming rights 319–20
National Advocate 92–3
National Motor Racing Museum 26, 302
Negus, Wayne 200
Neill, Dennis 132–3
New Zealand Grand Prix
  1954 143–4
Neylon, Chad 306
Niedzwiedz, Klaus 20
Nightingale, Brian 89, 285–6, 302
Nind, John 96
Norris, Lando 311–12

Oastler, Malcolm 300–1
O'Brien, Charlie 10, 18
O'Brien, Ian 'Fish' 307–9
O'Brien, James 233–7, 257
Ogden, Charlie 75–6
O'Halloran, Henry (Bernard) 92–3, 268
Olofsson, Anders 196
O'Neil, Laurie 154
Oran Park 177
Orange City Council 107, 109–11
O'Reilly, Kelvin 210
O'Shea, Michael 286–9, 291–4

Palmer, Les 231–2
Palmer, Ross 24, 231–3
Parramatta City Raceway 44
Parsons, David 194

343

Paton, George 149
Paton, Jack 149
Patterson, Bill 147, 153
Peck, Kerry 297–8
Penske, Roger 221–2
Perkins, Larry 'The Cowangie Kid' 22–3, 24, 31, 45, 161, 194, 198–9, 208, 217, 253
Perola, Monty 136
Peter Brock Trophy 212–13, 266
Peters, Tom 57, 64
Phillip Island racetrack 25, 32, 182
Phillis, Rob 133–4
Phillis, Tom 123–4
Pilbeam, Mike 299–300
Pleasance, Norman 105
policing *see* behaviour
Porsche's young driver development program 226–7
Porter, Mark 283–4
Pratley, Warwick 107, 301
Prendergast, Kevin 305
Prendergast, Nathan 305–7
Pretty, Greg 133
Pringle, Jimmy 55

Quinlan, Brock 295
Quinlan, Glenn 295

RAC TT 159
race promotion 42–8
race teams 217–22
RaceCam 46–8
racecraft 261–4
racing families 313–17
Ratel, Marie 227
Ratel, Stéphane 227–9, 236–7
Ratel, Victoria 227
Raymond, Mike 42–8
Raymond, Steve 43–4
Razor Gang wars 90
records 4, 8–9, 30, 242–64
REDeX 108–9, 152
Reed, Cam 301

Reed, George 74, 107, 301–2
Reed, Norma 301
Reid, Hugh xix–xxi
Reid, John B. 202, 298
Reid Park xxi
Reinke, Chris 238
Repco (Reconditioned Engine Parts Company) 141–2, 149
Revell, Barry 'The Phantom Chef' 101–2
Reynolds, Bill 86
Reynolds, David 260
Richards, Clay 216
Richards, Fay 217
Richards, Jason 206
Richards, Jim 23, 28, 31, 194, 197–9, 201, 213, 215–17, 281
Richards, Steven 215–17
Rindt, Jochen 156
Rizzo, Arthur 104
Rizzo, Valerie 104
RMS *Queen Mary* 84
Roberts, Kenny 13, 17
Roberts, Kenny Jr 17
Roberts, Tony 34, 40
Rosenthal, Bob 277
Rothmans sponsorship 12
Rush, Gary 320
Rust, Greg 213
Rydell, Rickard 214

safety 89, 91–3, 96–8, 270–1
Sampson, Brian 194
Sayle, Douglas 10
Sayle, Harold 11
Sayle, Jeff 10
Sayle, Marie 10–11
Sayle, Murray 10–11, 17, 127, 129, 250–1
Saywell, Jack 72, 78–80, 82–3, 243, 269
Scaysbrook, Jim 129
Schenken, Tim 213, 279–80
Schuppan, Vern 143
Scott, Gary 253
Scott, Glyn 167, 274

INDEX

Scott, Shirley 322
Scott, Toni-Lee 322–3
Seamer, Sean 220–2, 305–6, 318
Seeliger, Ern 'The Baron' 146–7, 269
Senior, Art 77, 85
Sesquicentennial Grand Prix Parramatta Park 91
Seton, Barry 47
Seton, Glenn 'The Baby-Faced Assassin' 21, 45–6, 47, 217
Shanks, John 118
Sheene, Barry 207–8
Shepheard, Reg 108–9
Sherrin, Les 61
Sherwood, C.O. 77–8
Sherwood, John xix, xxi, 44, 56, 63–6, 77–80, 91
Shmith, David 163–4
Shmith, Maurice 163
Sidecar Racers 134
sidecar racing 134–8
Simonsen, Allan 236
Sinclair, Alan 51–3, 62–3, 67, 68
Skaife, Mark 23, 199, 205–6, 217, 219, 255
Skaife, Russell 206
Skyline xx, 33
Slaughter, Les 135
Small, Les 253
Smith, Barry 117
Smith, Reg 271–2
Snow, Gwendoline 73
Snow, John 70–4, 77–81, 83–4, 86
Snow, Sir Sydney 71
South Australian Grand Prix 52
Spa-Francorchamps circuit 228
spectator anecdotes 286–8, 295–6
sponsorship 201–3
Spooner, Eric xvii–xviii, 60
sport chaplaincy 278–80
Sports & Entertainment Ltd (SEL) 210–11, 219–20
SS *Mariposa* 85
SS *Orford* 52

SS *Orvieto* 95
stakeholders 202–3
Stewart, Doug 110
Stewart, Jackie 156–7
Stewart, Max 153
Stibbard, Ivan 184, 208, 253, 279
Stillwell, Bib 147, 152–3, 160
Stone, Shane 211–12
Stump Cam 46
Sulman, Tom 5, 159, 274–5, 301
Sulman monument 275
Sulman Park 275
Sun-Herald 197
'superbike' 11
supercars 204–23
Supercars Australia 236–7, 290, 305–7, 311–13, 315, 330
Suzuka circuit 228
Swedberg, Paul 79–80, 85–6, 102
Sydney Harbour Bridge opening 89–90
Sykes, Geoff 124

Takai, Ikujiro 'The Little Giant' 117, 128–9, 249–51
Tander, Garth 259
Tate, Ian 183, 188, 192
Tauranac, Austin 155
Tauranac, Ron 155, 164
Taylor, Robert 105
Team Brock 195
Team Kawasaki Australia 16
Team Triple Eight 204–5, 213, 217–18
Telegraph newspapers 153
Tesoriero, Vincent 6, 11, 14, 21, 130, 138, 229–31, 282–3, 291–4, 327–8
Thompson, Bill 81, 88
Thornton, Ian 283
Tilke, Hermann 326
Tobin, Leo 55, 62, 79, 85, 103
Todt, Jean 223
Toombs, Mavis 125, 276
Toombs, Ron 14, 117, 125–7, 275–7
touring-car racing 162–78
track reference points ix–x, 32–3

Tresise, Rocky 153
Tronson, Mark 278
Tuckey, Mick 302–3
Turner, Al 173, 190

Uffindell, Ron 60, 64–6
unofficial racing 285–6

Vale circuit xiv–xvi
van Gisbergen, Shane 258
Van Praag, Lionel 75
V8 Consortium 202–3 *see also* Supercars Australia
V8 Supercar Events 211, 219–20
'Velocity' 330
Vincent, Phil 145
von Oertzen, Baron Klaus Detlof 52

Wada, Masahiro 128, 249–51
Waggott, Merv 165
Wahluu 319
Walker, Peter 'Skid' 59
Walkinshaw, Tom 46–7, 200, 206
Walsh, Kathleen xvii
Wannick, Eddie 76
Ward, Peter 99
Warwick Farm Raceway 124
Watson, Don 281–2
Weatherby, Cec xx, 61–2
Webber, Alan 262
Webber, Mark 261–3, 273
Webster, Wayne 39
Werner, Dick 226

West, Des 36, 40–1
Whincup, Jamie 212, 217–19
White, David 210
White, Ray xix, xxi
Whiteford, Doug 106–7, 142–3, 151, 159–60
Whitehead, Graham 69
Whitehead, Peter 53, 57–60, 62, 64–7, 68–9, 78, 91, 149, 162, 288
Whiting, Charlie 206
Wide World of Sports 45
Wilkinson, Arthur 'Bluey' xiv, 74–5, 85
Wilkinson, Garry 47
Wilkinson, Muriel 85
Williamson, Peter 46
Willing, Barbara 10
Willing, Brian 10
Willing, Glenn 10
Willing, Len 10
Willing, Rhonda 10, 11
Willing, Warren 4–17, 117, 128–30, 244, 249–51
Wiradjuri nation 320, 321, 323
Woelders, Henk 34–5
Woodley, John 276
World of Sport 45
World War II 80–1, 84–8, 92

Yamaha TZ750 8–9, 11–13, 249–51
Youl, Gavin 271–2
Youlden, Luke 260–1

Zehnder, Oscar 101, 104–5